"A POST-MODERN PERSPECTIVE ON CURRICULUM"

WILLIAM E. DOLL, JR.

D0103356

TEACHERS COLLEGE PRESS

Teachers College, Columbia University
New York and London

Published by Teachers College Press, 1234 Amsterdam Avenue
New York, New York 10027

The color image of the Lorenz attractor appearing opposite page 92 was provided courtesy of Art Matrix, Inc., Ithaca, New York.

Library of Congress Cataloging-in-Publication Data

Doll, William E., Jr.
  A post-modern perspective on curriculum / William E. Doll, Jr.
     p.   cm.—(Advances in contemporary thought series)
  Includes bibliographical references (p.) and index.
  ISBN 0-8077-3217-6 (alk. paper) : $32.00
     1. Education—Curricula—Philosophy.   2. Education—Philosophy.
3. Curriculum change.   I. Title.   II. Series.
LB1570.D616   1993
375'.01—dc20   92-35205

ISBN 0-8077-3217-6

Printed on acid-free paper

Manufactured in the United States of America

99 98 97 96 95 94 93   8 7 6 5 4 3 2 1

To Mary, my wife, and Will, our son. Both have played important
roles in my own transformation.

Contents

Foreword

During the twentieth century a quiet and sometimes not so quiet intellectual and conceptual revolution in Western thought began. Some mark its beginnings earlier; some view it as negative and destructive; and some see it only as the latest fad; but now, near the end of the century, many are coming to see it as a broad and pervasive mind shift that will bring with it challenges to find new ways of thinking and doing in all fields of human endeavor. William Doll is a sensitive educator who has a good feeling for what this conceptual revolution is about and a facility for describing it and applying its framework to curriculum theory. His book is a model of what the *Advances in Contemporary Educational Thought* seeks to provide.

Post-modernism means many things to many people. There is no simple, agreed-upon description of it. Its manifestations are different in different fields. Just as those at the end of the Middle Ages and Renaissance didn't know what they were in the middle of because the modern era had just begun, so too we at the end of the modern age can only dimly make out a possible future fundamentally unlike the past.

Doll begins his sketch of the emerging post-modern framework drawing our attention to a fundamental contrast between open and closed systems. The eighteenth- and nineteenth-century closed system view of physical reality was one in which cause and effect worked exchanges in the machinery of the universe. This was a deterministic system in which the laws of connection and relation could be discovered and used to predict and control. It produced a similar view of social reality for the new social sciences and the field of educational research and scholarship that developed in the nineteenth and twentieth centuries. But more and more the model of biology, of organism as an open system, is replacing the closed system model of pre-twentieth-century physics as a way to frame our understanding of change in both the physical and social worlds. Even physics itself has changed.

Not necessarily linear, uniform, measured, and determined, the model of organic change is one of emergence and growth made possible by interaction, transaction, disequilibrium, and equilibration. Systems are self-regulating and capable of transformation in an environment of turbulence, dissipation, and even chaos. Gone is the certainty of laws and uniform relations. Now transformation, multiple interpretations, and alternative patterning become the basis for understanding and constructing meanings. Open-endedness is an essential feature of the post-modern framework.

Doll is a sensitive and sympathetic reader of a wide array of pre- and post-modern works. He helps them speak to each other and to us about this new way to think and to perceive the world and the role of the educator in it. Piaget, Bruner, Dewey, and Whitehead get extended special treatment by Doll as prescient post-moderns, but the list of major and minor philosophers and scientists Doll brings to bear on his project is encyclopedic. In this comprehensive work weaving the pre-modern, modern, and post-modern into a new vision of curriculum, he skillfully draws on the ideas of such thinkers as Plato and Aristotle; Descartes, Galileo, and Newton; Kuhn, Rorty, and Bernstein; Heisenberg, Gödel, and Einstein; Gadamer, Heidegger, Habermas, and Ricouer; Lyotard, Dobzansky, Prigogine, and Weiss; Chomsky, Skinner, and Gould; and such curriculum theorists as Bobbitt, Charters, Taylor, Kilpatrick, Rugg; Tyler, Pinar, Kliebard, and Schwab. Never used as ornament, each contributes some piece of the rich fabric Doll weaves to display the fundamental metaphors and assumptions we have created to deal with the natural and social worlds and the curriculum.

For example, take the educationally central concept of mind. Replacing the metaphors of mind as blank slate, black box, immaterial thing, and more recently, information processor, mind itself becomes the post-modernist's metaphor for human consciousness, purposiveness, thinking, creativity, whimsy, and cognitive playfulness. Mind is not a passive mirroring of nature, but the human ability to actively interpret and transform concepts in ways that make lived experiences meaningful and useful.

From this perspective, Doll envisions a post-modern curriculum that will allow human powers of creative organization and reorganization of experience to be operative in an environment that maintains a healthy tension between the need to find closure and the desire to explore. Such an open system will allow students and their teachers in conversation and dialogue to create more complex orders and structures of subject matter and ideas than is possible in the closed curriculum structures of today. The teacher's role will no longer be viewed as causal, but as transformative. Curriculum will not be the race course, but the journey itself. And learning will be an adventure in meaning making.

Doll offers his own vision of a curriculum utopia "where no one owns the truth and everyone has the right to be understood," where the teacher is a leader, but only as an equal member of a community of learners. Metaphors will be more useful than logic in generating dialogue in this community. There also will be a new conception of educative purpose, planning, and evaluation that is open-ended, flexible, and focused on process not product.

Doll characterizes his imagined curriculum as one of four R's. It will be *Rich, Recursive, Relational,* and *Rigorous.* Its richness will come from its openness and tentativeness. This will make a multitude of areas available for cooperative dialogic exploration. Recursiveness will be important because, like Bruner's concept of the spiral curriculum, a rich curriculum grows in richness and sophistication by reflecting back on itself and providing opportunities, in Dewey's sense, for the reflective reorganization, reconstruction, and transformation of experience. Relational refers to the continual search for relations between ideas and meanings and the taking into account of the relation between the historical and cultural context and the ways relations are perceived. And finally, rigor becomes the purposeful seeking of alternative relations and connections.

In essence, Doll offers a post-modernist, process-oriented vision of teaching and curriculum built from the base of a constructivist and experiential epistemology where we engage ourselves in a conversation with each other in the context of our collective history and seek meaning through alternative interpretations and transformations. In this book he ably demonstrates the power of historical reflection to illuminate our present position on the cusp of change, and he provides a powerful vision of what might be.

Jonas F. Soltis
Series Editor

Preface

This book had its inception in an exchange of ideas I participated in with Angela Frawley and Wells Foshay at the 1987 AERA meeting in Washington, D. C. There, I presented a paper on an "unstable curriculum," combining ideas drawn from Piaget, Prigogine, and Schön. Both Angela and Wells were so enthusiastic about my expanding these ideas into a book that I seriously considered such for the first time. Serendipitously, I was teaching in California at that time and had, just prior to AERA, attended David Griffin's Santa Barbara conference on "Toward a Post-Modern World." This was one of the most exciting conferences I have ever attended and one which gave me a framework for my ideas about instability and the curriculum. I am deeply indebted to David for introducing me to both post-modern and process thought; and especially for introducing me to his associates at Claremont, John Cobb and Mary Elizabeth Moore. Over the past years, I have spent many enjoyable hours in their company and at their process conferences. I regret that my version of post-modernism, with its interest in post-structuralism and hermeneutics, may not be to David's liking (he calls this branch "deconstructive"), but I am quite convinced that Whiteheadian process thought (which David calls "constructive" post-modernism) needs to negotiate passages between itself and deconstructive, post-structural thought. In espousing this union, I have been both encouraged and chastised by Malcolm Evans, a process educator and founder-factotum of the Association for Process Philosophy of Education. To David, John, Mary Elizabeth, and Malcolm I owe much. They have had a formative effect on my thinking.

Any book of this scope has a genetic lineage going back beyond its inception. Here that lineage lies in my graduate education at Johns Hopkins University, where I studied with John Steven Mann and John Walton. These two wonderful mentors introduced me to John Dewey, on whom I did my doctoral dissertation, and to the then emerging field of curriculum theory. Upon graduation I tentatively and cautiously called myself a curriculum theorist—hoping no one would ask what it was a curriculum theorist did.

Two decades of attending curriculum theory conferences—at Milwaukee, Rochester, Kent State, Airlie, and Bergamo—have shaped my thinking about both curriculum and the role of a curriculum theorist. Those long drives from upstate New York (when I was at SUNY-Oswego) to Airlie, VA., almost always taken with Jim Wood, helped me develop my interpretation of Jean Piaget. At Airlie I also came to grips with my own sense of rationalism, one I hope is more mythopoetic now than it was then. I remember well Jim MacDonald's constant admonition that my writing was "not mythopoetic enough." I have tried to correct some of that in this book.

It was at SUNY-Oswego, where I taught and administered for 15 years, that I labored with the biological as well as pedagogical writings of Jean Piaget. Here, too, I wrestled with Jerome Bruner's continually flitting focus, and was introduced to the writings of Ilya Prigogine and the whole new world of "dissipative structures." To Terry Lindenberg, Lio Garzone, Jim Seago, and Bob Sidwell I am appreciative of the many conversations we had on these topics. Jim Seago helped me see Piaget from a biologist's perspective; Bob Sidwell introduced me to Prigogine; Lio Garzone kindly and critically read much of what I wrote (including early drafts of chapters in this book); and Terry Lindenberg did all the above and more, having been a friend, critic, and counselor for almost a quarter-century. My heartfelt thanks to all my Oswego friends.

It was in Redlands California that I began the early drafts of this book. Here (while administering the teacher education program) was a good place to think about Whitehead, post-modernism, and process theology. The proximity to Claremont was useful and I traversed the I-10 frequently. Our own Curricular Colloquia brought a number of exciting speakers to campus. But most influential for me, as I tried to develop insights into just what was a post-modern pedagogy, were the comments and support given me by Sam Crowell and Yasuyuki Owada—each was painstaking in the time and attention given to my stuggles. Sam has seen many versions of this book over the years and always has been supportive and insightful. It was with him and our student Ron Scott that I began trying out some of the ideas I describe in the book, those involving elementary and middle school students working in mathematics.

In 1988 I moved from the University of Redlands to Louisiana State University. I made this move to count as colleagues the outstanding curriculum theorists Bill Pinar had then assembled. For a period of two or three years, LSU had, I believe, more outstanding curriculum theorists than any other department in the country. In addition to Bill I am most indebted to comments and criticism from Jacques Daignault, David Kirshner, Spencer Maxcy and from a host of marvelous graduate students who, under the rubric of "Friday Friends," critiqued the chapters in their many and varied forms. Through this process the book acquired, more and more, its own character and here, too, it acquired certain poststructural and hermeneutic qualities. The graduate students and their contributions are too numerous to name but the work of John St. Julien and Wen-Song Hwu must be mentioned. John has scrutinized the wording and the argumentation, especially that regarding self-organization. Wen-Song has been insistent in his demand I read Serres, not to mention Lyotard and other post-structuralists. I thank John and Wen-Song for their contributions; the book is stronger for their time and attention.

During the past years at LSU, the book has indeed had its labor pains—final decisions on what would be left in, on what would be the wording. The midwifing process of the book's birth belongs to the editors—Jonas Soltis, Brian Ellerbeck, and Neil Stillman. This trio has always been supportive, insightfully critical, and continually generous. Jonas was astute enough in the early versions, back in Redlands, to see (potential) order in the chaos I first presented and wise in assigning Brian to help me develop that order (it did not emerge spontaneously). Brian was truly amazing in his perceptive insights and so good in encouraging but not pressuring me over two years of rewrites. Neil has helped me argue my case for those pecularities of form I like—such as my addiction to dashes. To all three my thanks and admiration. Teachers College Press is a truly wonderful "house," and no author could ask for better editors.

I also am indebted to a variety of friends who encouraged the union between the ideas the book expresses and myself: Nel Noddings, Elaine Atkins, Hugh Munby, Donald Oliver, Chet Bowers, Alex Molnar, Ted Aoki, Daiyo Sawada (who encouraged my telling of stories), Noel Gough, Bill Schubert, Roger and Alexandra Pierce, and Frances Klein to name but a few. I am far more indebted to them than they know.

Finally, I come to the two people, both women, who have shared with me virtually all the joy and pain which comes with birth. Jeanne Robertson, my graduate assistant for the past three years, has not only read every word and looked at every comma but has checked every quote and every reference. Her work goes well beyond that expected of a doctoral student. My wife, Mary, needs no introduction; a Beckettian scholar in her own right, she is as much a fixture at Bergamo curriculum conferences as I am. Whatever interesting features and phrasings the book has are due to her delicate and deft hand. I have loved her for over 25 years and in that love I have grown to admire her skills as a scholar, teacher, counselor, and fashioner of phrases.

With all the foregoing help, the book should come into this world healthy and vigorous. That judgement, of course, the reader will have to make. But definitely the book would not have been born without such help. I thank all those mentioned and hope they will not be disappointed in that to which I have given birth.

Introduction

CHANGING PARADIGMS

> To the question . . . What Knowledge is of most worth?—the uniform
> reply is—Science. This is the verdict on all counts.
> For direct self-preservation . . . Science.
> For gaining a livelihood . . . Science.
> For parental functions . . . Science.
> For good citizenship . . . Science.
> For the enjoyment of art . . . Science.
> For purposes of discipline . . . Science.
> Science . . . is the best preparation for all these orders of activity.
> —Spencer, *Education: Intellectual, Moral, and Physical,*
> 1859/1929, pp. 84–85

Herbert Spencer asked and answered this question in the year Charles
Darwin first published his *Origin of the Species* and the year John Dewey
was born. Spencer's answer, Science, Science, Science, not merely reflects the tenor of the times but also mirrors the foundation on which
the modernist paradigm has been built, a paradigm that framed American intellectual, social, and educational thought during the first seven
or eight decades of this century. Science is one of the dominant obses-
sions we have had as a people. Productively it has made America a
leader among the world's industrial nations; socially it has framed for
us the dream of a more leisurely life where machines replace people in
doing the drudgery of daily living; intellectually its methods have dominated areas well beyond its own domain—areas of philosophy, psychology, and educational theory. Science of this Spencerian type—a
modernist adaptation of Isaac Newton's empiricism and René Descartes'
rationalism—has become for the social sciences, and hence for education and curriculum, a paradigm. In Thomas Kuhn's (1970) terms, a paradigm controls the "methods, problems, and standards" (p. 48) a community uses as well as the broader "constellation of beliefs, values,
techniques" (p. 175) it cherishes. Modern science, originating with

Nicolaus Copernicus and Galileo Galilei and culminating with Albert Einstein, Neils Bohr, and Werner Heisenberg, has done just this. It has performed the task of control so well and so effectively that during this century science has expanded from a discipline or a procedure into a dogma, "mushrooming its methods into a metaphysic," hence creating *scientism* (Smith, 1982, p. 110).

Such *adoration of science*, its deification, probably reached its height of influence in the early 1960s, shortly after Sputnik and just at the beginning of the curriculum reform movement. The Fall 1963 issue of *Daedalus* praises science and its methodology—in the form of professionalism and expert knowledge—as "characteristic of the modern world as the crafts were of the ancient" (p. 649). At this time it was believed that professional, scientific knowledge would help us compete with the Russians in space, defeat the communists in Vietnam, eliminate poverty and improve health care at home, and increase the knowledge base of young people. Teaching machines, programmed learning, and a teacher-proof curriculum were the wave of the future, the road to social salvation. Donald Schön (1983) labels the thinking that underlies this "scientistic" view as "technical rationality." Here reason is bounded by and defined in terms of scientific technology. This type of knowing has made science truly the knowledge of most worth. One of its greatest contemporary achievements was placing a man on the moon in the late 1960s; one of its greatest failures was the loss of human life in the dramatic and tragic explosion of the Challenger shuttle two decades later.

In the intervening years, America began a disenchantment with technical rationality and the view of science it expounds—technical expertise did not win the war against communism (it collapsed of its own ineptitude), hunger, or drugs. Nor can technical rationality balance the federal budget, hold down inflation, or maintain our leadership as the world's premier nation. In the arts, literature, and philosophy, new voices and visions are being heard: voices and visions not based on Cartesian or Newtonian assumptions (Nielsen, 1991; Schmittau, 1991). Even in the sciences, a newness is emerging. The indeterminancy and relativism of quantum physics are finally having an effect beyond their own confines (Briggs & Peat, 1984). The rigid formalism of the modern paradigm is being challenged by the eclectic pastiche of a post-modern one (Jencks, 1987).

Today, in the last decade of this century and millennium, we are in the midst of forming this new paradigm. Hans Küng (1988) calls postmodernism[1] a "megaparadigm" to indicate the breadth of its epochal sweep. Not only has this paradigm spawned a "new" physics, chemistry, and biology, it has also brought forth calls for a new metaphysics, epistemology, and cosmology (Davies, 1984, 1988; Kitchener, 1986, 1988). In mathematics, chaos theory has burgeoned into the science of complexity (Briggs & Peat, 1989; Gleick, 1987; Pagels, 1988). In the humanities, especially in the arts and political theory, a strong debate has been waged for a number of years over the nature and stature of the post-modern (Foster, 1983; *Genre*, 1987; Jameson, 1991; *New German Critique*, 1981, 1984). While virtually all literary and social theorists agree with Jürgen Habermas (1983) that "modernism . . . is dead," (p. 6), having exhausted itself, no consensus has emerged on the condition or project replacing modernism. Indeed, maybe no one, all-encompassing project or vision will hold our attention in the next century as Enlightenment rationality has held it in the past two.

The implications of a post-modern perspective for education and curriculum are enormous but by no means clear. How the sweeping changes affecting art, literature, mathematics, philosophy, political theory, science, and theology—changes questioning the basic epistemological and metaphysical assumptions in those fields—will play themselves out in education and curriculum is yet unknown. I venture to propose, though, that the changes in these other disciplines are so great—so megaparadigmatic—that education, as the confluence of many disciplines, will also be affected. If this proposition "materializes" (a modernist word and concept), I believe a new sense of educational order will emerge, as well as new relations between teachers and students, culminating in a new concept of curriculum. The linear, sequential, easily quantifiable ordering system dominating education today— one focusing on clear beginnings and definite endings—could give way to a more complex, pluralistic, unpredictable system or network. Such a complex network will, like life itself, always be in transition, in process. A network in process is a transformative network, continually emerging—one moving beyond stability to tap the creative powers inherent in instability. In such a transformative network, prediction and control, key elements within the modernist curriculum model, become less "ordered" and more "fuzzy." Really what happens is that a whole new sense of order emerges: not the symmetrical, simple, sequential order classical science borrowed from medieval thought, but an asymmetrical, chaotic, fractal order we are now beginning to discover in the post-modern sciences. Needless to say, this gives science itself a whole new cast, moving it from its premier position within a closed system where its methodology dominated, to a more equitable position among many methodologies in an open system.

When this new and subtler form of order comes to schooling, the relations between teachers and students will change drastically. These relations will exemplify less the knowing teacher informing unknowing students, and more a group of individuals interacting together in the mutual exploration of relevant issues. As Donald Schön (1983) says, in this frame, students may well "suspend disbelief" in the teacher's authority, remaining open to the teacher's "competence as it emerges" through actions and interactions. The teacher, reciprocally, will be "readily confrontable by students" and will work with the students to probe the tacit understandings both teacher and students possess (pp. 296–297). In such a frame,[2] traditional methods of evaluation and assessment become irrelevant; authority shifts from an external beyond to a communal and dialogic here. The *quality* of the questioning as well as the appropriateness of the answer will need to be assessed; in fact, the former—not easily quantifiable—will frame the latter. Finally, curriculum will be viewed not as a set, a priori "course to be run," but as a passage of personal transformation. This change of focus and subject will place more emphasis on the runner running and on the patterns emerging as many runners run, and less emphasis on the course run, although neither the runners nor the course can be dichotomously split. Organization and transformation will emerge from the activity itself, not be set prior to the activity. This point is one John Dewey and Jean Piaget made continually, in their long and productive careers. Unfortunately, their words fell on deaf, modernist ears.

The foregoing comments about curriculum and its methods seem strange, even absurd, within a modernist paradigm. However, this paradigm is historical—the product of a particular, Enlightenment-oriented, Western mind-set—developed over the past three to four hundred years (Toulmin, 1990). From the vantage point of the newly emerging, post-modern mind-set, these curricular concepts seem quite natural, even normal.

Before outlining the book and the ways I intend to deal with the curriculum implications inherent in this new paradigm, I would like to make some distinctions between modernism and post-modernism. Assessing the former is prerequisite for understanding the latter.

MODERNISM AND POST-MODERNISM

We must reconcile ourselves to . . . the thought that *we no longer live in the "modern" world*. The "modern" world is now a thing of the past. . . . [Our post-modern world] has not yet discovered how to define itself in terms of what it *is*, but only in terms of what it has *just-now-ceased to be*. In due course, the change from modern to post-

modern science will evidently be matched by corresponding change
in philosophy and theology also.
                              —Toulmin, *Return to Cosmology,* 1982, p. 254

Stephen Toulmin makes two points here that are important to his, and
my, view of the post-modern condition. The first is that it is impossible
to give one overarching definition of post-modernism: The movement
is too new to define itself and too varied and dichotomous for any one
branch to be representative. Indeed post-modern thought has pervaded
the arts, humanities, literature, management, mathematics, philosophy,
science, the social sciences, and theology. The term has even become an
"in" word in popular culture, and pervades our society—often in contradictory ways. Toulmin's second point is that science will be the key
discipline around which the post-modern paradigm will eventually develop. In making this latter statement, of course, Toulmin is positing
contemporary science imbued with creativity and indeterminism, not
Newtonian or Laplacean science imbued with discovery and determinism. Toulmin thinks of science as open and transformative, not as closed
and predictable—a position he has only recently come to develop (1982,
Introduction).
    David Griffin, in his series on post-modern thought, (1988a, 1988b,
1989, 1990; Griffin, Beardslee, & Holland, 1989; Griffin & Smith, 1989),
acknowledges his indebtedness to Toulmin (1988a, p. 31) and places
scientific-theological dialogue under the rubric of *constructive* post-
modern thought. This thought unites that which Descartes rent asun-
der. As one of Griffin's former students has said, post-modern thought
"represents a critical reappraisal of modern modes of thought"; it calls
into question "the rigid dichotomies modernity has created between objective reality and subjective experience, fact and imagination, secular
and sacred, public and private"; it is an intellectual and moral reaction
against "the Cartesian straightjacket we have imposed" on ourselves
(Waters, 1986, p. 113). While this definition is designed to apply only to
Griffin's constructivist mode, not to his deconstructive post-modern category—that emanating from continental aesthetic, literary, and political theory—it is as good a general working definition as I have found.
I believe it fits the aesthetic, literary, and political forms of post-
modernism as well as the scientific, philosophical, and theological.
    Griffin (1988a) uses the term *deconstructive* in a pejorative sense, re-
ferring to that branch of post-modernism which "deconstructs or elimi-
nates . . . God, self, purpose, meaning, a real world, and truth as correspondence" (p. x). While this branch of post-modernism can be so
viewed—helping explain the vituperative and acrimonious debates be-

tween some modernists and post-modernists—I prefer to say that continental literary and philosophical theory transforms, but does not eliminate, God, self, purpose, meaning, reality, and truth. In fact, if we must dichotomize post-modernism—as we presently do in a modernist, Cartesian manner—I choose to do so along the lines of C. P. Snow, in his *The Two Cultures* (1964). Here the scientific and aesthetic communities exist side by side, neither superior to the other (although the *literati* have pretentions along these lines) but each having different histories and methodologies. From my view these two trends in post-modernism complement one another. Indeed, a curriculum that is creative and transformative must combine the scientific with the aesthetic; eclecticism is one feature that makes post-modernism such an exciting movement. In fact, as Katherine Hayles (1990, Ch. 10) suggests, we may do well to talk of post-modernisms, not of the post-modern.

Daniel Bell (1976, 1980) helps us understand some of the bitter animosity aesthetic post-modernism has created in its rebellion against the formalities of modernity. Bell (1976) traces the roots of modernity back to Newton and Enlightenment thought, where there "was a fundamental cosmological picture of the world . . . [with] a beginning, middle, and an end" (p. 109). The scientific cosmology of Newton provided "faith in the homogeneity of the universe and its systemic, rational order." This world view and the "contradictions" it spawned held sway for over three hundred years. One of these contradictions was the rise of the avant-garde: a deliberate attempt to fight against the norms of modernity, particularly in its bourgeois form. In the late nineteenth and early twentieth centuries, from the struggle between dominant bourgeois values and those of the radical avant-garde—a struggle the avant-garde "continually waged but never won"—modernity achieved its greatest artistic and literary triumphs. Harry Levin (1960/1966), writing on "What Was Modernism?," says that in the fifty-year period 1890–1940, modernism produced "the most remarkable constellation of genius in the history of the West" (p. 284). World War II changed all that; after the war there occurred a collapse of the intellectual, social, and moral standards that had sustained the bourgeoisie and provided a foil for the avant-garde. Nowadays, Bell (1976) says, "there is no longer an avant-garde, because no one . . . is on the side of order and tradition. There exists only a desire for the new" (p. 53). There is no longer a counterculture. In a sense, the avant-garde has won, thus eliminating not only bourgeois values but itself as well. We are now left with only a "psychedelic bazaar"—Bell's term for the pastiche he sees comprising post-modern art, architecture, literature, and culture.

Jürgen Habermas (1981) does not share Bell's neo-conservative call for a return to bourgeois values and views. But he agrees with Bell that modernity has exhausted itself—not so much in its avant-garde excesses as in its bureaucratization, which segregates life into components and removes it from "the hermeneutics of everyday conversation" (p. 9). In this sense "modernism is . . . dead"—it has little more to offer in its present form. Habermas, though, still believes in modernity's project: a better future for all members of society based on a specialized knowledge gleaned most particularly from science. And he believes the traditions of culture, including philosophy and art as well as science, can still play an important role in this unfulfilled project, if we can relink "modern culture with an everyday praxis" in a dialogic manner (p. 13). To make such a relinking will require limits on capitalism with its autonomous greed, on professionalism with its technical expertise, and on bureaucratization with its autonomous and segmented compartments. These are major shifts, ones Habermas does not see occurring soon or easily. However, he feels this alternative must be put forth lest modernity slip into the neo-conservative trends of antimodernity without so much as a whimper.

Jean-Francois Lyotard in *The Postmodern Condition* (1984) is wary of Habermas' desire to finish the unfulfilled project of modernity. Lyotard believes Habermas is really creating a "metadiscourse" based on an "explicit appeal to some grand narrative," and postmodernism should be incredulous toward any such attempt (p. xxiii). Such grand designs are, of course, the essence of Western philosophy from Plato through the nineteenth century, with particular contributions made by German philosophers. In Habermas' plan, Lyotard sees but another Germanic attempt to ground thought in "transcendental, ahistorical, universal principles" (Peters, 1989, p. 99). This attempt is just what post-modern thought challenges.

While I agree with Lyotard that post-modernism does have a healthy and needed "incredulity toward metanarratives" (p. xxiv)—dealing instead with particulars as particulars—I believe he has overlooked the potential power, in Habermas' dialogic conversation, of transforming both the participants and that being discussed. This open, interactive, communal conversation is key to a post-modern curriculum; it is the process by which transformations take place. Such a conversation need not be a screen for a grand metanarrative.

Charles Jencks (1987), art historian, believes that Bell, Habermas, and Lyotard in their debate are really focusing on extreme forms of modernism, not on post-modernism. Thus, he labels what they are describing as ultra, high, late, or arch modernism but not post-modernism (p. 32). This "confusion" is not a mere semantic difference; it represents "a difference of values and philosophy" (p. 34). For Jencks, post-modernism, as the hyphen indicates, looks to the past at the same time it transcends the past. This means the new is built, often literally, on the old. In this complex relationship, the future is not so much a break with, or antithesis to, the past as it is a transformation of it. Post-modern art and architecture are thus "double-coded" or Janus-faced, indicating a present entwined with its past and future.

A second feature of post-modernism is its eclectic nature. As Jencks (1987) says,

> Pluralism is the "ism" of our time. . . . [We must] choose and combine traditions selectively . . . *eclect* those aspects from past and present which appear most relevant for the job at hand. (p. 7)

When we are successful in this pragmatic task of choosing and combining, we produce "a striking synthesis of traditions"; we continue the tradition of the modern while at the same time transcending it. When we are unsuccessful, our eclectic mixture becomes a pastiche, in Bell's words, a "psychedelic bazaar." *Which outcome occurs depends on the choices we make.* Educationally, we need to be trained in the art of creating and choosing, not just in ordering and following. Much of our curriculum to date has trained us to be passive receivers of preordained "truths," not active creators of knowledge.

A third feature of the post-modern as Jencks sees it is the concept of multilayers of interpretation. His word is "double-coding." The post-modern looks to the past in order to code past remnants within a future vision. What one sees in a post-modern framework, thus, is a curious mix of two codes within one structural matrix. This matrix is, at once, paradoxical, dialectical, and challenging: a play of ideas. By choosing and combining traditions, Jencks says the post-modern is a deliberate mix that plays with such modernist principles as "history," "truth," and "consistency" as a way of demonstrating that abstract principles are only that—abstractions—selected or chosen (in a partly random, partly historical manner) to provide an "imaginative transformation of a shared symbolic system" (p. 38). Thus, our creations and our curricula should be multifaceted, mixing the technological with the human, the proven with the innovative, and the serious with the playful. Irony and parody need to infuse our work, lest we become so wedded to any one tradition or narrative that we deify it. This is what the Marquis de La place did to Newton's ideas, what the followers of Marx did, what the social scientists did to the doctrines of the natural sciences, and what the Tyler rationale did to the simple task of setting goals.

Figure I.1 The "Ruins in the Garden," the parking garage of the Neue Staatsgalerie in Stuttgart, Germany. Designed by James Stirling, it is an outstanding example of post-modern architecture.

Jencks chooses the Neue Staatsgalerie in Stuttgart, Germany (1977–1984) by James Stirling and Associates as a prime example illustrating these multivariate, post-modern qualities (see Figure I.1). Here an "Acropolis" sits on a base, high above the traffic. However, this Acropolis "holds a very real and necessary parking garage, one that is indicated by stones which have 'fallen' like ruins, to the ground" (p. 16). These holes in the wall have the essential "double code": On the one

Figure I.2   A second view of the Neue Staatsgalerie, showing the "Acropolis" above the garage.

hand they evoke memories of the classical; on the other they reveal steel construction and pipes for ventilation. Thus, Stirling's Acropolis says, "I am beautiful" just like the Acropolis in Greece, but I am "also based on concrete technology and deceit" (p. 19).

Modern architects like Charles-Edouard Jeanneret (LeCorbusier) or Mies van der Rohe would never have allowed functionalism to be combined with playful deceit. That would have violated "truth to materials," "logical consistency," "straightforwardness," "simplicity" (p. 19). Yet all these are present in the Neue Staatsgalerie, but with an ironic, self-mocking twist. The elders of the city like the noble past and classical lines the museum evokes (see Figure I.2),while the youth of Stuttgart love the handrails of blue and red (Figure I.3), which fit with their day-glo hairstyles. "This is a very popular building with young and old," says Jencks. "I found their different perspectives were accommodated and stretched" (p. 19). One of the educational challenges in the post-modern mode is to design a curriculum that both *accommodates and stretches;* a curriculum that (combining terms and concepts from both Kuhn and Piaget) has the essential tension between disequilibrium and equilibrium so that a new, more comprehensive and transformative re-equilibration emerges.

Figure I.3   A side view of the entrance to the Neue Staatsgalerie

ORGANIZATION OF THE BOOK

Although the element of spontaneity exists in teaching, effective
teaching is a result of a systematic, scientific approach. The class activities for the day must be planned, identified, and evaluated. This process insures sequential mastery of your objective.
          —*Faculty Handbook*, 1986, Jurcipa, California School District

This modernist interpretation of what constitutes curriculum planning
juxtaposed with the previously given Toulmin quotation on the demise
of modernism illustrates one of the main themes of this book. Modernism as an all-encompassing intellectual movement has outlived its use-
fulness, yet it lives on as *a*, if not *the*, force in curriculum practice. We
are in a new stage of intellectual, political, social development. It is time
to do more than re-form our methods and practices. It is time to question the modernist assumptions on which these methods and practices
are based and to develop a new perspective that simultaneously rejects,
transforms, and preserves that which has been.

This book has three foci. The first is recognition that we are on the
cusp of changing paradigms, not merely in the sciences but in the humanities as well. This paradigm change appears to be a megaparadigm
change, one bringing about new ideas in cosmology, epistemology,

metaphysics. While not all of post-modernism's ideas will be studied in this book, my intent is to present enough of them and with sufficient intellectual grounding that the reader will be able to generate individual, heuristic curriculum insights. In doing this, I will follow the lead of David Griffin and Stephen Toulmin and draw mostly on scientific-theological-ecological trends, not on aesthetic-literary-political ones. Partly this choice is one of preference: I know the disciplines of science and mathematics far better than I know those of art, architecture, and literary or political criticism. Partly the choice is practical: The history of the American school curriculum has been shaped by its modernist view of science more than by any other factor. What led us into a modernist curriculum may well lead us out. Finally, the choice is intentional: I agree with Toulmin that it will be a new version of science—more complex, indeterminate, and interactive than the classical version—that will dominate and be generative in this new paradigm. Here I believe the concepts of self-organization, dissipative structures, ecological balance, punctuated evolution, and complexity theory will prove heuristic in designing post-modern curricula. I hope that in looking to science from a post-modern perspective I will not commit the error past curricularists have made—that of deifying science and its methodology. Toward this end I will not use Auguste Comte's reductionist hierarchy of disciplines, with mathematics and physics acting as the foundation of all thought. Instead, I will look to each science as an entity in its own right. Nor will I look to philosophy, science's brother in the modernist tradition, as *the frame* for all analysis, as Immanuel Kant and his followers did. Rather, I will look upon philosophy as an "edifying" discipline in the tradition of Richard Rorty (1980), a discipline that can help us with our practical, situational problems. Finally, I will draw on continental thought—hermeneutic and phenomenological—to help establish a sense of community, dialogue, historical interpretation, and exploration of paradox, all of which I consider important to post-modern thought. In short, as a post-modernist, I will draw on and intermix a variety of contemporary movements.

The second focus of the book is the metaphorical application of post-modern characteristics to the curriculum. As an intellectual movement, post-modernism has revolutionized such fields as art, architecture, literary theory, management, mathematics, music, philosophy, political theory, the sciences, and theology. While none of these fields or disciplines should be used as a model for curricular development—an error of imitation curricularists have continually made—a look at assumptions and methods in these fields could well be heuristic for curriculum theorists and designers. Curriculum is its own field; as Herbert

Kliebard, David Tyack, and other historians have noted, it has its own story—one that is now being told. But lying at the heart of education (itself a crossroads for many other disciplines) curriculum is influenced by these other disciplines and can learn much from them. There is a need to study other disciplines and to abstract, metaphorically not literally, those ideas and ideals which have pedagogical potential.

In doing this I will consciously attempt to use language different from the "machine and productivity" language that now dominates curriculum discourse. Currently, we "gear up" for tasks, keep classes "on-track," and "produce results." So pervasive and controlling is this language that we have never really understood the meaning or implications of Jean Piaget's statement that "life is essentially autoregulation" (1971b, p. 26) or John Dewey's that "the educational process has no end beyond itself" (1916/1966, p. 50). Neither fits easily within a mechanistic mode; each comes from an organic frame, more biological than physical.

In the same vein, I will also make a conscious attempt to define curriculum not in terms of content or materials (a "course-to-be-run"), but in terms of process—a process of development, dialogue, inquiry, transformation. Such use is consistent with William Pinar's (1975) adopting the infinitive form of curriculum, *currere*, to emphasize the person and process of "running" the course, the experience an individual undergoes in learning, in transforming and being transformed. Such a view includes both content and process, with the content embedded within the process, forming part of it. This integration goes beyond the traditional curriculum–supervision split, which is too ends–means sequenced: ends chosen first, then means adapted or adjusted to those ends. In defining curriculum in terms of process, I am thinking more of Hans-Georg Gadamer's "conversation" or John Dewey's ends–means integration—neither supplanting the other, each needing the other. As self can, indeed must, be defined in terms of "other" (Bruner, 1990), so content must be defined in terms of process. The post-modern view of curriculum I will develop is one that moves beyond a spectator epistemology, beyond a process–product, subjective–objective split.

The third focus is on a reinterpretation of the writings of John Dewey, Jean Piaget, and Jerome Bruner, as these bear on education and curriculum. While I would not call any of these theorists post-modern, with the possible exception of Bruner and his work on both the "New Look" in perception and the narrative mode in thought, I will argue their educational views are better understood from a post-modern than a modern perspective. Dewey's concepts of experience and transaction, Piaget's of development and reequilibration, and Bruner's of learning and thought blossom more fully and richly in a post-modern milieu.

The book itself is partitioned into seven chapters apportioned among three parts: The first part focuses on the closed vision of the modernist paradigm; Part II examines the open vision of the post-modernist paradigm; and the third part explores the educational vision of building a post-modern curriculum matrix—one without "tops" or "bottoms," with no beginnings (in a foundational sense) and no endings (in a terminal sense). The distinction between closed and open systems is a viable one for describing the curricular differences between modern and post-modern thought. Prigogine (1961) defines thermodynamic closed systems as those which "exchange energy but no matter"—for example, water wheels or gears—while open systems "exchange both matter and energy"—for example, atomic reactors (p. 3). Prigogine is saying here that there are qualitative differences between closed and open systems. In closed systems, which are usually mechanical in nature, only exchanges take place; there are no transformations. Exchange (not transformation) is and has been a powerful curricular metaphor. In closed systems, stability, centers-of-balance, and equilibrium are key ingredients. These systems have centers. Open systems, on the other hand, have moving vortices or spiraling swirls and are by nature transformative; *change not stability is their essence.*[3] They are living, not inert, and are represented usually by organic, not physical, models. Growth, not stasis, is their defining feature; directionality, not centering, is their primary concern. By their nature, open systems need challenges, perturbations, disruptions—these are the *sine qua non* of the transformative process. Without them the process would not function. In Piaget's (1977b) model disequilibrium disturbs equilibrium in order to create re-equilibration: a new equilibrium organized at a higher level. "However the nonbalance arises, it produces the driving force of development. . . . Without the nonbalance there would not be 'increasing re-equilibration'" (p. 13).

Obviously, mistakes, disruptions, perturbations are looked at differently in these two systems. Closed systems, being centered, stable, and looping back on themselves, in a mechanistic, cause–effect, "negative" (equilibrium seeking) way, find disruptive qualities too decentering. Curricularly, these disruptive qualities take time from "the task at hand" and create "noise," which the system wishes to overcome or eliminate as quickly as possible. The current curriculum syndrome of setting goals, planning implementations, and evaluating results fits well within a closed systems model. Contrarily, open systems *require* disruptions, mistakes, and perturbations—these are the "chaotic mess" to be transformed. The system works via dissipation, iteration, and "positive" feedback that amplifies (Briggs & Peat, 1989, pp. 25–26). Curriculum goals here need be neither precise nor pre-set: They should be general and generative, allowing for and encouraging creative, interactive transformations. Their evaluation frame will not be in terms of deviations from a norm or standard—a deficit concept—but in terms of the quality of that generated—a heuristic but less easily measured concept. Regretfully, measurement as we know it in curriculum assumes a closed system, and "working away" from a pre-set ideal carries with it a sense of negation and failure. Even the A − or 90 is less than or "away from" the ideal.

The primary challenge in open systems is not to bring process to closure (to produce a "perfect" product) but to direct the transformations in such a manner that the becomingness of process is maintained. Every closure in this frame is a new beginning, and every new beginning is connected historically with its past. In Dewey's terms, every end is a "turning point," in the ongoing process of organizing activity and hence of meaning-making. Obviously, such a curriculum is teacher-dependent not teacher-proof, and its defining characteristic is a sense of movement or process. The quality of this movement and the uniqueness of its features is one of the themes running throughout the book. Here the teacher's planning and pedagogy—as Max van Manen (1988, 1991) uses this latter term—must be done in a reflective, interactive way. Pre-set plans can be only general guidelines, "fuzzy" by intent, not particulars to be implemented or followed.

The first part of the book has two chapters: one on the assumptions underlying Cartesian and Newtonian thinking, another on the carryover of these assumptions into twentieth-century American curriculum thought and practice from Franklin Bobbitt through Ralph Tyler. The second part analyzes aspects of the post-modern paradigm as this paradigm is developing in the fields of biology, chemistry, mathematical chaos theory, the cognitive revolution, and process thought. Chapter Three analyzes recent developments in biology, particularly organizational or hierarchy theory, and uses this theory as a basis for re-examining Jean Piaget's curricular recommendations and his equilibrium–disequilibrium–reequilibration model of development. Chapter Four carries forward this concept of organization into both Ilya Prigogine's thermodynamic, dissipative structures and mathematical chaos theory. Chapter Five describes the recent cognitive revolution, against the background of the demise of behaviorism, and explores a new epistemology—a hermeneutical, experiential, constructivist epistemology. Here, Jerome Bruner's curriculum ideas are reassessed, particularly those involving active meaning-making, the toleration of ambiguity, and development of the narrative mode of thought. Chapter Six focuses on recent and past works in process thought, notably those of John Dewey and Alfred North Whitehead, and on how these works connect with the hermeneutic tradition as outlined by Jürgen Habermas and Hans-Georg Gadamer.

The third part focuses on curricular practicality through a post-modern vision, especially as I interpret this vision in light of my own teaching in the schools and my reading of Joseph Schwab's "The Practical." Both Schwab's reflections and my experiences will be integrated into the concept of "emergence"—complexes growing naturally out of simples—which is, itself, now emerging from the "new" physical and natural sciences. I will also attempt here a set of curricular criteria alternative to the ones Ralph Tyler developed for modernist pedagogy.

Throughout my writing on the post-modern, I will speak of curricular possibilities in terms of a vision, not a model. There is no all-encompassing post-modern model; in fact, such a concept violates the openness of post-modernism's emphasis on each practitioner being a curriculum creator and developer, not just an implementor. If curriculum is truly a collaborative effort and transformative process, then "creator" and "developer" are far better descriptors than "implementor" for discussing what a post-modern teacher does.

We must all begin where we are, and so mathematics (and sometimes science) will be my entrée into post-modern curriculum practice—my pedagogic practicality. I hope, though, this book is written heuristically enough that other reflective practitioners will be able to use their own pedagogic practicalities to develop their curriculum matrices—ones applicable to their own fields. Such development is a challenge the book presents to the reader, one the reader must meet individually, yet in dialogue—with self, with others.

NOTES

1. Authors differ in their use of the hyphen with the word post-modern. I prefer the hyphen—to show connection with and transcendence of modernity—but in discussing a particular author will adopt the form chosen by that author.

2. I will use the concept of frame frequently to express a sort of mini-paradigm, personal yet situational. Donald Schön (1983) says frames "bound the phenomena" to which individuals pay attention. As such, frames are "ways in which individuals *construct* the reality in which they function" (pp. 309–310). Jacques Derrida says frames separate *what is* from *what is not*. Frames are

The decisive structure of what is at stake; [they lie] at the invisible limit between the interiority of meaning . . . *and* all the empiricisms of the extrinsic which [by their nature] miss the question completely. (*La Verité en Peinture*, 1978, p. 61. My interpretation of a personal translation by Denise Kuehne)

3. Technically, open systems do have stability: a complex stability which occurs across and through change. Chapters Three and Four will explain this nonstatic or nonequilibrium stability in some detail.

Part I

THE MODERN PARADIGM:
A CLOSED VISION

Using science, particularly physics and astronomy, as an organizing frame, it is possible to categorize the history of Western thought into three megaparadigms: pre-modern, modern, and post-modern. In this frame, the pre-modern covers the span of time from recorded Western history to the scientific and industrial revolutions of the seventeenth and eighteenth centuries. In this long duration, many smaller paradigms existed: primitive, Greek, Christian, medieval, Renaissance, Humanist. Different as these paradigms were, they all shared one distinguishing feature: a cosmological harmony that included an ecological, epistemological, and metaphysical sense of balance or proportion. A good deal of this existed and still exists in primitive societies, as writers like Gregory Bateson and Huston Smith remind us. However, it is also true that such a world-view permeated Greek and Western thought until the time of Galileo and Descartes. In this view, one worked with and in nature. While Plato and Aristotle separated qualities such as ideas from objects, they still believed that each category or quality needed the other. Justice for Plato was a sense of balance or proportion, and for Aristotle virtue consisted of the mean between the excesses of extremes. In general, the Greeks developed an epistemology, a metaphysics, and a cosmology[1] where qualities such as good/evil, up/down, light/dark, hot/cold could be conceived and defined only in terms of the union of these opposites. Reality and personal existence were made up of the struggle or balance between these opposites. In the ancient Greek myths, Odysseus was heroically successful as he was able to maintain a proper balance between these opposites; Oedipus was tragically unsuccessful as he was unable to maintain this balance. Phenomenologically, the Greeks viewed the educated person as one who possessed the wisdom harmony brings: one in tune with the universe and its forces. Four was considered the perfect number because it represented, in its geometric form as a square, the balance of sides and angles.

During the sixteenth and seventeenth centuries, this cosmology came to an end; it was slowly replaced by a new mathematical and mechanistic cosmology—a scientific one—begun by men like Nicolaus Copernicus, Tycho Brahe, Johann Kepler, and Galileo Galilei. All these men were mathematicians, and in the simple, ordered beauty they found in the mathematics of the time, they thought they were also discovering Nature's order—its Natural Laws. Galileo likened the universe to a grand book, "which stands continually open to our gaze." But we cannot understand this book until we first "comprehend the language and read the letters in which it is composed. *It is written in the language of mathematics,* and its characters are triangles, circles, and other geometric figures" (*Le Opere di Galileo Galilei* (Tomo IV), 1844, p. 171; personal translation, emphasis added). In short, Galileo saw mathematics as the alphabet God used in writing Nature's Laws.

Beginning in the late seventeenth century, Newton brought this new cosmology to its fullest fruition, expressed best in the final edition of his *Philosophia Naturalis Principia Mathematica* (1729/1962)—usually referred to by the simple but sweeping title, *Principia.* Chief among these "Principles" was that one of them, gravity, determined both the orbit of the planets around the sun and the falling of an apple to earth. This principle applied to the whole universe, uniformly—as Newton and both his predecessors and followers expected. Further, this principle could be expressed in one, simple mathematical formula:

$F = G \dfrac{Mm}{r^2}$, or gravity equals the multiplication of the objects' two

masses, divided by the square of the distance between them (commonly labeled r). This formula showed, Newton believed, that all Nature was consonant, "conformable to Herself and simple" (1730/1952, p. 397). It was the formula Newton's friend, Edmund Halley, used to predict the return of the comet that now bears his name. In fact, Halley was instrumental in having Newton write his *Principia* and underwrote the funding of the first printing.

Writing a century later, Pierre Simon, Marquis de Laplace, believed this conformity to be so great that in his own *Celestial Mechanics* (1799–1805/1966) he had no need of Newton's "God hypothesis" to explain the mechanical workings of the universe—mathematics would do it all. However, he did accede that Newton was "the most fortunate" of men who ever lived "in as much as there is but one universe, and it can happen to but one man in the world's history to be the interpreter of its laws" (In Burtt, 1932/1955, p. 31). With this presumed discovery of Nature's order, those scientists, philosophers, and other intellectuals following Newton (and before him Descartes and Galileo) adopted a new vision. In this vision, humankind was not to supplicate itself to Nature through ritual or prayer, nor to work in harmony with Nature. The discovery of Nature's Laws gave humanity (some will say men—Merchant, 1983) control over Nature. Adopting Galileo's sense of experimentation, Descartes' method of right reason, and Newton's principles, it was now seen as possible to bend, first Nature and then other people, to the will of those experts who knew what should be. Sociology and psychology were born in the aftermath of this vision, and the "scientific method" took on a mystical aura.

Such eighteenth-century social visionaries as Pierre Laplace, Claude Henri de Rouvroy (Comte de Saint-Simon), and Auguste Comte saw a new age aborning—an industrial, technocratic age. They believed that wealth would now be created not by war and plunder but by industrial production. A new breed of men would arise, "engineers, builders, planners," and these technocrats would not only follow Nature's Laws but actually improve them, as breeders were doing with plant genetics. No longer was the vision one of working in moderation with Nature; it was now that of civilizing nature, improving it. Progress and perfection seemed possible, even inevitable.

At one level this modern paradigm represented an open, not a closed, vision. Progress, perfecting, and continual material improvement in the lives of all were held out—in the Enlightenment and Industrial visions—as reachable goals. The vehicles for reaching these goals were Descartes' methodology and Newton's principles, particularly his sense of simple order. But at a deeper level, the vision was a closed one. Descartes' methodology for "right reason" was as certain and dogmatic as the scholastic one it replaced, and Newton's mechanistic science was predicated on a stable, uniform, cosmological order. The centerpiece of this vision, cause–effect determinism measured mathematically, depended on a closed, nontransformative, linearly developed universe. Stability was assumed, nature was in all ways "conformable to Herself and simple," and the disciplines were organized in a reductionist hierarchy from mathematics and physics through sociology and psychology. Albert Einstein—temperamentally at least, the last great Newtonian—expressed his view that there is not randomness in the universe, metaphorically: "God does not throw dice" (Heisenberg, 1972, pp. 80–81). In an intellectual time frame, Copernicus and Einstein represent the extreme boundaries of the modern paradigm, with Descartes and Newton as the medians. But, of course, as with any extremes, Copernicus and Einstein also represent the bridges between paradigms—one with the pre-modern, the other with the post-modern.

Chapter One in this part will explore Descartes' and Newton's world-views, especially in regard to the closedness of their vision. Chapter Two will investigate the educational and curricular "carry-overs" of these modern world views into twentieth-century America.

NOTE

1. Cosmology as a word and an idea is receiving increasing attention. Stephen Toulmin (1982, 1990) features it prominently in two of his books, while Donald Oliver and Kathleen Gershman (1989) make it a centerpiece in their book. Jeremy Bernstein and Gerald Feinberg (1989) have written a book, *Cosmological Constants,* referring to the seminal articles of those contemporary scientists having an interest in the universe's origins. Such interest, though, as I see it, takes one beyond the scientific into the metaphysical, religious, and metaphorical. Cosmology is a large umbrella concept covering all four of the fields of science, philosophy, theology, and literature. Oliver and Gershman (1989), following Alfred North Whitehead and his quest for a unifying perspective, call cosmology the bringing together of metaphysics and science "within the framework of a meaningful story" (p. 156). I, too, wish to tell a story: of our curriculum's intellectual origins, of the individuals who contributed to those origins, of their combining metaphysics with physics, and of possible ways to reconceptualize curriculum thought in our new, post-modern world.

Descartes' and Newton's World-Views

PRE-MODERN ORDER

> Moral virtue is a mean . . . a mean between two vices, the one involving excess, the other deficiency, and it is such because its character is to aim at what is intermediate.
> —Aristotle, *Nicomachean Ethics*, Bk. II, Ch. 9

This quote, opposite from the modernist view that more is better, represents the ancient Greek ideal of order—balanced, symmetrical, purposeful—an ideal that permeated the pre-modern paradigm of an earth-centered universe. This paradigm covers a long time span, from the ancient Greeks through the Renaissance—a period of almost two thousand years. During those years the paradigm was subject to a number of influences and modifications—Hellenic, Roman, Judeo-Christian, Arabic, pagan, Gothic. Still, the paradigm persisted, and in the fifteenth and sixteenth centuries the dominant patterns in astronomy, gentlemanly ideals, mathematics, metaphysics, poetry, and science were Greek, especially in the neo-Platonic and neo-Aristotlean forms adopted by the Renaissance. Thus, the philosophy and science of Plato and Aristotle formed the foundation modernist science played against as it developed its own paradigm. This paradigm came to fruition in the works of Descartes and Newton, who, like Plato and Aristotle, represent the rationalist and empiricist branches within the paradigm. The modernist paradigm is now the contemporary one post-modernism is playing against as it develops its own paradigm.

The Greeks' sense of balance can be seen in their statuary and architecture, especially in the Parthenon, built according to the "Golden Mean" with the length of a building approximately 1.6 times its width. As Aristotle said, this sense of proportionate order even carried over to justice and morality. In fact, for the Pythagoreans—whose motto was "all is number"—justice was the number four: even, perfectly balanced.

Whatever differences Plato and Aristotle had over the virtues of rational deduction versus empirical induction, they agreed on the point of balanced order. Proportionate order more than anything else came to represent the Greek ideal of culture: It was their *paideia* (Jaeger, 1939–1944). While anything was allowed, nothing was permitted in excess. Here lies the original concept of the Olympic Games as pure and noble amateur sport. For the Greeks, professionalism was a study in excess and hence represented failure—a loss of balance. Conversely, the modernist technocrat emphasizes excessive knowledge in one area while paying less attention to how that knowledge fits into a more holistic balance or overall harmony. Pandering after professionalism, a mark of the educational technocrat, is a modernist concept, not a pre-modernist one; it values specialized expertise and technique over a broader, wiser, more holistic approach to knowledge and life.

Along with balance the Greek concept of order also had a strong sense of closure and stasis. Boundaries were finite, immutable. To step over boundaries, out of one's destined position or class, was to court the fates and in mythology to risk the anger of the Gods. While Euclid was too much a rationalist to accept mythology, he did favor the finite and the closed in his geometry. His geometry is of closed circles and line segments, which he reluctantly agreed could be extended to lines if one chose. But all his shapes were straight, balanced, closed. Ptolemaic astronomy and cosmology, building on Euclid, also envisioned the universe as closed and circular. The presumed movements of the spheres was always circular, with the apparently irregular motion of the moon and other spheres accounted for by cycles within cycles, or epicycles. A similar belief in symmetry applied to arithmetic. The square root of two—a number "irregular" in its nonrepeating conversion to decimals—was called irrational. As Morris Kline (1980) says of the Greeks, "The concept of a limitless process frightened them." They shrank before "the silence of the infinite" (p. 57). The rectangular architecture of their buildings was not only harmonious but also finite and complete in itself (*propter se*). Its dimensions could easily be grasped. In this sense Greek architecture is categorically different from the Gothic church of later ages, where under soaring spires and immense space an individual is swallowed up in the cathedral's "dim interior," transported to another world.

Justice for the Greeks was not only "four-square," but depended on each person carrying out in a community (*polis*) that which the individual was born to perform. The Platonic definition of Justice—"to perform one's own task and not to meddle with that of others" (*Republic*, 433b)—did not allow for individuality or freedom. Choice, an essential ingredient of the post-modern paradigm, was not an option for a pre-modern. Nor was choice in any way reflected in the pre-modern curriculum. Plato's educational and social theories were based on each individual fulfilling a pre-set role for the common good. The roles for rulers, guardians, artisans—each class with its own metal—were prescribed and nonvariant. The Forms that these classes copied were absolute, permanent, unchanging.

Behind this notion of a just society as an ordered society lay a belief in the reality of ideals: the Forms. In this realm everything had an essence or internal quality. For the neo-Platonists of the Renaissance, this internal quality became the Christian soul. When, in the first book of the *Republic*, Thrasymachus keeps giving Socrates various examples of justice to stand for definitions, Socrates continues to press him for the essence of justice, for its essential quality apart from specific examples. Such an essence was found, Plato believed, in the soul of a person or object: that which partook of the world-soul. Each individual soul knew its place in the world order before birth and with recollection or contemplation could recall that role. This view allowed Plato (*Meno*) to think of knowledge as remembrance, as he demonstrates with Meno's slave boy, who under questioning recollects the relationship between a square's sides and its diagonal. Socrates' famous method of questioning—the Socratic method—is really recollection-oriented, not open-ended and progressive as in a true dialogue. Rather, it is designed to get at eternally existing and previously known truths. Interestingly, while in curriculum literature we call the Socratic method dialogic, we use the method in a manner remarkably close to its original intent—to help students discover known truths, truths teachers already possess.

Although Aristotle did not accept Plato's concept of a world soul, he did accept the concept of essence—transferring essence from the externality of idealized Forms to norm-referenced categories. Thus, in Aristotle's taxonomic classification systems there is a normative ideal for each category, even for virtue. The sense of an ideal and stable state, externally located but internally embedded within every object, gave an animism to Greek nature and thought. Every object "aims" for this ideal and natural state; this is its function and purpose—its teleology. In Aristotelean physics, fire rose because its essence was lightness; water coalesced because of its essence; and objects thrown into the air strove actively to return to their natural home, the earth—center of the universe.

Socially and educationally, the closedness of this view meant that individuals were not to overstep their bounds or rise above their class. In a more positive manner, it meant that harmony and integration should pervade all one did. Life and learning should be balanced. This noble ideal flourished in the Renaissance with its views on courtly behavior and well-rounded gentlemen and ladies. However, with the rise of industrialism, a new but still closed vision appeared.

Carolyn Merchant, feminist and ecologist, in her book *The Death of Nature* (1983) laments the change from the pre-modern to the modern paradigm. For her, this change was one from female nature to male machines, from an organic and holistic world view to a "system of dead, inert particles moved by external rather than inherent forces" (p. 193). Ecologically, this loss of balance and harmony has been a drawback, if not a disaster, emanating from the modernist paradigm. Unless a sense of balance is re-established, humans may well destroy themselves and the planet they live on. Indeed, there is a certain male aggressiveness that permeates the modern paradigm and works against restoring this balance. Further, the shifting emphasis from internal direction to external force has not been good for theories of learning. John Locke's *tabula rasa*, the spectator theory of knowledge, and nineteenth-century theories of association and mental impression are natural outcomes of this switch. Merchant, though, overlooks the fact that modern science and the industrial revolution did bring forth not only material benefits but also concepts of progress, freedom, and individual accomplishment not found in pre-modern thought. Modern thought opened up vistas not accessible by pre-modern thought.

However, the operation of this thought has assumed a closed, non-transformational frame. Hence, while it has accomplished near miracles in the fields of medicine and microbiology, it has been quite ineffective in dealing with growth, development, and personal or physical interactions looked at from a systems or network viewpoint. In short, modern thought has not provided a good model for the education of human beings. Its Cartesian methodology has assumed the attainment of certainty, and its Newtonian predictability has assumed a universe stable, symmetrical, and simple in its organization.

DESCARTES' METHOD

[There are] certain laws which God has so established in nature . . . that after sufficient reflection we cannot doubt that they are exactly observed in all which exists or which happens in the world.
—*Discourse on Method*, 1637/1950, p. 27

This quotation reflects Descartes' method for "rightly conducting reason for seeking truth"—faith in an external order, sufficient mental reflection to realize that order must be expressed in a manner we can understand, and accurate empirical observation of the order. All this is encased in a sort of naive idealism—in our abilities, in God's generosity, in the one-to-one relationship between what we think is reality and reality itself.

Descartes' statement also reflects the enormity of the world-view shift that accompanied Copernicus' positing of a sun-centered universe, and future scientists describing that universe in lawful, regulated terms. Louis XIV called himself the "Sun King" partly to reflect the grandeur of his reign but also to convey that he was the embodiment of a new order. By now the very concept of Nature itself had changed. In pre-modern times when earth was the center of the universe, Nature and her activities were seen in ecological and personal terms—of living and dying, growth and reproduction. However, once the earth was seen to be but a cog in a large, mechanized system, the metaphor shifted from organic to mechanistic, lawful terms—drawn from the new engineering that was then developing. The universe was no longer envisioned as "alive," but as filled with "dead, inert particles," atoms in a void. The planets, whose movement was measured with clockwork precision, were considered as gears in a vast machine. Even God took on machine-like qualities, losing the personal qualities found in the Old and New Testaments and becoming a *deus ex machina*. The dismissal of God as a working hypothesis, which Laplace did so easily, was but the final step in the march from organicism to mechanism, from inherent essences to mathematical formulae.

Such formulae still play a large role in our contemporary concepts of reality, and they play an overly dominant role in our view of what constitutes good education. Whereas the Greeks defined quality education in terms of essences, we follow the modernist tradition of defining education in terms of test scores. In fact, IQ—a central concept of intelligence for many educators—is defined by psychometricians only in terms of test scores, leaving out particular "knowledge, skills, talents, educational acquisitions, memory, and wisdom" (Jensen, 1981, p. 11). Thus defined, IQ becomes a hollow concept, useful only in predicting itself.

The megaparadigm shift from the pre-modern to the modern threw fear into the hearts of Europe's intellectual and power elite. On the one hand, these individuals were fascinated with the new and particular insights science and mathematics were bringing—which revolutionized astronomy, physics, medicine, commerce, and transportation. On the other hand, they worried about the loss of natural harmony and order the old paradigm posited. Control was now wrested from its natural place on earth and placed externally "out there." Measured causes and effects replaced abstracted qualities; physics, not biology, provided the dominant nonreligious metaphors—a change, incidentally, from the medieval, Christian times.

In these mechanical metaphors lay the foundations not only of modern science—seen in terms of external forces pushing and pulling—but also of our mechanistic and scientistic curriculum, one we might call "measured." In this machine-oriented curriculum the goals lie outside, and are determined prior to, the instructional process; once firmly set, they are "driven through" the curriculum. The teacher becomes the driver (often of someone else's vehicle); the student becomes at best a passenger, at worst the object being driven. This mechanical metaphor effectively removes the student from a meaningful interaction with the teacher involving the goals or planning of the curriculum. Further, adopting the mechanical metaphor—either tacitly or overtly—makes it hard for curricularists to understand Dewey's concept of goals and ends arising from within activity, rather than being set prior to activity. Dewey's notion that ends lie within, not outside, the process is understood best when one adopts an organic, ecological frame, not a machine-like, gear-driven one.

When the planet earth became but a cog in a larger system—a system humans could neither control nor supplicate—prediction became more and more important; it was predictable movement that provided assurance the universe was still orderly. The mathematics of measurement—a joy to all scientists from Copernicus to Newton—indicated the moon would not wander from its orbit, the winds would not die down, the clouds would not dry up, and the fruits would not wither on the tree (Merchant, 1983, p. 128). Such a fear was real for the populace of the seventeenth century, trying to adapt to a new and strange paradigm. As John Donne says, in his *The Anatomie of the World:*

> And the new Philosophy cals all in doubt,
> The Element of fire is quite put out;
> The Sun is lost, and th' earth and no man's wit
> Can well direct him, where to looke for it.
>
> 'Tis all in peeces, all cohaerance gone.
>   —1633/1968, lines 205–213

Shakespeare, in *Troilus and Cressida* (c. 1603/1936), states the same sentiments when he has Ulysses say:

> Take but degree away, untune that string
> And, hark, what discord follows
> —Act 1, scene 3, lines 109–110

Both poets express the tenor and terror of the times. The seventeenth century was filled with turmoil and discord—religious, civil, intellectual. Henry of Navarre (the IVth) was assassinated when Descartes was a youth, with the Thirty Years' War beginning shortly thereafter; in England, Charles the First lost his crown and his head, and Oliver Cromwell's "noble experiment" wreaked havoc on the traditions of church and state; and the rise of cities brought an onslaught of pestilence and crime. Add to this the new cosmology of an earth spinning freely in space and it did seem as if all was "in peeces, all cohaerance gone." As Stephen Toulmin points out, there was a great need at this time for metaphysical, social, political stability. In fact, he says, quoting another, "The central theme of Seventeenth-century Europe was a 'struggle for stability' " (1990, p. 92). Both Descartes and Newton contributed to the enhancement of this struggle, to rebuilding confidence, to showing that coherence was not gone, Nature indeed being "conformable to Herself," even though the paradigm expressing this unity was changing. By 1700 the rebuilding process was in place: The monarchies of France and England had been restored—albeit in altered form—and a new intellectual coherence was established. Descartes' method for "rightly conducting reason" and Newton's *Mathematical Principles of Natural Philosophy* played important roles in this process.

From our vantage point at the end of modernism's reign, it is interesting to note that control—so important a characteristic of the paradigm—was born of both a positive vision and a hidden fear. It is control which was key to the paradigm's productive success, a point the "new industrialists," or technocrats, understood well. However, the paradigm was also born of fear—fear that if we "take but degree away" then "tis all in peeces." Modernism, especially in its educational and curricular manifestations, has feared loosening the tautness of the string of control. Post-modernism helps us see that nature itself consists of flexible order, that order and chaos are not diametrically and irrevocably opposed but are embedded one within the other. This observation brings pressure on us to redefine both order and chaos: to see order not in terms of external imposition but in terms of internal harmony and balance, and to see chaos not in terms of absolute dissolution but in terms of a new type of order—a "lumpy," complex, multilayered order.

Descartes, born just prior to the seventeenth century, found himself at an early age "saddled with so many doubts and errors" that he could ascertain nothing that was not in dispute. He longed for certainty in a world filled with uncertainty. He found such in a "dream" he had on the night of November 10, 1619. Alone, in a stove-heated room in Germany while on duty with a mercenary group he had joined to remove himself from the temptations and distractions of Paris, he gave himself up to reflective meditation. The result of these meditations was a new "method of analysis" which completely reformulated philosophy. As Ernst Cassirer (1932/1955) says, this reformulation altered "the entire world picture" (p. 3), permeating all fields of knowledge: philosophy, literature, morals, political science, and even theology, "to which it imparted a new form" (p. 28). Although Catholic, and serving for the Catholic Duke of Bavaria in his fight against the German Protestant princes, Descartes formulated a thoroughly Protestant system—he would be his own priest and inquirer, accepting no one else's authority, not even that of the Church or his respected teachers. He would be a complete skeptic, with faith only in the certain laws of God, in mathematics, in geometrical deductions, and in the clarity and distinctness of his own reflective intelligence.

Descartes (1637/1950) devised four methodological rules for directing reason in the search for truth.

> *First Rule:* Accept only that which presents itself to the mind "so clearly and distinctly" that its truth is self-evident.
>
> *Second Rule:* Divide each difficulty "into as many parts as possible" for an easier solution.
>
> *Third Rule:* "Think in an orderly fashion," as did the geometers of old with their "long chains of reasoning," always proceeding by gradual degrees, from that which is "simplest and easiest to understand" to the more complex.
>
> *Fourth Rule:* Review all the foregoing to be "certain that nothing is omitted." (p. 12)

What is interesting about these rules from a curricular viewpoint is (1) their closeness to both the modernist "scientific method" as well as to the Tyler rationale, and (2) the rules' own allegiance to mathematical, especially Euclidian, thought. In advocating clear definitions, a reductionist methodology, and careful evaluation, Descartes was providing a skeletal foundation for the curricular methodology today's schools use—moving from the well conceived to the empirically valid. In such a methodology, ends are external to the process; there is not a dynamic between theory and fact, imagination and practicality; whatever is true, factual, or real is discovered, not created. The sterility of such a methodology is contrary to that now developing in post-modern science. Here the concept of self-organization, as in the Big-Bang theory of the universe's origin, encourages us to conceive a methodology based on creativity rather than discovery (Davies, 1984, 1988). In such a methodology, as both Dewey and Whitehead knew, ends emerge from within process itself; they are not external to it. This means that prior to the process' development the ends can be delineated only in general, even "fuzzy," terms. Precise determination of the sort Descartes sought is impossible, both in theory and in practice.

Applying this stable-set versus emerging-process analysis to Ralph Tyler's four fundamental foci for curriculum planning—(1) chosen purposes, (2) provided experiences, (3) effective organization, (4) evaluation—it is easy to see his framework as modernist, not post- or premodernist. While it is possible—as some argue—to define educational purposes in process terms, as long as these purposes are set prior to the process, with the other steps following in linear fashion, then the process becomes *de facto* the implementation and evaluation of pre-set ends. But such a view of process is severely limited. Tyler's framework encourages curricularists to develop steps three and four—means and evaluation—with more sophistication and precision than steps one and two—selection of purposes and experiences. Overall, Tyler's four foci are but a variation on Descartes' general method for "rightly conducting reason and seeking truth in the sciences." Learning, in both these models, is encased in a closed system—limited to the discovery of the pre-existent, the already known. Here there can be a transmission of information but not a transformation of knowledge.

The second curriculum point to be made about Descartes' method, its connection with Euclid's geometrical reasoning, is an obvious one, especially as shown in the first and third rules. "Clear and distinct" truths are direct carryovers from self-evident, geometric axioms. Descartes' "long chains of reasoning . . . proceeding by gradual degrees," are the deductive steps Euclid used in his proofs—steps, by the way, school students no longer deduce but memorize. In both Euclid's and Descartes' methods there is the assumption of an external reality—set by a rational, geometrical, undeceiving God, unaffected by our personal ruminations and activities. This categorical separation between the external and the personal—so contrary to Hebrew, Christian, and medieval thought—is part of Descartes' legacy to modernism, a legacy that has carried over into curriculum's separation of teacher from student, knower from known, and self from other.

In fact, Descartes—following Galileo and preceding Locke—even emphasized the separation of reality into primary and secondary qualities. The primary qualities, mathematical and objective in nature, are those of size, shape, motion, and position. The secondary qualities, inferior to the primary and indeed less "real" (because they are subjective), are those recognized through the senses—color, odor, taste, texture, sound. This distinction is one Edwin Burtt (1932/1955) says we should pause on for a moment, "for its effects on modern thought have been of incalculable importance. It is a fundamental step toward banishing [humanity] from the great world of nature" (p. 89). In this banishing, nature becomes less than it was; it becomes an object to be manipulated by "reason." In the pre-modern (Greek through Christian) eras, humans and nature were "integral parts of a larger whole." This larger whole provided a framework that both tempered human actions and gave dignity to them. In Descartes' categorical separation of the objective from the subjective, humans—at least in terms of their senses—became a tangled bundle of secondary qualities. Personal feelings, intuitions, experiences were not a source of knowledge. Knowledge existed "outside"—immutable, unchangeable—residing within the great Laws of Nature. Knowledge could be discovered, but not created—the system was closed. Descartes bequeathed to modernist thought a method for discovering a pre-existent world, not a method for dealing with an emergent, evolutionary one. Analagously, the same comment can be made about the curricular "discovery method" of the 1960s—it helped students discover the already known; it did not help them develop their own powers of dealing with the indeterminate. Like Descartes' method, its use was limited.

Michel Serres offers intriguing insights and comments on Descartes' methodology. As a French post-structuralist, Serres uses metaphor to make his points and analyzes all in terms of language and the "language games" authors play. Serres' first move is to bring forth LaFontaine's fable of the sheep and the wolf drinking at a stream. The sheep positions itself downstream of the wolf so as not to offend the stronger beast, not to "muddy His drink." However, after some dialogue over who has what rights and powers, the wolf carries the sheep off into the woods and eats it, "without any other form of *proces*" (1983, pp. 15—16). The fable's moral is: "The reason of the stronger is always the best." Living by this proposition, says Serres, is to play a dangerous game, for one must then *always* be the best. It is possible for the shepherd with his dogs to come looking for the lost sheep (to upstream the wolf, as it were), and then the wolf becomes the object eaten, not the one eating:

In a contest, a competitor is not always assured of winning. A player stronger at a given moment because of a given move can later fail when his opponent discovers the means or obtains the power to pass upstream from him. (p. 22)

Thus, the player needs to make "a maximal move," one that "freezes the game-space in a single pattern of order and hierarchy." It is just this maximal move, Serres says, that Descartes has made in his methodology for "rightly conducting reason." Descartes begins his game by doubting all, by accepting only the optimal, rejecting all that is not "entirely certain," of believing only the "indubitable," of distancing himself from "everything" in which he has "the least doubt" (p. 26). In the maximalist game, this is a minimalist move: After all this maximum doubt, what is left is the minimum—the I, the I am, the I am who doubts. From this minimalest position, Descartes makes a brilliant move, a "maximum *maximorum*" move. From the depths of doubting, from the minimalest of all minimal positions he enlists the aid of another player, an all-powerful player: God Himself. Now the minimum "I" becomes impregnable—I and God become one. "I always wins." "God is a point without an upstream." "I can no longer lose . . . everything becomes possible." "In the game of truth, *error has been checkmated*" (p. 27; emphasis added).

In this metaphorical playing lies a powerful and trenchant critique of modernist epistemology. Philosophy in the positivist vein and science in the scientistic vein have set themselves up as arbiters of the rules in the game of knowledge. They have, like Descartes, checkmated error by allowing nothing upstream of themselves. Scientific rationality has become the supreme Wolf. Here lie the intellectual foundations of modern thought. This position Alfred North Whitehead (1925/1967) labels as "one-eyed reason, deficient in its vision of depth" (p. 59). Paul Feyerabend (1988) says this tradition illustrates the need to "protect science from its ideologies" (p. vii); while Richard Rorty (1980) says this concept of philosophy becoming a "super science" is one of the conceits of Western egocentricism (p. 359 ff). It is a conceit which underlies our modernist concept of curriculum—we allow only one type of knowing: a rational, definitional knowing.

NEWTON'S STABLE UNIVERSE

Nature does nothing in vain . . . for Nature is pleased with simplicity.
—Book Three: "First Rule of Reasoning," p. 398

This most beautiful system of sun, planets, and comets could only proceed from the counsel and dominion of an intelligent and powerful Being . . . [who] governs all things . . . as Lord over all.
—Book Three: "General Scholium," p. 544

I offer this work as the mathematical principles of philosophy, for the whole burden of philosophy seems to consist in this.
—Preface to the First Edition, p. xvii

These passages, from the *Principia Mathematica* (1729/1962), give a sense of Newton's metaphysical view about Nature and its order. In this view, nature is beautiful in the uniformity of its simple symmetry; and buried within that symmetry is a set of necessary, linear, causative relations accessible to exact mathematical description. Richard Westfall (1968) calls this view "peculiar" (p. 77), for it asserts not only that nature is a set of necessary relationships but that it must present itself, to our observation, as such. Reality for Newton is both simple and observable. Ironically, while this concept of nature as a set of necessary relationships is ultimately dependent on God's goodness, the translation of this concept into mathematical terms elevated mathematics to an exalted, Godlike, position. This allowed Laplace to dispense with God as an "unneeded hypothesis." This mathematization of science also allowed Laplace to develop his concept of the exact predictability of all future events. Thus, Newton, a religious individual who saw in nature's beautiful symmetries God's design and who wrote as many theological as scientific tracts, unwittingly provided the foundation for the separation of science from religion.

The real "peculiarity" of Newton's metaphysics, though, lies not so much in itself as in our wholesale acceptance of it as the "natural" order of the universe. We consider chaotic or complex order, indeterminacy, transformation, internal direction, and self-generation as unusual, not because they are so in themselves but because they violate our "natural" acceptance of Newton's world-view. It is this clash of paradigms which so bothered Heisenberg and Bohr, leading to moments of confrontation, depression, and exhaustion while they struggled, in the 1920s, to develop the "Copenhagen interpretation" of quantum physics. Heisenberg (1972) was especially bothered by this clash (Chs. 5, 6).

It is Newton's metaphysical and cosmological views—not his scientific ones—that have dominated modern thought so long, providing a foundation in the social sciences for causative predictability, linear ordering, and a closed (or discovery) methodology. These, in turn, are the conceptual underpinnings of scientific (really scientistic) curriculum making.

In the pre-modern paradigm, there is no way to order the opposites, for each has its own qualitative essence. There is no quantitative scale, no central norm to which all corresponds. Measurement is impossible. The mathematical scientists of the sixteenth and seventeenth centuries changed that. They ordered all on one linear scale with an ideal at the top and a practical norm in the middle—all other positions related to these two. Events, activities, experiences could now be quantified. Newton's great contribution to this concept was in deriving one formula $(F = G\frac{Mm}{r^2})$ for ordering the mutual attraction of physical objects, a formula that measured the "force" holding the universe together. Newton proposed gravitational "force" as an alternative to Descartes' "vortices." The formula's statement is that objects' atomic masses have a gravitational pull on one another in inverse ratio to the squares of their distance. In simpler terms, this means that apples falling from trees and planets revolving around the sun follow the same rules—a single uniformity pervades the whole universe. And this uniformity can be mathematically abstracted from observation, as in the orbiting of Halley's comet.

Aristotle, in the Greek tradition, separated earthly motion with its constant change and corruption from the harmonious order of the immutable heavens. He made this separation at the orbit of the moon—beyond the moon one order existed, below the moon another order existed. Newton showed this bifurcation to be unnecessary, since a simple and symmetrical mathematical order underlay all motion. That this order was a metaphysical abstraction from empirical observation, that there were always "small errors" between the mathematical ideal and observed reality, did not bother Newton or his followers. The ideal and the real merely took on a rational–empirical split, not the heavenly–earthly one of Aristotle. This split has remained with us, with mathematics and the *theoretical* maintaining a privileged position over the observational and *practical*. As both Joseph Schwab (1970) and Donald Schön (1983) point out, in this split the practical and experiential are seen not as viable entities in their own right but as applications of the theoretical. Professionalism, of the technical-rational variety, espouses this split, downgrading an individual's own sense of competence in favor of copying or applying the performances others have devised. Curricula from elementary school through graduate degrees are based on this set-performance model. Deviation from this model is considered "irrational."

The concept of an abstracted, uniform order that can be measured—fictitious as it may be—has played an immensely important role in the modern paradigm. The presiding concept has spawned other concepts—all of them important for the framework we have built to house curriculum as a series of tasks or materials to be mastered. Three of these other concepts are linear sequencing, cause–effect relations, and the negation of qualitative change over time.

Linear sequencing is, of course, the heart of mathematical order—at least of the simple, linear, calculus order Newton devised. This sequencing sees 1, 2, 3, 4 proceeding in a series of uniform steps, each a composite of preceding ones. Such gradualism pervaded Charles Darwin's concept of evolution, just as it pervades our concept of curriculum. Both see change and development in uniform, incremental steps. Textbooks use a serial, graduated order, as do course syllabi; even homework assignments and instructional methods evidence this order. It is a hidden but dominant aspect of contemporary curriculum, from first grade through college. Only kindergarten and doctoral seminars seem able to develop more interactive, dynamic, and complex forms of order.

The concept of causality, present in pre-modern thought in terms of proximate causes, efficient causes, necessary causes, and the ubiquitous First Cause, received a new formulation in the hands of Newton—a formulation that remains with us today as our natural way of looking at change. For every effect there must be a prior cause; effects do not happen spontaneously and the same cause will always produce the same effect. In his "Second Rule of Reasoning," Newton (1729/1962) says: "To the same natural effect we must . . . assign the same cause" (p. 398). In a closed, mechanistic universe this has meant that same effects will *always* follow same causes. Predictability is not only assured, it is complete and absolute. Jacob Bronowski (1978) points out that this postulate of causality has "been elevated to the rank of the central concept of science" (p. 40), becoming modern science's "guiding principle," the very "centre of scientific method" (p. 59). More than this, it has "become our natural way of looking at all problems"—including those in economics, philosophy, psychology, and education. This postulate is that of the machine: "From the same beginnings will follow same ends." Such a mechanistic causality is what underlay Laplace's determinism, behaviorism's principle of stimulus–response, educators' faith in the predictive value of IQ, and teachers' faith in repetition as a vital, if not *the*, method of learning. But, of course, the principle is false: "Nature is not strictly a succession of causes and their effects" (p. 75). Such a view is viable only if one posits, as Newton did, a closed, mechanistic universe.

Ilya Prigogine and Isabelle Stengers (1984), in their book *Order Out of Chaos*, comment that in presenting his vision of a set universe, Newton managed to give us a view that "escapes the clutches of time" (p. 213). For Newton (1730/1952) time was unimportant; the established Order of Nature was formed by "God in the Beginning . . . as never to wear or break in pieces" (p. 400). Neither time nor development are part of such a picture. This stable, indeed static, view of nature was challenged by Charles Darwin a century and a half later. However, while time then became a factor—acquiring an "arrow"—as development moved toward higher and more complex forms of organization, the basic pattern of the Newtonian paradigm was so entrenched that this development was seen to occur in sequential, gradual steps. The stability Newton posited was only slightly, not fundamentally, altered; there were no gaps, punctures, breaks in the sequence of evolution. Fractals, the geometry of brokenness, were not part of this vision.

The gradualness of progress and the linear connectedness of development have carried over into educational and curriculum theory. It was and still is assumed the curriculum must be organized in sequential steps. Gaps, breaks, punctures are not only absent from the curriculum, they are seen only in negative terms. Time itself is seen exclusively in cumulative terms, as a co-relation with what is learned: the longer the time, the more learning accumulated. Time is not seen as an active ingredient, necessary for developing the creative possibilities inherent in any situation. In a post-modern view, development becomes not merely cumulative but qualitatively transformational; transformations occur as interactions expand, increase, mature—over time. Piaget could never understand why Americans so strongly wished to "speed-up" time; in so doing they were destroying the very frame within which the process of stage transformations occurs.

Educationally, we have yet to realize the potentialities inherent in time as a frame for transformations. Methods of reflection, reorganization, and interactive play need to be part of our curriculum construction—these methods are congruent with the processes post-modern science tells us nature uses in bringing to actuality the creative potential inherent in the universe. We need to consider time in ways that move it beyond the linear and cumulative which see it as a necessary and essential ingredient in qualitative transformations.

Another of Newton's metaphysical concepts that has had an influence on curriculum is that of individual atoms forming the ultimate reality or "building blocks" of nature. In Newton's (1730/1952) words, from his *Opticks*, "God in the Beginning formed Matter into solid, massy, hard, impenetrable Particles" (p. 376). These particles were seen as autonomous units, touching each other in a mechanistic manner but operating independently. Newton's "attraction at a distance" (gravity) operated through these units, much in the manner of a machine comprising interconnecting gears. This is the visual model Newton used when thinking of how gravity works.

In the modernist paradigm, the concept of curriculum as autonomous but interconnected units is ubiquitous. From the first grade on, curriculum is considered in terms of units arranged in linear order. Learning, itself, is defined in terms of the number of units covered, mastered, accumulated. Such a view does not facilitate considering curriculum as a transformative process, one composed of complex and spontaneous interactions. In considering curriculum as a transformative process, we will need to view curriculum as more than a series of contingent units—to see it as a mixed and multivariate integration of rich, open-ended experiences; as a complex mosaic ever shifting its center of attraction as we shift ours.

CHAPTER 2

Curriculum Carryovers

AMERICA AND TECHNOLOGY

One can hardly believe there has been a revolution in all history so rapid, so extensive, so complete . . . [it] overshadows and even controls all others . . . [it is] *writ so large that he who runs may read.*
—Dewey, *School and Society*, 1915/1956; pp. 8–9; *emphasis added*

These statements refer, of course, to industrialization—the concrete embodiment of the modern vision. Those holding this vision believed that through industrialization a new society would be born—one utilizing the tenets of science for the economic and social benefit of all. Following these tenets, America, after the Civil War, moved from a second-level agricultural power to a first-level industrial one. By 1900 America not only led the world in industrial production, it virtually outproduced the second, third, and fourth countries combined (Tyack, 1974, p. 29). This revolution has been a dominant force in twentieth-century society, shaping our values, including the way we envision education and schooling, and giving our society its particular technological cast.

By the time Dewey singled out industrialism, the social vision of Comte de Saint-Simon—father of technocracy and premiere theoretician of industrialism—had both faded and been realized. His particular socialist vision, called by one commentator "authoritarian socialism" (Markham, 1952, p. xxviii), was expounded by his followers as "From each according to his capacity, to each according to his performance" (in Bell, 1973, p. 77). This phrase, altered slightly but significantly by Frederick Engels (whom Saint-Simon influenced), is more akin to the capitalist philosophy of Henry Ford than to the socialist one of Karl Marx. Failing to gather a strong following after the mid-nineteenth century, the socialist vision of the Saint-Simonians quickly died out; although it did influence, at least indirectly, utopian communities in New York, Pennsylvania, and Indiana. The only ones of these, though, that continued to exist into the twentieth century were similar to the Oneida, New

York, community, where the vigor of individual leaders made the community part of the American entrepreneurial spirit (Lockwood, 1965).

On the other hand, the technocratic aspect of Saint-Simon's (1825/ 1952) vision—that of a new society, organized around the technical competence of a new breed of men: "scientists, artists, industrialists" (p. 78)—became both the ideal and the reality of American social and political organizations. The values and practicalities of this technocratic vision were promoted during the century by such men as Frederick Taylor, Thorstein Veblen, B. F. Skinner, and Robert McNamara. Today this vision, founded on what Donald Schön (1983) calls "technocratic rationality," has reached its limits.

Saint-Simon held a passionate belief in industrialism. Machines, by increasing production and lowering the cost of manufactured goods, would provide all with a better life. He believed that in this new society the plunder, waste, and pompous display characteristic of the pre-revolutionary *ancien regime* in France would be replaced by efficient production, "scientific" decision making, and orderly behavior. This new society demanded new leaders, drawn from art, science, industry: leaders who had technical expertise, not political connections. Without this "new breed of men" the new society could not function. Saint-Simon was too much an aristocrat and had seen too closely the excesses of the French Revolution to believe in the autonomy of the proletariat. His socialism was, indeed, "authoritarian." The populace, he believed, needed to be led—by those with expertise. Through the writings of both Veblen and Skinner, Saint-Simon's vision became part of the social literature of twentieth-century American thought. It was, though, woven into the warp and woof of our society by Frederick Taylor in his "scientific management" of workers at Bethlehem Steel Company in Baltimore, Maryland, in the 1890s.

At the time, it was common for day laborers to work in groups under the direction of a foreman. Decisions were made collectively or sometimes through default by the laziest worker. Taylor found the pig-iron crew at Bethlehem Steel moving about 12 and one-half tons of lead, per man, per day, from a scrap yard to a waiting boxcar. This was a bit above average for pig-iron handlers on the East Coast. After doing time-and-motion studies, Taylor and his associates concluded that through scientific management pig-iron handlers should be able to stack 47 or 48 tons per day. While this was a surprising figure, Taylor adopted the attitude that it must be reached. The "couldness" of the figure, derived theoretically, now became a moral imperative; Taylor (1911/1947) saw it as his "duty" to be certain the boxcars were loaded at the new rate. A further "duty" was to see the work done "without bringing on a strike" and in such a manner "that the men were happier and better contented when loading at the new rate" than they were when loading at the old rate (p. 43).

To accomplish this mission, Taylor chose a man he called Schmidt, a small Pennsylvania Dutchman who often trotted home from work and was known to be "close" with his money. "A penny looks about the size of a cartwheel to him," said his foreman. But most important, Schmidt was "stupid" enough to be well suited for his boring and physically draining task—"so stupid . . . that he more nearly resembles an ox" than a man (p. 59). The dichotomy between Taylor's public pronouncement of Schmidt as a "first class, high priced" man and a belief in his inherent stupidity is reflected in his interview with Schmidt. There he taunts Schmidt about being "high priced," finally saying in mock exasperation that Schmidt well knows "a high priced man has to do *exactly as he's told* from morning till night . . . right straight through the day. And what's more, no back talk" (pp. 45–46; emphasis added). Such language, Taylor concedes, may seem a bit "rough" to our ears, and well it would be even to "an educated mechanic or . . . an intelligent laborer." But with a person of "the sluggish type of Schmidt . . . it is appropriate and not unkind," especially since it fixes his attention on that which will help him—his extra wages—and away from what he might consider "impossibly hard work." For his 400% increased productivity, Schmidt received an extra 70 cents a day.

Taylor believed that "laws" of scientific management underlay all he had Schmidt do—this is why he had a duty to be certain the boxcars were loaded at the new rate. One of these laws was the time relation between Schmidt "on-load," carrying pig-iron bars, and "off-load," either resting or walking back to the scrap pile. This ratio needed precise measurement, if the "highest state of efficiency" was to be reached. To bring about such a state was Taylor's mission. Toward this end, he formulated four duties or principles to which management needed to pay attention. *First,* "a science for each element of a man's work" must be developed to replace "the old rule-of-thumb method." *Second,* the workmen must be "scientifically selected and trained," not left to their own methods, as was done in the past. *Third,* attention must be given "to insure all of the work being done in accordance with the principles . . . developed." *Fourth,* an "equal division of the work and the responsibility must be drawn between management and the workmen." This last principle, Taylor says, is important enough to "require further explanation" (pp. 36–39).

What Taylor means by equal division of responsibility is that each group, management and workers, must do that for which each is best suited. Management's task is to plan out fully "at least one day in advance" the work each man is to do. Further, each workman must receive these work orders "in writing and in detail" every day. These orders specify "not only what is to be done but how it is to be done and the exact time allowed for doing it." This pre-ordering of tasks, by managers for workers, is "the most prominent single element in modern scientific management" (p. 39). It is an element Franklin Bobbitt (1918) and Elwood Cubberley (1916) incorporated into their views of how curriculum should be designed and used. It is an element that remains intrinsic to the lesson planning devices taught prospective teachers in their methods courses. It assumes ends should be fixed prior to the implementation of means. Efficiency, then, is measured in terms of the number of *specific* ends achieved and the time needed for achievement. Such a linear and closed system tends to trivialize the goals of education, limiting them only to that which can be particularized (Doll, 1972, 1973).

These dual foci of specificity and quantification—the "scientific" aspects of the "technical rationality" model—swept the country. Not only did American industrialism become synonymous with efficient production, but American life took on the same hue. The maxim "Save the Minutes" became a motto not only in the factory and the classroom but in the home as well. Popular magazines such as *Outlook* and *The Saturday Evening Post* ran features on "Scientific Management in the Home" (Callahan, 1962, p. 44). One clergyman, Dr. Shailer Mathews (1912), even wrote a book advocating the need for scientific management in the churches. He believed church workers needed to be taught to "work under direction according to plans" (p. 1), even if such a procedure meant a certain loss of initiative. "The philosophy of efficiency demands" this. Joseph Mayer Rice, who in the 1890s despaired over the incompetence and corruption he saw in the public school system—leading to dull, mechanical, and repetitive teaching, as well as to dehumanization of students—twenty years later saw scientific management as the remedy for these ills. His second book (1914/1969) has the words *scientific management* in its title and confidently asserts that he has "discovered not only the fundamental cause" of these ills but the remedy as well—namely, "the introduction of scientific management into the conduct of our schools" (p. vii). Such a "scientific system of pedagogical management . . . [demands, incidentally] . . . the measurement of results in the light of fixed standards" (p. xv). Rice saw a management system, not teachers' own growth, as *the way* to educational reform. In this move educational reform started on a path it has remained on to the present day: defining reform in terms of "improved" management systems, not in terms of teachers' personal growth and power.

An intriguing aside in Rice's book is that in measuring the efficiency of memorizing spelling words—the number right correlated with the time spent—it became apparent that a threshold was reached around 10 or 15 minutes per day; more study time, often up to 50 minutes per day, correlated with lower, not higher, scores (p. 87). This fact was treated as an example of the way scientific management could point out and help eliminate waste in education, rather than as a spur to question the efficiency model itself. The concept of students' innate organizing abilities or of teachers' roles in setting a challenge for such organization—lest boredom easily set in—was not seen. Nor was the concept of transitional thresholds seen. The "scientific" model did not allow such a fundamental question to be asked. It was merely noted that too much time spent on one area produced inverse results; and, as Rice says, the efficient use of time is indeed "the point around which the entire problem of educational reform revolves" (p. 65). So began the pattern of devising curricula in small, measured units.

Technical efficiency, especially on the assembly line, increased productivity during the 1920s, 1930s, and 1940s. Schools adopted this assembly line model as multipurpose, and multileveled classrooms gave way to discrete, but contiguous, grade levels. The holistic school day was broken into separate time units of thirty-five- to forty-minute segments. This latter factorization was brought into the public schools by U.S. Steel Company when it established the model city of Gary, Indiana, on the shores of Lake Michigan, in the early years of the twentieth century. By standardizing instructional time, Superintendent Wirt could ensure that all rooms were being utilized efficiently. Thus, U.S. Steel Company gave mechanized clocks to every classroom.

World War II provided America with an opportunity to demonstrate visually the value of technical efficiency both on the battlefield and on the production line. The development and delivery of the atomic bomb represented a crowning achievement. The tremendous destruction the bomb wreaked and the enormous loss of life it caused were justified in the modernist terms of rational choice—ending the war, limiting the loss of American deaths. Other ways to achieve these goals were hardly considered; means became locked into ends. The virtue of ends implied the virtue of means—or, in being dichotomously separated from ends, means became incidental to ends.

The postwar years brought technical rationality to its apex. As John F. Kennedy drew around him "the best and the brightest"—including Robert McNamara, who created a revolution in the defense department by structuring it along new lines of cost-effectiveness—Saint-Simon's vision of a technocratic and professional society became reality. The Introduction to the Fall 1963 issue of *Daedalus* proclaims that "everywhere in American life the professions are triumphant" (Lynn, p. 649). With this vision of expertise and this technical methodology America would lead the world—in eradicating poverty, containing communism, and exploring outer space. The dark clouds of war in Vietnam seemed but a small blotch on a very sunny horizon.

The triumph of the professions was based on two [Saint-Simonian] assumptions: (1) the special knowledge the professional possessed, (2) the moral type of person the professional was assumed to be. In-depth knowledge utilized for the common good provided the basis for modernism's social vision. The knowledge the professional possessed was, by definition, knowledge the layperson did not and *could not* possess. Not only did the professional possess technical skill, the professional possessed technical "skill premised on an underlying theory" (Lieberman, 1970, p. 55). This feature of underlying theory means one cannot become professional on one's own but, rather, must be trained and certified by other professionals. Professionalism is thus based on (1) technical skill, (2) theoretical knowledge on which the skill is premised, and (3) acceptance by a community of other professionals.

The basic training model for professionals is the medical one of theoretical science (chemistry, biology, zoology), followed by applied science (anatomy, physiology), culminating in clinical experience (internship, residency). This model forms the general pattern for premedical and medical programs. It also forms the pattern for the professional training of teachers—foundations, followed by methods, followed by student teaching. This program mirrors the Comtean hierarchy of mathematics as fountainhead of all theory, with physics as the premier science, followed by chemistry, biology, psychology, and the other social sciences. Such a hierarchy sees the abstract and fixed sciences or disciplines as foundational, with the lesser sciences taking their direction from this rationality. Schön's term, "technical rationality," is most appropriate in describing this linear, reductionist, "scientific," and taxonomic view of knowledge, from which follows the concept of practical knowledge as no more than an application of theoretical knowledge. As Bernard Barber says in the Fall 1963 issue of *Daedalus*, knowledge the expert professional possesses is not experiential knowledge, refined and reflected; rather, it is "generalized and systemized knowledge" (p. 672).

The second [Saint-Simonian] assumption is that professionals, as a new breed, will be motivated by altruistic community interest, not by personal or petty preferences—their orientation will be primarily "to community rather than individual interest" (p. 672). Thus, the professional, through personal detachment, is a natural leader, one to be revered in the community. Such a leader should receive a "system of rewards" both monetary and honorary. While the medical and legal professions have received these rewards, the education profession has not. In fact, for all their struggles to acquire the status of professionals, teachers are still considered more as workers like Schmidt—followers not leaders.

Jethro Lieberman, in his book *The Tyranny of the Experts* (1970), states that in "putting the experts in charge" we, as a society, have made the wrong choice. The professional's primary allegiance, rhetoric of service aside, has been not to the people but "to the maintenance of the profession itself—its image, health, membership, reputation" (p. 5). Professional organizations are ultimately responsible to, and exist for, themselves. This framework, Lieberman says, makes the "expert the wrong person to define his job or evaluate how well it is performed" (p. 275). Such must be done publicly in an open manner with input from a multitude of sources. Frederick Taylor would not approve; Saint-Simon, with qualifications, might.

Daniel Bell (1973) , popularizer of the term "post-industrial," sees the professional technocrat in two lights. In one of these the professional is the "new working class" of the post-industrial society, a society Bell sees as moving from the production of goods to the rendering of services. In this society the professional is the cultural focus. This new class is the embodiment of Saint-Simon's "new breed." But Bell recognizes that the "technocratic mind-view" in which the professional has been trained—emphasizing "a disciplined approach to objectives" with reliance on "precision and measurement," and deeply Newtonian in character—does not lend itself to leadership (p. 349). Leadership requires skills in polity—those drawing on "religious, aesthetic, intuitive modes." Polity skills are developed by dealing with people, not with machines. Thus, Bell is indeterminate on the role this new class will play. On the one hand, the expert professional has knowledge a post-industrial society needs; on the other hand, people in that society want participatory democracy. Technical rationality focuses on efficiency of production, not on "bargaining between persons." The latter requires decisions of value and choice; the former believes these are unnecessary since, Cartesian like, one and only one "best way" exists.

This dilemma surfaces in education, influencing the type of curriculum we practice. In the modernist framework, which both Saint-Simon and Taylor accepted, there is a "natural order" or "best way" on which all methodology is based. Once discovered, this best way should be, indeed must be, followed. This explains, in part at least, why Taylor felt a moral imperative to see the boxcars loaded at the new, "scientific" rate.

Such an absolutist view encourages the very categorical separation between managers and workers Taylor exhibited in his dealings with
Schmidt. Clearly, this is not a good model for developing inquiring
minds.

Donald Schön (1983, 1987, 1991), in his books on the reflective practitioner, attacks technical rationality not only for mechanizing
thought—emphasizing implementation of means over choice of ends—
but for negating the real world of lived practice. Schön, in his study of
competent practitioners, finds demonstration of a different model and
development of a different sense of professional—a "reflective practice"
model with a practically oriented practitioner as its ideal. This model,
experientially based, hones and refines the practitioner's personal and
individual competence—a competence generated not through certified
courses of study but through reflections on and in lived experience.

When a practitioner reflects experientially, three events not found
in the theory-to-practice model occur. First, the practitioner approaches
problems not as copies of generalized theory but as unique, personal
instances. Here, the practitioner pays attention to the non-confirming
or anomalous aspects of a problem—those characterized by "uncertainty, instability, uniqueness, and value conflict" (1983, p. 50). The
practitioner's art is that of working through this "mess," not by applying
universal rules but by employing intuition, analogies, metaphors.

Such employment forms the second aspect of this practical methodology. The practitioner uses intuition, analogies, and metaphors to
help "frame" or situate a problem. Frames[1] are the assumptions and
connections in which a problem is ensconced. As Schön (1983) says:

> When a practitioner becomes aware of his frames, he also becomes
> aware of the possibility of alternative ways of framing. . . . He takes
> note of the values and norms to which he has given priority. (p. 310)

The practitioner's ends as well as means are now open to public scrutiny. This leads to the third aspect of practical methodology—a dialogue
the practitioner maintains with the situation, always listening for "back
talk" (p. 164) from the situation and employing the language of metaphor in discussion with the situation. Such an open dialogue—with
oneself, with others, with the situation—is key to developing a reflective methodology. Not all practical methodologies become reflective, but
all reflective methodologies originate in practice. This is a key point for
Schön, as it was for Dewey, Piaget, and Joseph Schwab.

In proposing such an alternative methodology—one that has direct
and immense implications for curriculum—Schön is beginning to de-

velop what Hugh Munby and Tom Russell (1989) call an "epistemology of practice" (p. 71). Such an epistemology—quite different from the sense of practice Taylor used—conceives of knowing in terms of the process of "becoming," not in terms of the discovery of "being." From the viewpoint of this new, post-modern epistemology, the technical rationality model "appears," Schön (1983) says, "incomplete" (p. 165); it attends only to problem-solving, not to problem-finding or problem-framing. In our contemporary and rapidly changing world these latter two are more important than the former.

THE SCIENTIFIC CURRICULUM

Work up the raw material into that finished product for which it is best adapted. Applied to education this means: Educate the individual according to his capabilities.

> —Bobbitt, "The Elimination of Waste in Education," 1912, p. 269

Our schools are, in a sense, factories in which the raw products (children) are to be shaped and fashioned into products to meet the various demands of life.

> —Cubberley, *Public School Administration*, 1916, p. 338

These quotations reflect how thoroughly the language and thought of industrialism permeated American social thought and school curriculum.

In the nineteenth century, America, with its social roots in agriculture, focused its educational thought and attention on the teacher, particularly on the personal qualities the teacher should possess. As Horace Mann (1867), Secretary to the Massachusetts Board of Education, says in his "First Annual Report" (presented in 1838): all teachers need to be paragons of virtue—exerting their "best endeavors to impress on the minds of children and youth committed to their care and instruction" the principles of "sobriety, industry, frugality, chastity, moderation and temperance" (p. 421). This view of the teacher as a personal role model maintained a pervasive influence during much of the twentieth century. Charters and Wapples (1929), for instance, admonish teachers to show moderation in pleasures: not to play bridge too often nor to attend clubs or dances too frequently (p. 229), and it was not until World War II that married women were commonly employed as teachers.

Nonetheless, the turn of the century did show a switch in emphasis—from the teacher (epitomized in nineteenth-century rural America by Mark Hopkins sitting on the end of a log) to the curriculum, particularly the "scientific" curriculum. The schools were growing too rapidly for education to focus on the particularities of individual teachers—the high school population was doubling every decade; and the teachers themselves were a varied lot, especially in the cities where immigrants soon outnumbered duly registered Americans. This was America's melting pot era, a time of vast and rapid change. To handle the problem of change, particularly social change, America turned to its schools, and the model it used was that which made its factories productive—scientific management. Curriculum became a "national preoccupation" (Kliebard, 1986, p. 2), one might even say a national obsession; and the scientific curriculum was based on efficiency and standardization. These two qualities are the ones America, following the lead of Herbert Spencer, associated with science. "Save the Minutes" became a maxim not only for the New York school teacher who uttered the phrase to Joseph Mayer Rice, but also for those appointed to serve on two national commissions to study the "Economy of Time in Education" (Cremin, 1961, p. 193).

More time could be saved and more goods produced if workers, including teachers, would do as told—this was the key to efficiency and standardization. Thus, William Torrey Harris (1891)—Hegelian, founder of the *Journal of Speculative Philosophy,* St. Louis school superintendent (1869–1880), U. S. Commissioner of Education (1889–1906)— stated the "cardinal virtues of schooling" to be "regularity, punctuality, silence, and industry" (pp. 196–197). These four would produce a good factory worker and a good student, provided "good" was defined to mean faithful obedience to others' procedures, not the development of one's own—as in a "good" child. In this manner the "raw material" of youth could be molded into the "finished products" of adulthood.

While this curriculum model did focus on efficiency and standardization, both calibrated in measurement terms, the learning model underlying the curriculum posited what Bruner (1973) calls a "deficit hypothesis" (p. 452). This hypothesis—Calvinist in tone—assumes that humans by nature have deficits. For a Hegelian such as Harris these deficits kept individuals chained to their primitive selves, unable to appreciate the higher values of thought and culture. For industry leaders these deficits prevented the immigrants, usually raised on farms, from being good factory workers. For teachers and administrators these deficits kept school children sick, unclean, impoverished.

Franklin Bobbitt (1918) saw the curriculum focusing on deficits or the "shortcomings of individuals" (p. 45)—whether cultural, personal, or social. Deficits could be ascertained by measuring the gap between the practical "forms of knowledge" that "make up the affairs of adult life" and those "abilities, attitudes, habits" possessed by students on any given assessment. Toward this end, Bobbitt (1924) drew his curriculum inspiration from the "fifty years of adulthood, not the twenty years of childhood and youth" (p. 8). Since it was sometimes impossible to have agreement "as to the characteristics" of the "best" work, or "on what constitutes social efficiency" (1918, p. 51), Bobbitt felt it important to go to the workplace itself and measure these in scientific terms. For him, science was precise facts and detailed procedures. Thus, he listed the desired or needed characteristics in specific, not in general or "vague," terms. For the mathematics curriculum he turned away from the history and structure of number and shape—a failing the "new math" of the 1960s tried to remedy—to the practical mathematics used in commerce, mining, manufacturing, meat packing, insurance, and banking. Here, the workplace of the industrial society became idealized with the curriculum constructed from the errors students made on simulated work exercises. Here lies the origin of curriculum goals stated in precise, practical, and measurable terms. These goals represent the ideals of an industrial society.

Presaging both Skinner and needs assessment, Bobbitt (1924) advocated a curriculum that focused exclusively on errors students made. As he says in a list of curriculum recommendations:

10. A diagnostic study of the language-abilities of each individual student needs to be made. Where he reveals weakness, he is to be trained; where he is already sufficiently strong, he is not to be trained.
11. Spelling drills for each individual should be centered upon the errors which he makes. (p. 248)

Jean Piaget and Noam Chomsky also developed diagnostic studies of language abilities. While these two disagreed on the origins of language abilities, each put performance deficits aside to focus on potential powers—competence: powers which could both transform and be transformed, powers which could generate other powers in a never-ending, evolutionary cycle. Even allowing for the modernity of Chomsky's categorical separation of mind from matter and of Piaget's rigid separation of stages, these models can be understood best in a postmodern frame. The primary emphasis in any competence model is not on the deficits of Being but on the powers of Becoming. In such a model performance deficits are not denied but are placed within the frame of competence powers. Errors do not become *merely* wrongs to be corrected; they also become insights into powers to be developed and transformed. The relationship between competence and performance is now seen as complex, one not equatable with the other—a point the "competency-based" curriculum movement of the 1970s never understood (Doll, 1984). In Chomsky's (1971) words, we must be "devious and clever" (p. 36) in assessing competence from performance, and such assessment requires our conceiving of curriculum as a conversation between "from" and "toward," not merely as a deficit from "toward." Such a conversation, of course, forces us to reconsider the concept of grades, which is nothing but a device for expressing, indeed measuring, the performance deficit.

In the early decades of the twentieth century—when modernism was in its golden age—the schools were filled, as William Schubert (1986) says, "with a flurry of work in 'scientific curriculum making'" (p. 76). Edward L. Thorndike (1913) provided the intellectual basis with his massive three-volume *Educational Psychology;* W. W. Charters demonstrated the science of curriculum construction in his 1923 book; and Henry Harap developed a popular how-to curriculum manual in 1928. Both of these 1920s works as well as Thorndike's (1921) "word-lists" drew up job analyses of practical, everyday, industrial activities. It is interesting to note that in justifying this position, Charters criticizes Plato for not coordinating his educational aims with practical job activities. If he had so done and not left "ideals isolated from activities," then Plato "would powerfully have influenced the education of the next two thousand years" (pp. 9–10). For Charters, curriculum thought must emanate from a matching of ideals with activities. However, in practice, the industrial activities themselves became the ideals of education: the precise and proper goals curriculum advocates and measures. Education and curriculum were now thoroughly grounded in the industrial society; goals and ends could not be separated from society's activities, nor could they be mentally "abstracted from activities" within the society" (p. 32). Ideals became hollow words, not guiding beacons. Goals and ends became no more than rephrased job analyses of industrial occupations and professions. Concepts of transformation, growth, development, and evolution were either nonexistent or severely limited. Again, in dichotomously separating ideals from activities and then replacing ideals with activities, the modernist mind saw ends as practicalities and means as vehicles for delivering ends. Charters was right: Plato did err in separating the Forms from practical life; but he, Charters, committed the same error by substituting the industrial workplace for Plato's Good.

While there were strong countermovements to this trend in the form of child-centered, humanist, and progressive thrusts—which did ameliorate the more narrow and excessively behaviorist versions of curriculum (Doll, 1983b)—all movements ultimately succumbed to the allure of this "scientific" framework. With its emphasis on control through standardization and progress through efficiency, it both answered America's needs in a rapidly changing society and provided a methodology for the future. Scientific knowledge was not merely the knowledge of most worth, it was the only knowledge of worth. Even Harold Rugg (1927/1969), a strong advocate of a curriculum progressive in nature and child centered in approach, called for a more scientific, specialized, and professional approach. This is evidenced strongly in his summary chapter for the *Twenty-Sixth Yearbook of the Society for the Study of Education, Part II* (pp. 147–162), a work whose preparation he directed. And, of course, John Dewey's continual critique of the old traditions and quest for new alternatives put forth the scientific method as the basis for such alternatives. While Dewey's view of science was more complex and multifaceted than the one used by most curricularists, he still contributed to science's simplistic and seductive allure. In short, America, its schools, and its traditions, both traditional and progressive, were captivated by a modernist view of science—a view Stephen Gould (1981) labels as "clouded" and myopic (p. 262). The myopia of this vision came from the mistaken belief that physics is the "ultimate science," and that by reducing all to physics and "quantifiable causes," one is dealing with the basic principles underlying reality.

In portraying the school curriculum as shrouded in the cloak of modernist science, I am not negating Herbert Kliebard's (1986) observation that the American curriculum, eclectic in nature, was born from a "not very tidy compromise" among opposing ideologies (p. 29). Rather, I am saying these ideologies had more effect at the level of rhetoric and discourse than at the level of classroom activity, and that even within the competing ideologies there was a general obeisance to the tenets of modernist science. Kliebard himself makes this same point both in his 1986 book—"efficiency, in later years, became the overwhelming criterion of success in curriculum matters" (p. 28)—and in a 1975 article, "The Rise of Scientific Curriculum Making and Its Aftermath." In the latter, he stresses that educators, while rejecting the research results of the Bobbitt-Charters model, have for over a half-century retained, even revered, the model itself. Kliebard (1975b) is incredulous, as we all should be, that this has happened. He concludes his article with the following observation:

To be critical of scientific curriculum making . . . is not to be critical of science or even the importance of scientific inquiry into the educational process; it is to be critical of a simplistic and vulgar scientism. Its persistence is a source of embarrassment. (p. 37)

THE TYLER RATIONALE

1. What *educational purposes* should the school seek to attain?
2. What *educational experiences* can be provided that are likely to attain these purposes?
3. How can these educational experiences be *effectively organized*?
4. How can we determine whether these purposes are being *attained*?
               —Tyler, *Basic Principles of Curriculum and Instruction*,
                                   1950, pp. 1–2; *emphasis added*

At first glance these questions seem reasonable, and indeed are so within a modernist, linear, cause–effect framework. The questions have had a wide, long lasting, and popular appeal. William Schubert (1986) points out that many educationists consider Tyler's *Basic Principles of Curriculum and Instruction* (1950) to be "one of the two most influential books on curriculum thought and practice" (p. 171), the other book being Dewey's *Democracy and Education* (1916/1966). While grouping Tyler with Dewey in terms of curriculum thought and practice seems incongruous, it is not an incongruity Tyler recognizes or accepts. As Schubert has recorded, Tyler believes his work was a synthesis of the curriculum thought which preceding him—that of Franklin Bobbitt, W. W. Charters, John Dewey, Boyd Bode, Harold Rugg, and Henry Harap (p. 172). Such a broad synthesis, encapsulated within four foci—more compact than Bobbitt's thousands of objectives, or even than Ruggs's eighteen questions—does explain, in part, the popularity of Tyler's rationale. However, a close analysis of the four foci, as Kliebard (1975a, 1975b) has done, shows them to possess less than they purport; they assume a modernist, stable-state universe, as well as a discovery epistemology.

The predetermination of objectives, the selection and organization of experiences to reflect those objectives, followed by evaluations to determine whether the objectives have been attained, appear to place prime emphasis on the choice of goals. In fact, Tyler states that the selection of objectives is not only the first act that must be done in curriculum planning but the key to the whole process, and he devotes approximately the first half of his book to this selection. In reality, though, the linear nature of the sequence allows the goals or ends to exist apart from the means of implementation and evaluation, with the evaluation referring only to the success of the implementation, not to the question of the appropriateness of the ends. Being pre-selected, objectives as ends are elevated beyond or made external to the process itself. Tyler does talk of "an acceptable educational philosophy" (p. 13), which is to act as a screen in the selection of objectives, lest unsuitable objectives be chosen. However, as Kliebard points out, Tyler says nothing about the composition or criteria of this screen; he just assumes a consensual ideological framework will emerge, both within a given school or among schools in a system. Handled in this manner, the values underlying this process become hidden. The assessment appears value neutral but is really linked to ends that are value laden, with no criteria set forth as to how the choice of ends is to be made. As Dewey continually stated, criteria for the choice of ends are essential to any educational enterprise that considers itself to be more than training or indoctrination, to any educational enterprise associating itself with democracy. In a democratic society, "ends arise and function within action. They are not . . . things lying outside activity." As such, ends are not fixed; they act rather as "terminals of deliberation," as ends-in-view, as "turning points *in* [not prior to] activity" (1922, p. 223). Here lies a basic value difference between John Dewey and Ralph Tyler. Dewey sees educational ends arising within the process of experiential activity, with learning as a by-product of that activity; Tyler sees educational ends set prior to experience, with learning a specifically intended, directed, and controlled outcome—one that can be measured. This difference, although crucial, is not always perceived; it is seen more clearly when curriculum is looked at from a post-modern, process perspective.

The linear separation of goals from the experiences designed to foster those goals allows Tyler and his followers to distinguish educational goals from curriculum goals. Educational goals can be broadly based and written in general, even fuzzy or vague, terms—for example, education should prepare one for life, or education should foster critical thinking skills—thus winning support from a large segment of society. For curriculum goals Tyler turns to Bobbitt's notion of framing these in terms of the practical and professional work needs of contemporary society. Like Bobbitt, he talks of "needs" as "gaps to be overcome" (p. 6). While Tyler does not use contemporary society as the only source of needs—student interests and the nature of subject matter are also studied—contemporary life-needs dominate. When he talks of identifying "needed changes in behavior patterns of the students which the educational institution should seek to produce" (pp. 4–5), Tyler is really using contemporary standards as the basis for these needs or gaps. Further, he uses technocratic experts as the ones to assess and even to determine these needs, which then take on a moral imperative. Needs, of course, as Tyler recognizes, become meaningless without "some conception of a desirable norm"; they represent "the gap between what is and what should be" (p. 6). As such, needs tacitly assume a stable-state universe wherein the oughts are agreed to, categorized, and measured. Such a stable-state assumption brings with it a positivist epistemology, one where knowledge exists independent of the knower and can be both discovered and validated.

This concept of standardized norms lying within a stable-state universe lies at the very heart of the modernist paradigm; it also is a concept the post-modernist paradigm, in all its variations, challenges, and rejects.

The Tyler rationale found expression in school curricula through the behavioral objectives movement of the 1960s, the competency-based education movement of the 1970s, and the Hunter model of the 1980s. In all of these the pattern is the same: pre-set goals, selection and direction of experiences, evaluation. Along with the linear ordering of this sequence and its dichotomous separation of ends from means there exists an instrumentalist or functionalist view of the nature of education. Here education is not its own end, growing from within itself; it is directed toward and controlled by purposes outside itself. In an industrial and capitalist society this has taken the form of acquiring jobs. Given this orientation it is only natural Tyler and his followers focused on job analysis as the source for curriculum inspiration, for the skills, knowledges, attitudes students should acquire. It is also understandable why, within this framework, the goals or ends of curriculum are not as important as the means for implementation—as with Schmidt. William Reynolds (1987), in critiquing Madeline Hunter's "Seven Steps," states this nicely when he says: "She does not question where the long-range goals originate. . . . [This] seems relatively unimportant to her . . . the important aspect is to implement effectively" that chosen (p. 7). Then Reynolds goes on to show that the heart of the Hunter model is really an expansion and evaluation of Tyler's second and third steps.

Ted Aoki (1983), on whom Reynolds draws, carries this concept of instrumentality in the Tyler rationale even further. He points out that the "scientific" tradition in curriculum is really a utilitarian orientation rooted in interest for "intellectual and technical control of the world" (pp. 11–12). This desire for control is embedded in the metaphysics of modernist science and in the scientism American curriculum thought has embraced. It has little to do with the methods and procedures of science itself, as both Kliebard and Gould have pointed out. Rather, its roots lie partly in modernism's fear of uncertainty and in its utopian vision of a better world through order and control. As a desire to gain control over nature, including human nature, such positivism is a continuation of the "scientific" legacy left by Laplace and Saint-Simon. B. F. Skinner (1953) expresses his version of this legacy when he states: "If we are to use the methods of science in the field of human affairs, we must assume that behavior is lawful and determined," that the actions people exhibit are the "result of specifiable conditions," which once discovered can be both anticipated and determined (p. 6). Madeline Hunter (1982) picks up this same theme when she says: "Teaching [is] one of the last professions to emerge from . . . witch doctoring, to become a profession based on a science of human learning," itself only recently "translated into cause–effect relationships of use to teachers" (p. 169).

These two quotations not only demonstrate instrumentalist aspects of the modernist-scientific view, they also bring forth the cause–effect framework underlying this view. Jacob Bronowski (1978), in his book *The Common Sense of Science*, says the concept of cause with its linear relationship to effect "has been elevated to the rank of the central concept of [modernist] science"; It is "what makes Newton's world different from that of Aristotle" (p. 40). "Cause and effect has taken [such a] powerful hold on our minds" that "we have the greatest difficulty in freeing ourselves from its compulsion . . . unconsciously, we fall back on it at every turn." It "has become our natural way of looking at all problems" (p. 59). But in spite of our allegiance, "the principle itself is mistaken; nature is not strictly a succession of causes and effects" (p. 75). Embodied within nature, defining its very essence, is the powerful force of creation, of spontaneous action, of self-organization. Neither the mysticism of an *élan vital* nor the mechanism of a determinist environment— alike in that both deny intention and dialogue—can define life and nature; only self-regulation with its dynamic and transformative interactions can do this. Here is the message post-modern science is sending us; it is a message we need to hear and use if curriculum is to enter a new and long overdue epoch.

Note

1. For a definition of how I am using the word *frame*, see Note 2 in the Introduction.

Part II

THE POST-MODERN PARADIGM: AN OPEN VISION

As Ilya Prigogine (1961) points out, in thermodynamics it is common to refer to systems as isolated, closed, or open. Isolated or perfectly stable systems—the universe was once imagined to be one of these—"exchange neither energy nor matter" (p. 3). Such systems may move, as the universe does, but this movement is purely cyclical within a set frame that itself does not change. It is this type of system that Socrates envisioned in his concept of knowledge being recycled; that Plato envisioned in his concept of reality lying eternally in the Forms, with humans partaking of it during their lifetimes; and that Aristotle saw in the process of acorns growing into oak trees, which in turn refertilize the earth with more acorns. Closed systems, on the other hand, a development of the modernist paradigm, "exchange energy but no matter" (p. 3). Thus, in such mechanical devices as gears, pulleys, waterwheels, there is a transference and concentration of energy but no spontaneous development of energy nor any transformation of matter into energy. However, in this transference and concentration, as in wind funneling into a well-wrought sail or human power increased by the gear structure of a bicycle, there is a transcendence beyond the purely physical. If matter is to be transformed into energy, at least the energy present is focused and harnessed, thus yielding increased results. Open systems, very much predicated on Einstein's $E = mc^2$, "exchange both energy and matter" (p. 3). Here these two quantities can be transformed into one another, as atomic explosions so dramatically illustrate. The key point, both metaphorically, in educational terms, and factually, in terms of the systems themselves, is that isolated systems exchange nothing, being at best cyclical; closed systems *transmit and transfer*; open systems *transform*.

Education and curriculum have borrowed some concepts from the stable, nonexchange concept—for example, children following the pattern of their parents, IQ as discovering and quantifying an innate potentiality. However, for the most part modernist curriculum thought has adopted the closed version, one where—through focusing—knowledge is transmitted, transferred. This is, I believe, what our best contemporary schooling is about. Transmission frames our teaching–learning process. We define good teaching (resulting in good learning) as the transfer of knowledge—often in the form of the noble works and accepted procedures of the Western, humanist tradition. Until now, the thermodynamic concept of an open system—one that transforms through dissipation—has not been explored for curriculum considerations.

The rest of this book will explore just such a transformative curriculum. Part II will look at the nature of open systems in a number of disciplines: biology, chemistry, mathematics, philosophy, and psychology, as well as the open or process thought aspects of the curricular theories of Jerome Bruner, John Dewey, Jean Piaget, and Alfred North Whitehead. As was said in the Introduction, none of these four could be called post-modern: Three of the four died before the movement became culturally popular in the 1980s. However, in hindsight, the struggle all four had with the tenets and assumptions of modernism can be understood better from a post-modern, open systems, process perspective. Part III will explore, in as practical a way as possible, the development of an open systems curriculum, one that can be labeled transformative or process oriented. One of the premier arguments in both parts will be the biologically oriented one that human beings per se are living systems, and that living systems per se are open systems. Thus, educational development would occur best when based on the type of system that characterizes being human.

Being human, though, is not modeled simply by equating living systems with open, thermodynamic ones. Being human means to go beyond both biological and thermodynamic structures. Purposiveness is a major part of being human, and part of purposiveness is a desire for and action toward closure, resolutions, definitions. This is the way we make sense of the "bloomin', buzzin', confusion we call life." Thus, human openness carries its own paradox, a desire for closure, resolution, definiteness. It is the complex interplay between openness and closure at a number of levels (conscious, biological, molecular) that appears key for transformations to take place. Further, as a paradox of the paradox, once we look at human activity in this transformative frame we see analogies with other systems, biological and chemical, where the concepts of purpose, self-organization, communication now seem apparent. Thus, the original separation of systems into a simple open-closed dichotomy leads not only to a realization of another, or second, way of cosmological framing but also to an alternative third way, which transforms each of the first two frames and provides a new level of complexity with openness and closure embedded within each other. Much in the following chapters will be devoted to exploring this third way, that which Jean Piaget called a *tertium quid*, and which John Dewey called a *definite alternative* to the extremes of both traditional behaviorism and romantic progressivism.

Past and recent curriculum discourse, though, has not paid attention to the complexity of human thought; rather it has adopted the behaviorist paradigm that, as J. B. Watson (1913) so well put it, "recognizes no dividing line between man and brute" (p. 158). Thus, the complex activities that humans engage in and the abilities they possess above and beyond, or in qualitatively greater degree than, brutes have been downplayed or neglected. This view has contributed strongly to a concept of curriculum where training in pre-chosen activities has superseded the development of transformative abilities—those abilities which in Jerome Bruner's (1973) phrase allow us "to go beyond the information given" (Ch. 13). It is these abilities (purposiveness, self-organization, communication) that educators and curricularists now recognize need to be developed and that characterize the quality of being human.

In part, the view modernism has held regarding human potential and the best way to develop this potential comes from modernism's own social and epistemological visions—the cosmology in which the paradigm has been framed. Founded on Enlightenment thought, itself based on Cartesian certainty and Newtonian stability, and particularly on the union of this thought with industrialism, modernism developed definite social and epistemological visions. The intersection of these visions lay in the concept that improvement, progress, betterment for all would come through technology and *right reason*. This was the vision Pierre Laplace had, the vision that inspired both August Comte and Henri de Saint-Simon; it even inspired Karl Marx and Andrew Carnegie, albeit in different ways. For all its real-world contradictions, this social-epistemological-metaphysical vision held sway during the nineteenth century and even well into the twentieth. It shaped the scientific thought of Frederick Taylor and Joseph Mayer Rice, giving to their work a sense of moral imperative. Underlying this cosmological vision was a belief or faith in certainty—that certainty was attainable through "right reason," and that once attained it would be lasting. Once the *real* structures—of mathematics and the sciences, of social and psychological situations, or reality itself—were understood, the stability of the cosmos was such that one could be certain forever. This was Laplace's utopian vision and the "sweet dream" of modernist reason.

In many ways, the twentieth century has been a century of disillusionment, an age of uncertainty and anxiety. Early in the century, Werner Heisenberg and others subscribing to the "Copenhagen interpretation" of quantum physics showed that certainty does not and cannot exist in the micro world of the subatomic (Gribbin, 1984). A few years later Kurt Gödel showed that the foundations of mathematics could not be proven in terms of consistency and completeness. Any mathematical, especially arithmetical, system rests on basic assumptions that seem intuitively correct but are logically unprovable (Kline, 1980, Ch. 12; Gödel, 1931/1963). At the social and political level the holocaust of two world wars has shown us that the sweet dreams of reason have not led us to a better, more just, or more moral society. Just the opposite! Finally, in this decade of the 1990s we are finding ourselves hounded by the economic, personal, political, and social decisions made in the 1980s. What seemed minor and unimportant then, decisions made in an almost cavalier way, have now grown into monstrous problems. We face the twenty-first century, the third millennium, gripped by strong elements of doubt and fear. If we have a faith, and I hope we do, it is a faith based on doubt, not on certainty. What we do—and we must do—we do with the realization that it may be wrong; no longer do we have the feeling of certainty and rightness in the universal and metaphysical sense the modernists posited. Such an absolute right (or truth) does not exist. Instead we make particular decisions which we hope will be right for now, for a local time and place.

Jean-Jacques Rousseau is generally acknowledged (Berman, 1982; Cox, 1984) as the one who gave shape to our historical concept of modern when he referred to *moderniste* as that which broke with the entrenched patterns of the past—in religion, politics, social affairs, knowledge. James Evans (1990) says that *moderniste* represented "novelty, discontinuity, and independence" (p. 209). It is, of course, this notion of independent thinking that Descartes, the Protestants, and the "new" scientists of the seventeenth century expounded and feared. This historical break with a settled cosmology was done in such a way as to bring into play a schizophrenic view of culture and reality—one where modernism asserted and honored certainty amid a hailstorm of social and intellectual turbulence (Toulmin, 1990). This dichotomous split is obvious in René Descartes' mind/body bifurcation, as well as in the vageries of his own life—to be explored in Chapter Five. Intellectually it can also be found in John Locke's empiricism, especially regarding primary and secondary qualities, and in Thomas

Hobbes' skepticism about our ability to know reality. The schizo-phrenic aspect of this split, though, comes out most strongly in the romantic tradition that ran counter to the scientific tradition. In his novel *Julie or the New Eloise*, Rousseau (1761/1900) has the young hero, Saint-Preux, experience *le tourbillon social* (the maelstrom of social life) with its exhilarations and frustrations. After a few months of this Saint-Preux says:

> I begin to feel the drunkenness into which this agitated, tumultuous life plunges me. With such a multitude of objects passing before my eyes, I lapse into dizziness. . . . I forget what I am and to whom I belong. (p. 249; *personal translation*)

As he grasps for something solid to hang on to, only phantoms appear, which he, "floating from caprice to caprice," finds disappear as soon as he tries to clasp them. Saint-Preux is caught between self-enlargement and self-deflation (pp. 249–250). It is in such an atmo-sphere that modernism developed its concept of self—a point realized and exploited by both Karl Marx and Sigmund Freud, albeit in quite different ways. Looking back on eighteenth- and nineteenth-century versions of modernism, James Evans (1990) says the movement has "sought to make us comfortable with a dualistic, and essentially schiz-ophrenic culture" (p. 211).

Post-modernism posits a quite different social, personal, and intel-lectual vision. Its intellectual vision is predicated not on positivistic certainty but on pragmatic doubt, the doubt that comes from any deci-sion based not on metanarrative themes but on human experience and local history. Acceptance of this (troubling) situation may well cause us pangs of fear but it also provides us with a motive to be better negotia-tors—with ourselves, our concepts, our environment, others. The loss of certainty encourages if it does not cause us to dialogue and commu-nicate with others. In turn, this frame of dialogic communication can lead to a different social vision, one applicable to teaching as well as to foreign policy decisions. Such a vision recognizes the rights of others and eschews the concept of "one best" or "one right" way. It accepts the indeterminacy inherent in complexity and multiple perspectives (Joseph Schwab, 1978b, uses the phrase "polyfocal conspectus," p. 342 ff). At the same time post-modernism strives for an eclectic yet lo-cal integration of subject/object, mind/body, curriculum/person, teacher/student, us/others. This integration, though, is a living process; it is negotiated not preordained, created not found. And this integration depends in part on us and our actions. We have a responsi-bility for our futures as well as for the futures of others. In this sense, carrying out an open vision may well bring us to an ecological perspective and cosmology. And within this perspective, we may find a personal vision, one which helps us recognize that our sense of self and reality as independent objects is meaningless. We are able to discern ourselves only in terms of others, reality only in terms of imaginations. Both self and reality are found in relations, a point John Dewey and Alfred North Whitehead understood well. Since self and reality are relational, we must, as Richard Rorty (1980) says, "keep the conversation going" (p. 377).

I wish to close this introduction to Part II with some comments about methodology. In discussing contemporary movements in mathematics, philosophy, psychology, process thought, and especially the sciences, I am not suggesting curricularists copy these movements or even use them for a foundational base. Such an essentialist, copy-model methodology lies at the heart of modernism, not of post-modernism. Rather, I am setting forth these contemporary movements to help us, as individuals caught between paradigms, develop a new paradigmatic frame. The contemporary movements, analyzed here, in other disciplines are meant to be used heuristically, to generate concerns about our own curricular thoughts and assumptions. We realize the historicity of basic assumptions—those we consider natural—only as we analyze and contrast these assumptions with others. As we question the historical roots of our contemporary beliefs, I hope we can free our inventiveness and creativity. The obverse of the post-structural dictum "to know is to kill" (definitional knowing aborts unborn thoughts) is that "inquiry frees" (opens up possibilities). In this vein the following chapters are meant to serve as heuristics not as models or foundations.

For the past few years, I have used the approaches described in this part of the book in my own classes (Doll, 1989a, 1989b). My reflections on these methods will, I hope, be generative for others as they think about and discuss curricular issues. As Donald Schön (1983) says, it is through dialogue, conversation, and public inquiry that we begin to "reflect on [our] own tacit understandings," thereby starting the dual process of (1) bringing these understandings to consciousness and (2) changing them at the same time (pp. 296–297). Such a process is transformative, not only in bringing our thoughts from taken-for-granted assumptions to explicit affirmations but also in providing us with a (process) frame whereby those affirmations can be studied, shared, critiqued, changed.

CHAPTER 3

Piaget and Living Systems

THE BIOLOGICAL WORLD-VIEW

[Those] who work in the so-called soft sciences . . . have often suffered from "physics envy." They have strived to practice their science according to their clouded vision of physics.
—Gould, *The Mismeasure of Man*, 1981, p. 262

Most general histories of "science" have been written by historians of physics who have never quite gotten over the parochial attitude that anything that is not applicable to physics is not science.
—Mayr, *The Growth of Biological Thought*, 1982, p. 14

All science is either physics or stamp collecting.
—Rutherford, in Gribbin, *In Search of Schrödinger's Cat*, 1984, p. 79

These quotations make two obvious points and one not so obvious point: First, in modernist thought, physics has been the canonical model for *all* science; second, the social sciences, including education, in trying to "scientize" their disciplines have adopted a shallow and mistaken view of what constitutes science. The less obvious point is that in using physics as the model, whether seen clearly or "through a glass darkly," the social sciences have excluded the concept of interaction. This has had devastating effects on curriculum, for, as both Dewey and Piaget have pointed out, it is interaction that forms the heart of growth. Physics, at least in its Newtonian, mechanistic form, has no view of growth and a most limited view of interaction—that of machines running down through friction and of objects moving through external force only. As Newton's first law of motion states, objects at rest stay that way—as do objects in motion—*until an outside force inflicts itself.* The cause–effect relationship implied here is an apt metaphor for the modernist concept of teaching and learning: One precedes and causes the other. Teaching becomes didactic, directing; not aiding, helping, stimulating, or challenging natural, self-organizing processes. Machines do not self-organize, compensate, grow—although a number of people in the artificial intelligence field are hoping to make machines that will perform these functions (Putnam, 1988).

An open, biologically oriented model, though, sees humans and their learning processes allied with self-organizing, living systems (Piaget, 1971a). One of the essential characteristics of living systems is that of interaction. In a living system, parts are defined not in isolation from one another but in terms of their relations with each other and with the system as a whole. This is one of biology's unique features, a feature which makes it both more appropriate as a model for human development and categorically different from Newtonian physics.

Aristotle, as a scientist, was basically a biologist, a categorizer and classifier. However, while he thought in terms of pre-modern balances and harmonies, he did not think in terms of systems, certainly not organic, living systems: those which show transformative, open-ended growth over time. This did not come until Charles Darwin and Alfred Russel Wallace did their seminal work on evolution. Further, Aristotle's classificatory bent was turned into dull and rigid categorizations by the scholastic logicians. Thus, the concept of biology as a discipline studying living organisms within an integrated, hierarchical systems frame was not a part of either pre-modern or modern thought. This concept arrived only in the twentieth century, at the end of the modernist period.[1]

The scientific revolution of the seventeenth century was based, though, not on Aristotle's classificatory scheme nor on the scholastics' logic but on Ptolemy's mechanistic concepts. The complex movement of the planets, which Ptolemy posited and Nicolaus Copernicus simplified by placing the sun, not the earth, at "the center," was mechanistic (Kuhn, 1959). It is still portrayed that way in school classrooms throughout the country, with their gear and pulley models of the solar system. This leaves out, or bypasses, the issue of the universe as a pulsating, creating, dynamic system.

A simplistic, non-quantum view of physics has been, as the quotation from Stephen Gould states, at the heart of the social sciences' view of what science is about. However, even at a more sophisticated level there is a tendency to accept Lord Rutherford's statement: All science can be reduced to physics and physical chemistry. Only in the mid-twentieth century was there a concerted effort by respected scientists to establish biology as its own discipline, to insist on its own "autonomy" with its own "way of thought." Here the work of J. H. Woodger (1948), Morton Beckner (1959), F. J. Ayala and Theodore Dobzhansky (1974), and Ernst Mayr (1982, 1988) has been outstanding. Mayr especially has been prodigious in his quest to establish biology's "autonomy." This word is a bit of a misnomer—it is not intended to convey a modernist, dualist split between biology and physics-chemistry. Rather the word means that biological concepts cannot be explained exclusively within the laws of the natural sciences; while the concepts of biology do not violate physical laws neither are they completely reducible to these laws (Davies, 1988; Peacocke, 1986).

Today, it is generally accepted that biology has its own characteristics, ones not *usually* found in physics and chemistry, certainly not in modernist physics and chemistry. There is an addendum to this last statement. In the work of Ilya Prigogine, Gregorie Nicolis, and others of the "Brussels School" there are indeed connections between contemporary biology's characteristics and aspects of post-quantum physics and chemistry. In fact, it is not unfair to say that these scientific theorists have relied, in part, on insights gained from the "new" biology to posit their concepts of the "new" physics (Davies, 1984, 1988; Hayles, 1990; Peacocke, 1983, 1986). However, this work—extremely exciting, as Chapter Four will show—is controversial and longer on metaphysics than on experimental verification. As one sympathetic critiquer has said, the Brussels School, in spite of Prigogine's 1977 Nobel Prize in chemistry, has produced "more philosophy than results" (Hayles, 1990, p. 10). Nevertheless, this philosophy might well help us produce a new, more relational or ecological metaphysics and cosmology, which, in turn, will guide us in new ways to view and interact with our environment. Results may well be forthcoming.

The characteristics of the new biology that give it a sense of autonomy, compatible with but not reducible to physico-chemical laws, are (1) complexity of organization, (2) genetic history or coding, (3) plurality of causes, (4) directionality or purpose (*telos*), and (5) self-organization. Complexity is the most comprehensive, exciting, and far-reaching of these characteristics. In Chapter Four, complexity will be looked at from the perspective of mathematical chaos theory; here it is viewed from an evolutionary perspective where, over time, hierarchical systems or networks of organization develop that cannot be reduced from one to the other. One such evolutionary structure, which J. G. Miller (1978) uses in his monumental *Living Systems*, is cell-organ-organism-group-society-world. Another one biologists commonly use is that of atom-molecule-macromolecule-subcellular organelle-living cell-multicellular functioning organ-whole living organisms-population of organisms-ecosystem (Gerard, 1957). A third, and more common, hierarchical structure is the relationship between cells that constitute the brain and the brain as a functioning whole system. At the cellular level, the brain is "a ceaseless change of detail," there being about 10^{10} such cells, with each cell making about 10^9 network connections for a total of 10^{19} system interconnections. Not all of these connections operate at any one time; the brain uses only a small fraction of its capacity. This allows the brain to substitute one set of connections when another is damaged—for example, a blind person hearing better. Further, on any one given day 10^3 cells are decaying or dying. Yet within this ceaseless change of detail, our basic behaviors, our memories, our sense of integral existence as individuals retain "their unitary continuity of pattern" (Weiss, 1970, p. 213). At one level the brain is "chaotic"; at another it is complexly patterned. These two perspectives cannot be substituted for one another, nor reduced to one another; instead, they are complementary, indeed integrated. A curriculum aligned with the brain's complex structurings would include hierarchical orderings, integrated and complementary functionings, and pattern recognition. Chapter Seven will attempt to outline such a curriculum. I say attempt, for these concepts are not easy for our modernist-oriented minds to grasp, let alone develop.

Another concept implicit within hierarchy theory, itself part of complexity, is that of emergence: new structures emerging spontaneously, self-generatively, unpredictably from old ones. As Ernst Mayr (1988) says:

> When two entities are combined at a higher level of integration, not all the properties of the new entity are necessarily a logical or predictable consequence of the properties of the components. (p. 34)

And as Howard Pattee (1973) has said:

> Biological organizations . . . have an indefinite capability to evolve new functions and new hierarchical levels of control while maintaining a relatively fixed set of elementary parts at each level. (pp. 106–107)

This transition from one level to another, from one set of functions to another, is not entirely obvious; in fact, as Pattee and others have pointed out, there is an element of mystery about the transition. However, we do seem to know some facts: Living systems maintain a sense of balance with their environment. In Piaget's famous phrase, they "assimilate and accommodate." Further assimilations and accommodations occur through the need to overcome problems or perturbations. That is, problems and perturbations put these systems into play, into operation. As was said earlier, open systems actually need problems and perturbations in order to function. Even further, while the systems will try to maintain their sense of equilibrium via slight accommodations and assimilations, there comes a time, a threshold or bifurcation, when the perturbations become so great that the whole system needs to reorganize, to "generate 'emergent' properties in the *new context* of a larger set" (Pattee, 1973, p. 133, *emphasis added*). The emergence here is that of properties not functional at a lower level suddenly coming forth to develop at a higher level. Curricularly, this suggests teachers need to assess not only what performances and operations have been learned at one level, but what structures are in the embryonic stage of development ready to burst forth at a later time: a difficult but necessary task. As John Dewey (1916/1966) has said:

> Experience as an active process occupies time and its later period completes its earlier portion; it brings to light connections involved but hitherto unperceived. (p. 78)

This biological concept of emergence within hierarchy theory underlies much of Jean Piaget's work with children. In *Judgment and Reasoning in the Child* (1924/1976, Ch. 4) he describes the difficulties "young Weng" (age 7) has with some operations in multiplication and division. Weng does not see 4×3 as an isolated multiplication fact but as three sets of doubles $(2 + 2, 2 + 2, 2 + 2)$. As Piaget questions Weng he finds the boy not operating via memorization but groping with the operation of doubling (and of halving).[2] When Weng moves from a preoperational stage to a concrete one, the concept of relations will become paramount—seeing relations is one of the key factors in this latter stage. In Weng's gropings it is possible to see the beginnings of this emerging new stage; but only, I believe, if one is attuned to the concept of emergence.

At least four points, important for curricularists, are inherent in the foregoing discussion. One is that biology—with its concepts of complexity, hierarchy, and network relations—is heuristically a rich metaphor for curriculum thought. Another is that the generativeness of this thought is probably available only to those able to move beyond a closed (modernist) frame to an open (post-modernist) one. A third is that any sense of development that moves beyond mere accumulation to transformation will need to pay attention to the role problems and perturbations play—these are, as Piaget has said, "the driving force of development," at least of internal development. Fourth, the teacher needs to be aware of more than one level of operation: the not-yet-conscious, groping level as well as the performance level.

This latter point is worth more exploration. In his second essay on "The Practical: Arts of Eclectic," Joseph Schwab (1971/1978) talks of a "polyfocal conspectus," one that looks at any item or object from a multiple perspective. While it is not known whether he had read Howard Pattee's work on hierarchy theory, it is probable that as a biologist Schwab was familiar with the concept. At least the two are similar. Pattee (1973), distinguishing between systems theory of a closed type with its strong sense of the linear and hierarchy theory, which focuses on multiple perspectives, says of the latter, "It must be formulated to describe at least two levels at a time." Further, "it must allow interactions between alternative levels" (pp. 149–150). This latter point is most important: A polyfocal conspectus does not alternate between perspectives but rather allows perspectives to interact. In this interaction lies the key to transformative development. As young Weng begins his move from the isolated memorization inherent in the pre-operational stage to the elemental relations inherent in concrete operations, it is the interaction between memorization and relational patternings that is key—for example, 8×3 seen as twice 4×3. I believe this interaction as it develops will allow Weng to integrate that with which he is comfortable (adding two's, then doubling) with that which is new and challenging (the acquisition of more multiplication facts and the generation of newer patternings). As he achieves a comfort level with these new facts (16×3 as twice 8×3) and procedures (tripling/tripartiting not just doubling/halving) he can build a multifocused matrix of facts and operations— for example, seeing 16×3 as 8×6 or even as 4×12.

The foregoing procedure, which I have used with second- , third- , and fourth-graders (Doll & Robbins, 1986), has encouraged me to teach from a polyfocal curriculum, one deeply rich in perspectives and problematics (Doll, 1989a, 1989b, 1991). Such an emphasis is, I believe, the beginning of an alternative to the precise, clear (but limited) goals we usually associate with a well-constructed curriculum design—particularly one drawn in the Tyler, Hunter, or behavioral objectives mode.

While complexity of organization is the most important of the characteristics defining the new biology, the other four—genetic coding, plurality of causes, purpose, and self-organization—are also heuristic for curricular thought. Unlike machines (modernism's chief metaphor), living organisms have a genetic code built into them. This code, found in DNA (deoxyribonucleic acid), provides a guide for future development and experience. This means that future experiences and behaviors will emerge from present experiences and behaviors just as the present ones have emerged from past ones. Life, indeed our working reality itself, is made up of interconnected experiences. Obvious as this statement is, developmentally simple in its approach, it has not played an essential role in curriculum development. Many curriculum critics, including Oliver and Gershman (1989), point out that current curriculum design is based on fragmentation, isolation, atomization—not on the *flowing of experience.* Curricular subjects, class schedules, grade levels, lesson plans, even teaching strategies are represented in particle form. Commenting on the metaphysical assumptions underlying such a view, Alfred North Whitehead (1933) remarks:

> Newtonian physics is based upon the independent individuality of each bit of matter. Each stone is conceived as . . . alone in the universe, the sole occupant of uniform space . . . described without reference to the past or future . . . *fully and adequately . . . constituted within the present moment.* (p. 158; also in Oliver & Gershman, p. 21)

With this cosmological frame, it is only natural for teachers to advocate that students "do their own work," and that the curriculum be envisioned in terms of Carnegie units and individual course syllabi. A model based on biologically oriented assumptions would develop a different frame, more interactive and transformative.

The final two characteristics of biology I have picked to characterize its autonomy are those of purpose and self-organization. These two are conjoined: purpose as telos is evidenced in self-organization, while self-organization is itself a type of purpose. These two are also among the more controversial characteristics of biology—self-organization because it has many unexplained aspects; telos because it carries the historical association of pre-set, fixed ends. As individuals who seek both certainty and free will, we wish neither mysticism nor overdetermination.

Biology has been plagued, since the time of Aristotle, with the concept of *telos.* As Aristotle used the word, *telos* has a cosmic sense. In Mayr's (1988) words, it is the *final cause,* one of Aristotle's four, "responsible for the orderly reaching of a preconceived ultimate goal" (p. 29). This wording is reminiscent of Plato's language, with, however, the preconceived ultimate goals moved from the external Forms into the internal nature of the physical objects themselves, hence "causing" these objects to work toward a final state. This change from externality to internality is, of course, the change Aristotle wrought on his teacher's concept of Form. The inherent desire to move to a final end was Aristotle's explanation of the physical phenomenon Newton called gravity: here, physical objects' continual return to earth after being thrown into the air. What Newton "explained" with a mathematical formula, Aris-

totle "explained" metaphysically: an object's active seeking due to teleology of its natural resting place, earth—the center of the universe.

Christian theologians, especially Thomas Aquinas, building on
Greek metaphysics, associated *final cause* with their God, who in his Will
and Power was the originator and controller of all. "Thy Will Be Done"
is a phrase in the Lord's Prayer the medieval Church interpreted literally. In this closed system, the ultimate cosmic power remained outside,
not only external to lived life but often aloof from it—receiving human
supplication but not entering into dialogue with the supplicants.[3] This
was one of the many "protests" raised against the medieval Church.
Such an abstract God was in sharp contrast to both the Old and New
Testament versions of God–human relations. Even the Greeks, with all
their abstractness of God as an unmoved mover or prime Form, had a
cosmic binding between the natural and supernatural.

The scientific revolution of the seventeenth and eighteenth centuries only intensified externality and aloofness: God became mathematical, the Great Geometer, and the universe became mechanized, a clockwork. By the early nineteenth century, Laplace felt he needed only
numerical calculations for his cosmology. Aristotle's teleological cosmology was replaced by a mechanistic one. However, in the more humanist, romantic, alchemical traditions that formed a countermovement to
modernist mechanism this teleological tradition stayed alive. But in
neither tradition, the teleological nor the mechanistic, was the concept
of self-organization advanced in any way. This concept emerges in post-
modern, new biology thinking.

The tradition most likely to have advanced a self-organization thesis is that of late-nineteenth- and early-twentieth-century vitalism—or
neo-vitalism, as it is often called to distinguish it from the earlier vitalism of such ancients as Galen and Erasistratus (Birch & Cobb, 1981, pp.
75–77). In this neo-vitalist movement, Hans Driesch (1905, 1914) and
Henri Bergson (1911) are undoubtedly the two best known proponents.
Both were convinced that purely mechanistic accounts of life left something out, especially when looking at life's origin and development.
Driesch, an embryologist, was amazed at the ability of embryos to reform themselves into wholes when a single cell was broken off from a
2-, 4-, 6-, 8-, even 32-cell organism. However, instead of advocating self-
development, Driesch advanced his *entelechie* thesis, that, as Aristotle
had said, there exists a final end toward which organisms naturally as-
pire. Bergson (1911) in *Creative Evolution* advances the thesis that there
exists within all of us a vital force, an *élan vital*, that gives purpose and
direction to our development. In this frame, life itself becomes "a result
or biproduct of the vital process" (p. xii). Obviously, this movement
went too far with its sense of *telos*, so when no evidence of an internal

force or *entelechie* could be found the movement died. Remnants of it live on, though, in the organicist and anti-reductionist biological movements (Dialectics of Biology Group, 1982; Koestler & Smythies, 1970).

It was not until the seminal work of another embryologist, C. H. Waddington, appeared (1957, 1975) that the idea of self-organization began to emerge; and only with the further seminal work of Ilya Prigogine and his colleagues (Nicolis & Prigogine, 1977; Prigogine, 1980; Prigogine & Stengers, 1984) that it came directly to the fore. One of the key points in Waddington's "epigenetic" view (added on to genetic structures) is that living organisms develop genetic pathways (*chreods*) for future growth. Through interaction with the environment, where both genes and environment play conjoint roles, there occur at the molecular level certain thresholds or bifurcation points at which new pathways develop. While each new pathway is influenced by its own genetic history, the actual development of that pathway is open-ended due to the particular nature of the interaction between the genes and the environment. It is truly epigenetic. In terms of Jacques Monod's (1972) phraseology, it expresses an interaction of chance (environment) and necessity (genetic structure). The interaction between these two explains, for Waddington, evolutionary development. It is also this interaction that Jean Piaget (1952), coming from a biological background influenced by both Bergson and Waddington, uses to explain human learning. The learner's structures, as they interact with the environment, first do simple assimilations and accommodations but eventually—at a nonpredictable threshold or bifurcation point—combine to make a sweeping change (*tout ensemble*), transforming themselves into new and more sophisticated structures. In Piaget's (1971a) word, the structures "autoregulate" (p. 26). This literal translation of the French *autoregulation* is unfortunate since the English implies a sense of nonhuman, machine-like, nonpurposive balance not found in the French. Self-regulation, with its emphasis on that which is alive and purposive, might be a better translation; although here the risk is in anthropomorphizing this process. There is simply no way to capture the French connotation in English.[4] For Piaget, the autoregulatory process is life oriented and progressive, not mechanical and cybernetic. Development, as he conceives it, leads to progressively higher and more complex levels of structuration, which he calls stages. The following quotation from Piaget (1977b) emphasizes this point:

> We can observe a process leading from certain states of equilibrium to *others qualitatively different,* and passing through multiple "nonbalances" and reequilibrations. (p. 3; *emphasis added*)

Prigogine goes beyond Piaget and Waddington. He openly uses the word "self" not "auto"; further, he moves beyond regulation with its attendant concept of pre-set or teleological structuration to open-ended organization. Thus, Prigogine's key phrase is *self-organization* not *auto-regulation*. Self-organization is not teleological (moving to a predetermined end); it is not even teleonomic (purposeful adaptation to the environment, as in the preservation and function of life). Self-organization, rather, is open-ended. The future evolves from the present (and the past) and is dependent on interactions that have happened and are continually happening. To borrow a simple but powerful statement from Birch and Cobb (1981): "Development is thus an ecological succession in which one stage prepares for and initiates the next" (p. 25). The open-endedness of this process is in its initiation of a next stage; the past does contribute but only partially to this initiation. It is the dialogue between the present construct and the problems of the environment that determines the emerging, next stage. Such a becoming process is determined but unpredictable. A curriculum model designed along these transformational lines has the potential to be rich in generation.

Biology is a more heuristic model for curriculum generation than the mechanistic one we now use. Self-organization is, I believe, an essential attribute of this biological model. The details of how such self-organization occurs are still a mystery—as are the details of gravity, electricity, and quantum mechanics. But it seems evident that the process depends on reflective action, interaction, transaction—key points in the curriculum theorizing of Jean Piaget, Jerome Bruner, and John Dewey.

EVOLUTION AND ENTROPY—PROBLEMS AND PROMISES

It would appear that all nature exists in a state of perpetual improvement . . . that the world may still be in its infancy and continue to improve forever and forever.

—Erasmus Darwin, *Zoonomia,* 1794–96/1974, p. 254

All the labours of the ages, all the devotion, all the inspiration, all the noonday brightness of human genius, are destined to extinction in the vast death of the solar system . . . the whole temple of Man's achievement must inevitably be buried beneath the debris of a universe in ruins.

—Russell, "The Free Man's Worship," 1903, p. 67

These two quotations, strikingly different in thought and tone, show that modernism's "discovery" of change, via evolution and entropy, had its problems as well as its promises. Newton's world-view, one of clockwork order, saw Nature *always* and in *all ways* "conformable to Herself and simple." Such simple stability, even stasis, was so great that Carl von Linne (Linnaeus), the eighteenth-century Swedish taxonomist who catalogued plants and animals with the system we use today, never dreamed of movement up or down the "chain of being." Rather, he assumed each species fixed in its order by the Creator (*Systema Naturae*, 1735/1964). As Loren Eiseley (1961) so well phrases it:

> He [Linnaeus] had assumed that all species come from original pairs created on a small island which, in the beginning, had constituted the only dry land, the original Eden of the world. (p. 25)

Linnaeus held to this view even though he worked in the botanical gardens of his patron, where he saw the "sportiveness" of nature— abnormal plants derived from normal ones, by the skillful hands and fertile minds of the gardeners. To such "confusion" Linnaeus responded by distinguishing between the true Species of the Creator and the disorderly creations of the manipulative gardeners. The same perspective is evidenced by Linnaeus' great rival, the Frenchman Georges Louis Leclerc (Comte de Buffon). Buffon possessed many of the key ingredients of Darwin's theory of evolution: a tendency for life to multiply faster than the food supply, variations within a single species, a similarity of structure among different animals, a lengthened time scale needed to account for life's history, the extinction of some species, and the power of experimentation.

Buffon was not, though, able to synthesize all these particulars into a grand design, a metanarrative, as did both Charles Darwin and Alfred Russel Wallace. In fact, Buffon's vast *Natural History* (1797–1807/1968) is a 20-volume collection of the accounts of individual animals, not the elaborated synthesis of a theme. As Eiseley (1961) says, "Buffon never seems to have been able to get from artificial to natural selection" (p. 45).

Just how important artificial selection was to Darwin's grand design is a point of debate. He did come from English landed gentry, a people known for their animal breeding, and was himself a pigeon breeder. Thus, he knew firsthand how to breed a bird for subtle but important changes—stamina, quickness, wing span. Still, he was steeped in a strong religious tradition. He embarked on the voyage of the Beagle believing in the fixity of the species, in a literal interpretation of Gene-

sis, and in "the Bible as an unassailable authority" (*Autobiography,* 1929/
1959, p. 85). However, after he saw the Galapagos Islands with their
abundant variety of birds all "filling the same place in Nature," he began
to suspect "the stability of Species" (Keynes, *The Beagle Record,* 1979, p.
299). In short, Darwin, a modernist, was caught in the contradiction
between his zoological experiences and observations and his religious
upbringing. The voyage of the Beagle was a traumatic one for him.

Returning from the voyage in 1836, Darwin slowly became convinced of evolution—"descent with modification" is the phrase he
used, preferring it to his grandfather's more euphoric "improvement
forever." Conceiving of a grand evolutionary design, though, and decid-
ing on the mechanism that makes the design work are two different
issues: issues that separate Charles Darwin from Jean Baptiste Lamarck.
Both were evolutionists of their day. But Lamarck, along with Erasmus
Darwin, believed in the inheritance of acquired characteristics, while
Charles Darwin, following them by two generations, believed in "natural selection." At its most basic level, the phrase is no more than a
tautology: Those organisms better suited to survival will survive better.
As such, it is a *post-hoc* statement, describing what has happened but
offering no help in predicting what will happen. What are the charac-
teristics of those organisms better suited for survival? Sexual proclivity?
Strength? Cunning? Adaptation to changing environments?

For Darwin, two characteristics were essential to evolutionary survival: superfecundity and the ability to win in life's competitive struggle.
For superfecundity, Darwin meant not only that organisms should
reproduce but that they should reproduce with just enough slightly
different phenotypic variations that each member could find its niche.
This Law of Divergence, as it came to be called, was most important to
Darwin and was expressed by him in a letter to Asa Gray (September 5,
1857) as follows:

> The same spot will support more life if occupied by very diverse forms
> . . . [for] varying offspring of each species try to seize on as many and
> as diverse places in the economy of nature as possible. (1856–57/1990,
> pp. 448–449)

By this breadth of divergence a specie's offspring would be more likely
to survive. There is a strong sense of randomness here, as well as the
assumption that life is a continual combative struggle; "Nature red in
tooth and claw" is the phrase Alfred Lord Tennyson (1850/1975, p. 65)
has made so famous.

Like his contemporaries William Paley (1822) and Charles Lyell

(1830–33), whom he studied extensively, Darwin was strongly influenced by Reverend Thomas Malthus' pamphlet *"Essay on the Principle of Population,"* published in 1798. Here Malthus (1798/1914) argues that human populations left uncontrolled soon outgrow their food supplies. While populations "increase in a geometrical ratio, subsistence only increases in an arithmetical ratio" (p. 7). Only the strongest survive this scenario of "misery and vice." Darwin extrapolated this argument from human populations to all populations and in his *Origin of Species* (1896, sixth edition) proposed his metahypothesis:

> Owning to the high geometrical rate of increase of all organic beings, each area is already fully stocked with inhabitants; and it follows from this, that as the favored forms increase in number, so, generally, will the less favored decrease and become rare. . . . [So that] as new forms are produced . . . many old forms must become extinct. (p. 133)

In short, new species appear as randomly varying organisms and compete with one another in the struggle for existence. The "naturalness" and inevitableness of this process, though, speak more to the Victorian mind-set than to the empirical validity of the thesis.

In fact, the thesis was so strongly attacked that in his later works Darwin (1894) agreed he had "perhaps attributed too much to the action of natural selection" (p. 61). It was Fleeming Jenkin, a Scottish engineer, who raised the objections that caused Darwin to retreat from his bold stand on natural selection. Jenkin (1867) pointed out that rare, mutant, single variations would not survive in cross-breeding but would be "stamped out" through interunions—just as the traits of a white man cast ashore on an island inhabited by dark natives would have his white traits blackened out. Not knowing of Gregor Mendel's work with the inheritance of individual traits through successive generations, Darwin fell back to the sort of inheritance of acquired characteristics favored by his grandfather and Lamarck.

Gregor Mendel's work with genetic characteristics, showing that features such as color and size are passed on genetically as *units* (hence not able to be blackened out as Jenkins maintained), was not discovered until the year 1900—thirty-five years after Mendel first described his work and after his own death and that of both Darwin and Jenkins (Iltis, 1932). Even with the discovery of Mendel's papers it was another three to four decades before the contemporary neo-Darwinian "synthesis" was put together by such men as Theodore Dobzhansky (1937), Julian Huxley (1942), and Ernst Mayr (1942). The latter, in his recent works (1982, 1988, 1991), has defended the "synthesis" vigorously against a number of attacks—one of which was mounted by Piaget (1971a, 1978). The heart of the synthesis, a combination of Mendel's genetics and Darwin's natural selection, lies in two propositions, expressed by Francois Jacob (1974) as follows:

> First, all organisms, past, present or future, descend from one or several rare living systems which arose spontaneously. Second, that species are derived from one another by natural selection of the best pro-creators. (p. 13)

Ancillary to these two propositions but important for both education and neo-Darwinian evolution is the concept of gradual, linear progression. Darwin (1859/1964) talked of Nature having no "gaps" (*Natura non facit saltum*). He was so committed to this gradualist perspective that he saw the fossil record's nonconfirmation of his assumption only as an indication of "the extreme imperfection of the geological record" (p. 280). He realized, of course, that for the theory to have validity the fossil record would ultimately have to so confirm. He believed this confirmation would show a "finely graduated organic chain." In common with Newton, Darwin could not conceive of Nature as being anything but "conformable to Herself and simple."

Such a graduated perspective, one of modernism's key tenets, also underlies contemporary curriculum design. Curriculum materials are so structured that the "learning" students do is framed not in terms of their own self-organizing processes—which will have "gaps"—but as the result of following others' pre-set, logically designed, simply ordered, sequential steps. This premise, too often unseen, lies at the heart of Frederick Taylor's time-and-motion studies, of the scientific efficiency movement's basic methodology, of B. F. Skinner's operant conditioning, and of Madeline Hunter's "Seven Steps." Of this particular learning frame and the teaching methodology that accompanies it, Dewey (1938) says:

> Perhaps the greatest of all pedagogical fallacies is the notion that a person learns only the particular thing he is studying at the time (p. 48).

Such a particularist perspective flies in the face of what is known about the brain's normal functioning. As Leslie Hart (1983) says: The brain is "an amazingly subtle and sensitive *pattern-detecting* apparatus," designed or shaped "to deal with *natural complexity*, not neat 'logical simplicities' " (pp. 60, 76). If one wishes to develop a curriculum that facilitates the brain's abilities, bringing forth "higher order thinking skills," I propose the curriculum be rich in natural complexity and delivered in a manner sensitive to the brain's pattern-detecting devices. Few, if any, curricula have taken this as an explicit goal.

Niles Eldredge and Stephen J. Gould, together (1972, 1977) and separately (Eldredge, 1986; Gould, 1982, 1989a, 1989b), have challenged Darwin's notion of evolutionary progress via gradual steps. They assert that the nonconfirmation of his assumed gradualism is due not to the "extreme imperfection of the geological record" but to Darwin's own metaphysical assumptions. In place of his "phyletic gradualism" they propose "punctuated equilbria." The heart of their argument lies in their own belief that change and order are codeterminants of each other, each integrated into an evolutionary pattern. At the practical level, their argument is that the fossil record shows evolutionary growth as a series of equilibrium states, punctuated by a sudden "rapid transition between [these] stable states" (Gould, 1982, p. 139). Such a notion, akin to C. H. Waddington's "epigenetic assimilation," does not necessarily challenge the broad theme of neo-Darwinism, but it does reframe the concept of "natural" within natural selection, thereby opening the question as to whether neo-Darwinism is the *only* vehicle for explaining evolutionary change. Evolutionary change probably is more complex than simply the strongest, or most sexually prolific, surviving in a competition for food and mates. As Gould (1989b) phrases it:

> Progress by competition may occur in normal times, but episodes of mass extinction undo, disrupt, and redirect this process . . . [so much that] the rules for survival change in these extraordinary episodes. (p. 8)

This latter statement, rules changing in extraordinary episodes, combined with the earlier statement of nature's complexity including extraordinary episodes as part of its naturalness, provides a mega-metaphor: one found in Thomas Kuhn's concept of how paradigms change and in Jean Piaget's concept of how personal growth follows an equilibrium–disequilibrium–reequilibration model. This can be a heuristic device for teachers and curriculum designers interested in working with the concepts of self-organization and the brain's natural pattern-detecting or pattern-creating abilities.

At the time Lyell, Wallace, and Darwin were beginning to wonder about the nature of evolutionary change, others, notably Jean-Joseph Fourier, Sadi Carnot, and William Thompson, were dealing with a different concept of change—born of James Watt's newly invented steam

engine.[5] Here matter was actually transformed into energy (at least at
the macro or aggregate level); and when the energy dissipated by boil-
ing water was harnessed and put under pressure, it provided civilization with a new source of power, one that ultimately transformed society itself. Dynamic, or mechanical, change—that of gears, levers,
pulleys—is incremental, linear, easily controlled. Above all, it is reversible and nontransformatory. Thermodynamic change, that brought
about by heat, is not incremental, linear, or easily controlled. But it is
irreversible and transformatory; further, it is dissipative, seeming to
require dissipation for transformations to occur. Some energy is always
"lost" in the transformation process, or, put in a way that has heuristics
for curriculum, transformation occurs when there is a certain amount of
excess in the transformative relationship between matter and energy. It
may well be, as Piaget has argued, that any mode of operation may
need to be overdeveloped before another mode (or stage) can emerge.
And, as Bruner (1973, Ch. 10) points out, there may also need to be an
excess in *time*, actually a "waste" of time according to the scientific efficiency model, for transformations to take place. That is, an individual
may well need to feel comfortable in regard to the knowledge possessed
and the amount of time available before a new set of insights can
emerge. Here pressure, overdirection, and goals too narrowly defined
are all counterproductive.

Time added a new dimension to the Newtonian models of mechanics and space. In Newton's frame, time is irrelevant, machines are reversible—both automobiles and movie projectors can be run backward.
Time becomes important only when irreversibility enters the scene.
Then time acquires a direction or "arrow," a direction that modernists
hold cannot be reversed. Evolution, with its "positive arrow," has one
direction: toward increased perfection or higher order complexity. Entropy, with its "negative arrow," has the opposite direction: toward equilibrium or the even dispersion of all energy. These two arrows, opposite
each other, become one of modernism's many dualisms and contradictions. But both arrows share in the sense of unidirectedness and gradualism they espouse. Change, posing a challenge to the Newtonian
frame, was handled by making it as slight and even as possible—
once a direction was chosen it was set, with all change incremental and
gradual. Both evolution and entropy adopted this view. But in neither
of these nineteenth-century movements was change looked at in terms
of self-generation, transformation, or nonlinearity. This latter view of
change, an essential part of the post-modern paradigm, particularly in
regard to the newer sciences, had to wait for quantum theory, computers, and nonlinear mathematics. As Eldredge and Gould have played a

major role in challenging the gradualist and conformist assumptions underlying neo-Darwinian evolution, so Prigogine and his colleagues have challenged the assumptions underlying the second law of thermodynamics—namely, that in our universe entropy always increases over time ("strives towards a maximum"). Or, as stated in Rudolf Clausius' (1865) famous phrase, "Die Entropie der Welt strebt einem Maximum zu" (*Annals of Physics*, p. 400).

Before studying Prigogine's seminal work more closely, let us look at Piaget's (1971a) biological model of development and learning—that which he expounded in the latter years of his life, beginning with his *magnum opus, Biology and Knowledge*.

PIAGET'S EQUILIBRIUM MODEL

> Equilibration is by far the most important of Piaget's many original concepts. It is the missing link, or better, the keystone that holds together—both logically and psychologically—the edifice of his theory.
> —Furth, *Piaget and Knowledge*, 1981, p. xiv

Furth recognizes what many have missed: the importance to Piaget of a biological model of development and the role the process of equilibration plays in this model, particularly in the formation and transformation of structures. Piaget attained international fame for his psychological work with young children and for his philosophical work in outlining a genetic, or constructivist, epistemology. However, both of these endeavors were rooted in Piaget's lifelong commitment to biology, especially the developmental biology of organic systems. Piaget's first published writings—done as a teenager—were in biology (really zoology), as was his doctoral dissertation at the University of Neuchâtel. During his lifetime he collected plant specimens when he traveled to give lectures, and in his later years he entered the evolutionary debates with *Biology and Knowledge* (1971a)—his *magnum opus*—and *Behavior and Evolution* (1978)—the best expression of his genetic "phenocopy" theory. This genetic theory in turn became the basis he used for developing his theory of cognitive growth. C. H. Waddington, the developmental biologist and nontraditional evolutionist, in his own book, *The Evolution of an Evolutionist* (1975), devotes a whole essay to Piaget's work on lymnaea (snails). In this work, an outgrowth of his doctoral thesis, Piaget argues that phenotypic or character feature changes in lymnaea, brought about as they react to new environmental stresses, occasionally result in genetic modifications: The phenotypic changes become genetically assimilated, converted, or "copied" (pp. 92–95). Other biologists, though, have generally ignored Piaget's work in their field, partly because developmental biology, with its strong emphasis on organic holism, has been overshadowed by reductionist biology, and partly because even within the organicist framework, Piaget's ideas have a teleological, almost vitalist, bent. However, in the realm of the philosophy of science a number of biologically oriented theorists other than Waddington have paid attention to Piaget's ideas—notably Ludwig von Bertalanffy, Michael Polanyi, and Ilya Prigogine.

The heart of Piaget's theories—biological and cognitive—lies within his *intermediary concept* of "phenocopy" (or genocopy, for it is the genes that actively do the "copying"). This concept is simply explained in one of Piaget's "conversations" with Jean-Claude Bringuier (1980, Tenth Conversation). More depth on the issue, though, can be found in *Behavior and Evolution* (1978, Chs. 3 & 6). Piaget begins his "conversation on phenocopy" with his oft-quoted remark that knowledge is neither a copy of reality nor an imposing of *a priori* forms on reality. Instead, it is an intermediary between the two—a "perpetual construction [or reconstruction] made by exchanges between the organism and the environment" (Bringuier, 1980, p. 110). The word "copy" is a bit misleading here, especially if it has the sense of imprinting. What is really being said is that the genetic system itself changes (autoregulates) during certain interactions between itself and the environment. When and how such changes occur is a mystery, but it can be said that Piaget believes the changes to be neither random nor imposed. There is a sense in which the genome must "will" the change, want to change and be actively seeking a change. Here Piaget's vitalist tendency comes to the fore.

For Piaget, the central problem of biology—and analogously of any epistemology interested in knowledge in terms of its development and not just its verification, a genetic epistemology—is the *interaction* between the pressures the environment places on the organism and the reaction the organism has to those pressures. The Lamarckians and Darwinians, including their neo-advocates, put a different frame on this problem than does Piaget. Lamarckians see the environment's pressures and the habit-forming responses to those pressures as being directly transferred or imposed on, or inherited by, the organism's internal structures, its genome. Piaget believes the psychological behaviorists, such as those influenced by B. F. Skinner, with their strong emphasis on the effects of the environment, to be the inheritors of this tradition. The Darwinists believe that the environmental pressures (food, survival) are responded to purely by chance, the strongest or fittest surviving. Piaget rejects both of these: one being too mechanistic, the other too purposeless (especially at the human level). He develops his own frame, his *tertium quid* or "third way." This "third way" focuses on the *interaction* between the organism and its environment, particularly on the way the organism both actively seeks to respond to the environment and at the same time resists any pressures to change its own patterns. For this he draws heavily from C. H. Waddington's (1968–72, 1975) theoretical work on developmental change. In this frame, disturbances of an established equilibrium are key to the equilibration process; they are the stimulus or burr that excites organisms to reshape themselves. However, the environment does not shape the organism; organisms shape themselves. They are not as passive as the Lamarckians or behaviorists assumed—the mind is not a *tabula rasa* for Piaget. Instead organisms (including humans) make "positive reactions" to environmental pressures (1971b, p. 106).

This "third way" frame allows Piaget to bypass the usual dichotomies of choosing between environment and heredity, between nurture and nature (epistemologically between realism and idealism), or even of assessing a proportionality between them; rather his frame focuses on how heredity and the environment interact, how "nature is nurtured." Pedagogically, this *tertium quid* focuses on the interactive, dialogic relationship between the learner and the learning environment, including the material presented by the teacher. This relational focus, too often missed, underlies all of Piaget's child study writings—those describing the child's understanding of such concepts as space, time, causality, geometry, logic, and morality.

Piaget (1978) criticizes both the Lamarckians and the Darwinians—the former for being simplistic, the latter for being purposeless. But he saves his harshest words for the neo-Darwinians, those of the present dominant tradition. They hold, he asserts, a strong sense of purpose at the level of species organization—new species are always stronger and better than the ones they replace. But they believe this teleonomy (their linguistic replacement for teleology) occurs via purely random changes at the individual level:

> In other words, the nonrandom character of organization and of adaptation . . . are to be ascribed to . . . an "accumulation" of small variations . . . every one of which owes its existence entirely to chance.

Piaget (1978) goes on:

> The inconsistency of this account is flagrant. . . . Selection may have been responsible for retaining only the most desirable traits; but it has not *produced* these traits. (p. 30)

In fact, Piaget argues, the neo-Darwinians have sidestepped the issue of new trait production with their use of "natural selection." Natural selection is only *post facto* explanatory; it does nothing to help us understand what will emerge.

Like Gould and Eldredge, Piaget is interested in focusing on those occasions when new traits (or cognitive stages) emerge, not on how one keeps the traits already produced. While Piaget has, I believe, focused on the right issue here, his answer to the question of emergence is vague —how the child progresses from stage to stage is one of the issues baffling all Piagetians. Still, a look at his concept of phenocopy will provide an insight into the direction Piaget believes we should move in and the issues he believes we should study—biologically and cognitively.

Phenocopy occurs not because environmental changes impress themselves on the genetic system but because this system itself is active, always seeking a harmony within the organism and between the organism and the environment. When the external pressures are sufficiently disturbing to the internal equilibrium already established, the genes will actively (and voluntarily) reorganize themselves. As Piaget (1978) says:

> Where the disequilibrium is far-reaching, it eventually makes itself felt at the level of the regulatory genes, or at that of the genome's overall regulatory mechanisms. (p. 80)

When this occurs, the genome becomes aware that "something is not functioning normally," and in reaction "tries out variations." There is here a sense of purpose, a type of teleology—not the external, all-encompassing, end-directed teleology of Aristotle but an internal, indeed actively seeking, problem-processing teleology.[6] Due to this "looser" teleology, to use Michael Polanyi's phrase (1975, p. 162), with its semi-vitalist attitude, Piaget (1978) believes "total randomness is ruled out"; the "idea of 'trials' " is a "more appropriate" concept (p. 80). The neo-Darwinians, those accepting the "standard synthesis," are wrong—at least to the extent they accept "random variation as both necessary and sufficient to account for all of evolution" (Ho & Saunders, 1984, p. x).

Transposing this model to cognitive structures, Piaget proposes an equilibrium–disequilibrium–reequilibration model of individual development. Here again, disequilibrium plays a key role—it is "the driving force of development" or the motor of evolution, to use a modernist and mechanist phrase. In trying to overcome disequilibrium—here perturbations, errors, mistakes, confusions—the student reorganizes with more insight and on a higher level than previously attained. Along with the sense of Enlightenment progress that Piaget assumes here, it is important to note that this disequilibrium must be deeply felt or "far-reaching." The disequilibrium must be one that is structurally disturbing before reorganization will occur. Drawing on Waddington's notion of "chreods" or pathways of activity, Piaget believes that organisms (including students) will continue in past patterns as long as possible, indeed maybe longer than they should, before reorganizing. Thus, the perturbations and confusions must be ones that genuinely bother in a deep, structural sense—they must ask the student to doubt in a fundamental way the procedures being used and assumptions being made. This is akin to Dewey's sense of "real problems," not the artificial ones found in so many textbooks.

The teacher's art, along with helping disequilibrium occur, is that of constraining this disequilibrium—of not letting it turn into unbridled disruption. For the teacher and curricularist this is a greater problem both theoretically as well as practically than for Piaget. Waddington's developmental theory, epigenetic in the sense it adds purposeful choice onto the accepted neo-Darwinian frame, always has the genome choosing among alternative pathways. Thus, Piaget speaks of the "idea of trials" as the appropriate way to describe what the genome does when faced with perturbations of a disturbing nature. There is here the notion of limits already built into the theory. Piaget did not emphasize this when talking of cognitive development, and any first-year teacher is aware of the ease with which a class without some concept of constraints can become unbridled. This is an area post-modern teachers and curricularists will need to work on if they wish to generate practical curriculum procedures from Piaget's equilibration model.

Important as disequilibrium is as "the driving force" in development, it is not the crucial factor. This lies in the nature of action itself—the true "motor of evolution." Piaget's oft-made statement that every transformation or reorganization is "always an endogenous [internal] reconstruction of exogenous [external] givens" (In Bringuier, 1980, p. 114) harkens back to his belief that the phenome does not automatically impress itself on the genome, but rather the genome in its manner, way, and time responds to these exogenous pressures. In Waddington's (1957) terms, the genes have their strategy. Analogously, learners have their active strategies. These come into play not merely to overcome perturbations but because their nature is to be active. In his stage theory, Piaget emphasizes the role of action both as the defining characteristic of the first or sensory-motor stage and as the quality that permeates change throughout all the stages. Many educators, though, interpret such actions only on a superficial level, that of "hands-on" doing. Piaget is thinking more of actions that involve intellectual re-structuring, as the mathematician Dieudonne did when, as young boy, he realized that counting ten stones from left to right would produce the same number as counting them from right to left (Piaget, 1972/1977a, p. 727). In this activity Dieudonne left the world of stones for the world of relations; he left the physical world for that of mental activity. Better yet, he transformed the world of the physical into that of the logical and abstract, beginning his own transformation into a logico-mathematical thinker. Such a restructuring and transforming of reality is, for Piaget, the teleonomic end of all education, intellectual growth, and personal development. This restructuring is akin to Dewey's con-cept of education being the continuous reconstruction of experience, a process that has no end outside itself.

As helpful as Piaget's model of equilibration is for the development of a transformatory curriculum—a model that emphasizes the role played by disequilibrium, as well as the role of choice and purpose in internal restructurings—an important question still remains: How do the restructurings occur?

NOTES

1. E. A. Burtt (1932/1955), in the revised edition to his seminal work, *The Meta-physical Foundations of Modern Physical Science*, remarks that recent changes in the sciences, especially biology with its particular phenomena of developmental growth, will force "physical science itself . . . to break away from its Newtonian moorings and consider its foundation afresh" (p. 304). It took scholars another generation or two to recognize the import of this statement.

2. I have done more with Weng's gropings than Piaget has. As Weng uses "the addition of two's" to solve 4×3 and $4 - 2$ as well as $12 - 3$, I see the emergence of doubling (and halving). I have also tried this movement from the addition of two's to doubling/halving with success in my own research with children (Doll & Robbins, 1986). Piaget, true to his structuralist bent, was more interested in children's difficulty with introspection. Consequently he saw Weng's "fumbling" only as an inability to be logical. I see it as the beginnings of a logic yet to emerge.

3. Medieval times were, of course, filled with humans having religious con-versations with or "mystical visions" of God. But these were not the dialogues God had with Abraham, Isaac, or Job, nor that Jesus had with his disciples, nor even those represented by the Holy Spirit filling an individual soul, room, or community. In these mystical visions, God still remained aloof, inhabiting, as it were, the upper realms of those vast cathedrals the medievalists built to house His presence.

4. Humberto Maturana and Francisco Varela (1980) coined the word "auto-poiesis" to deal with this issue of a living system that regenerates itself but is neither mechanistic nor teleological; hence it can destroy itself as well as regenerate itself. They say an autopoietic system is

> a network of processes of production (transformation and destruction) of components that produces the components that through their interactions and transformations continuously regenerate the network of processes (relations) that produced them. (p. 79)

The emphasis here is on a system that can regenerate itself but, when it does not receive enough perturbations to perform transformations, will disintegrate.

5. It is interesting to note that Adam Smith, studying at Cambridge while James Watt was doing his experiments with steam there, could think of no other use for coal than "to provide heat for the workers." The turbulent and transformative thermodynamic possibilities of coal were beyond Smith's ken (Prigogine & Stengers, 1984, p. 103).

6. Obviously, this sense of a problem-processing teleology is more evident in human actions than in genomic ones. As a biological model this view is problematic. However, this does not, I believe, lessen its power as a heuristic for curriculum thought.

CHAPTER 4

Prigogine and Chaotic Order

CONCEPTS OF CHAOS

In the beginning there was Apsu the Primeval, and Tiämat, who is Chaos.
> —"Babylonian Creation Story," in Colum, 1930/1976, p. 17

Lo, thy dread empire, Chaos is restored;
Light dies before thy uncreating word:
Thy hand, great Anarch lets the curtain fall
And universal darkness buries all.
> —Pope, *The Dunciad*, 1728/1830, lines 653–656

A. A violent order is disorder: and
  B. A great disorder is an order.
    These two things are one.
> —Stevens, *Poems*, 1938/1947, p. 97

These quotations, from time periods roughly equivalent to the premodern, modern, and post-modern paradigms, show three views of chaos that the Western world has embraced. To us, imbued with modernist thinking, it is the second quotation that seems so "natural." Here chaos is envisioned as the antithesis of order: disorder run amuck. It is the *bête noire* every teacher fears, a beast that once unchained devours all it sees. Such a view of chaos, while natural in a modernist paradigm, is unnatural in both pre-modern and post-modern frames.

In virtually all creation myths, those of the ancient cosmologies, chaos was the "messy" primordial source from which all being and organization sprang. Hesiod tells us that "First of all came Chaos; and then broad-breasted Gaia" (*Theogony*, lines 116–117). Ovid, following Hesiod, states:

Before the sea and the land had formed,
  there was one face of nature, called Chaos;

it was just a rough and inharmonious mass.
Nothing had its own shape,
   and everything got in the way
   of everything else.
           —*Metamorphoses*, lines 5–7, 16–18

Tiãmat, the Babylonian goddess of primordial matter, creativity, and the chaotic void or abyss, likes her realm, where "everything gets in the way of everything else." She becomes angry when the offspring who spill out of her formless fecundity begin to give order and structure to the universe. She unleashes her fury via "formless monsters" who destroy all the nascent gods but Marduk, the "most able and wisest" of her offspring. In a titanic battle, he manages to slay but not defeat her. He does this when, as she opens her mouth to roar at him, he drives in "the evil wind that she close not her lips." Then he releases an arrow that "tears her belly" and "cuts through her sides, splitting her heart." Slain, Tiãmat is not defeated—her generative powers are rich indeed. Marduk needs to find a way to reharness those powers in a productive manner. He does so by plucking out her eyes, whose blood "runs as the Tigris and Euphrates rivers"; her breasts he turns into mountains, and her belly into the night sky. Finally, he masses her marrow into bones and fashions "man" (Colum, 1930/1976, pp. 17–19).[1]

This movement to a newer and higher level of order is the "artful skill" Marduk possesses. He can never totally defeat Tiãmat, nor bring stultifying order to creation, nor would he wish to—such would mean the extinction of life itself. Instead, he redirects Tiãmat's fecund properties into a more complex sense of order, a redirection that breathes new life into the universe. This allegorical tale brings forth a basic truth about creation—order, particularly imposed, external order—can easily become dull, routinized. The transformative skill Marduk possesses each teacher would also like to possess. Of course, even in a metaphorical manner, few students have the creative organizational powers Tiãmat does. However, as Noam Chomsky (1959/1984) emphasizes and as he points out in his critique of B. F. Skinner's *Verbal Behavior* (1957), the very nature of being human implies the ability to organize, generate, create. As Chomsky says, there is the "remarkable capacity of the child to generalize, hypothesize, and 'process information' in a variety of . . . complex ways" (p. 563). A transformative curriculum, then, is one that allows for, encourages, and develops this natural capacity for complex organization; and through the process of transformation the curriculum continually regenerates itself and those involved with it.

In the great myths of the Western world—those from Babylon,

Greece, Israel, and Rome—chaos is seen in two perspectives: (1) as the rich, primal, amorphous mass from which order is fashioned—either by God or by a "kinder Natural Order"; and (2) as the continual interplay (often physical intercourse) between the created order and the primal mass from which it evolved. Curriculum, particularly of the progressive or liberal variety, has paid some attention to the first of these frames, espousing the need for a rich if messy environment, naively believing that such an environment not only would allow creativity to occur but would actually bring about its presence. It is, though, the second frame that is the more interesting, the one which holds the greater heuristic power for curriculum. In this second frame, the titanic contest between Tiãmat and Marduk cannot be won by either; Tiãmat is too generative to be fully subdued and Marduk is too young and powerful to be denied. Rather, resolution comes only when Marduk is able to transform Tiãmat's powers into more suitable and less destructive ventures. Analagously, creativity occurs by the interaction of chaos and order, between unfettered imagination and disciplined skill. This is the art Marduk possesses, inherited in part from Tiãmat herself—a process whereby chaos and order are enfolded within each other, uniting to form a more complex, comprehensive, and sometimes "strange" new order. This new vision, complex and chaotic, is part of a post-modern view. But before studying it and its strangeness, a look at modernist order seems appropriate—the order that bifurcates, considering itself superior to and the antithesis of disorder.

The Renaissance brought with it a re-look at the ancient texts, often with a new twist. Chaos emerged as a lack or loss of order, sometimes as order's antagonist. Shakespeare has Othello tell Desdemona:

> Perdition catch my soul, but I do love thee!
> And when I love thee not, Chaos is come again.
> —*Othello*, Act III, Scene III, lines 90–92

And he has Venus, mourning Adonis, say:

> Beauty dead, black chaos comes again.
> —"Venus and Adonis," line 1020

Sir Thomas Elyot warns:

> Take away order from all things,
> What should then remain? . . . *Chaos!*
> —*The Boke Named the Governor*, 1533/1962, p. 2

And finally Pope, again from *The Dunciad*, says:

Then rose the Seed of chaos, and of Night,
To blot out Order and extinguish Light.
                              —1728/1830, lines 13–14

The scientists and mathematicians in the seventeenth, eighteenth, and nineteenth centuries viewed the universe as a marvel of simple symmetry. Newton's great accomplishment, of devising one equation to "explain" both the rotation of the planets and the falling of apples, was testimony to the clockwork order God impressed on the universe. This order showed nature to be "comfortable to Herself" and stable over time. Take away this order and the chaos left was not a fecund mass rich with new generation but a formless, frightening void. In this view, chaos is essentially the antithesis of order, the work of the devil, or of human ignorance. As the *Primer in Private Prayers* of 1559 says, Chaos is "That old confusion . . . without order, without fashion" (quoted in the Oxford English Dictionary, 1989, p. 273). In all these representations, chaos is seen not as an important and necessary part of creation—actually that out of which creation is generated—but as the dark side, the "unnatural" aspect of naturalness, the anti-Christ, or Black Beast—the source of all disruption and confusion.

To change from this still-pervasive view to one contemporary science is now showing is a shift of megaparadigmatic proportions. It is a change which reorients our whole cosmological focus. It is represented, as Prigogine and Stengers (1984) say, by looking into the night sky and seeing not just permanence—of the sort that so filled Newton's and Kant's (and even Einstein's)[2] hearts with joy and feelings of certainty— but seeing also other objects: strange ones, such as "quasars, pulsars, galaxies exploding and being torn apart" (pp. 214–215), stars collapsing into black holes. This dual, paradoxical, contradictory focus becomes schizophrenic from a modernist perspective, but integrative, complementary, and holistic from a post-modernist one.

Explaining this new, post-modern, cosmological frame—one James Gleick (1987) equates with a "new science" and Paul Davies (1988) has called "nothing less than a brand new start in the description of nature" (p. 23)—might best be approached through a story and an example. The story is of Henri Poincairé's response to the King of Sweden's challenge, in 1890, for someone to solve "the three-body" problem by proving that the problem could not be solved—at least not with the mathematical knowledge then current. The three-body problem involves calculating the gravitational effect three bodies—such as the sun, earth, and moon—have on one another's orbital cycles. The importance of this problem is that in terms of Newtonian equations only two of the three bodies' gravitational attraction can be calculated, and hence predicted, with certainty. When a third body enters, the problem is that the moon's attraction of the earth causes perturbations in the earth's orbit around the sun, which in turn alters the moon's previous orbit. This change, of course, alters the moon's attraction of the earth, in turn causing yet another perturbation in the earth's orbit around the sun. The prediction of orbital cycles on a long-term basis cannot be precise; there is always a bit of error. Mathematicians and theoretical scientists of the day assumed, from the prevailing metaphysics, that these "small errors" were unimportant since the universe was replete with a simple, stable order. But Poincairé raised the spectre of what Edward Lorenz (1963) demonstrated almost three-quarters of a century later—that small perturbations over time lead to major changes. Nature is not perfectly conformable with itself nor is the universe's order simple.

A new mathematics and a new science would be needed to solve the three-body problem. Max Planck's discovery of the quanta, Neils Bohr's and Werner Heisenberg's formulation of the Copenhagen interpretation of quantum reality, and Kurt Gödel's challenge to the foundations of arithmetic—all in the early decades of the twentieth century—intensified this need. But it was not until the 1970s, with the advent of the computer to help solve nonlinear mathematics and with the birth of chaos theory, that this need was finally met. Meeting one need, though, created another. If the Newtonian assumption of a mechanistic, clockwork universe is not a good metaphor for describing the reality and workings of the universe, what can be a better metaphor? What is a better concept of reality?

Katherine Hayles (1990) suggests that we categorize the eighteenth century in terms of clockwork order, the nineteenth century in terms of organic growth, and the twentieth century in terms of turbulence. These seem useful classifications, although the nineteenth century might better be thought of in terms of positive and negative "arrows of time"—evolution and entropy. And some have suggested that in focusing on turbulence as the key metaphor for the twentieth century, we may well need to develop not only new mathematical and scientific concepts but also new epistemological and metaphysical ones (Kitchener, 1988). It could even be said we are in need of a new cosmology—using this word to indicate not only our deepest metaphysical and spiritual beliefs about our origins but also to indicate the methods of ritual, story, and myth whereby we express and develop these beliefs. The new paradigm we are seeing emerge from the insights of chaos theory requires of us nothing less than *a brand new start in the description of nature*—a start which will affect our metaphysics as well as our physics, our cosmology as well as our logic.

A swinging pendulum—first between two magnets set in a plane, then among three magnets set in a plane—is a dramatic illustration of this sudden transformation from simple to chaotic order. In swinging between two magnets, a pendulum's movements are rigid and repetitive. When three magnets are placed on a surface equidistant from each other and the momentum (speed × weight) is low, the pendulum swings between two of the three magnets as if the third did not exist. With a slightly stronger push, increasing the momentum, the pendulum will swing between alternative sets of twos— △ —first a↔b, then either b↔c, or a↔c. With a still stronger push, though, a "radical new behavior" evolves. At first the pattern is the one just mentioned—an a↔b oscillation followed by an a↔c or b↔c oscillation. Then, at some critical point the movements break into chaos, oscillating wildly among the three magnets. As John Briggs and David Peat (1989) say about turbulence:

> Nature's systems will often undergo rigid, repetitive movements and then, at some critical point, evolve a radical new behavior. (p. 33)

Here the radical new behavior, no longer regular, implies the nonexistence of a pattern. But there is one. It is just not observable to the naked eye, nor is it a simple, symmetrical pattern. In fact, the pattern lies not in the movements themselves but in the abstractions of the movements onto a graph that correlates the movement's variables into a single point and looks at these points over periods of time. By using such a graph—called a "phase space" graph—it is possible to focus on something other than the particulars of the movement itself, namely on the coordination of the movement's variables as these relate as a system over time.[3] In short, *it is in these abstract relationships that the patterns emerge.* This last sentence should be read again, for here lies one of the important changes contemporary concepts of chaos have brought to our life—to look at objects in our universe, indeed reality itself, not in terms of individual particulars or incidents or occasions but in terms of the patterned relations any grouping of particulars, incidents, or occasions has. As Katherine Hayles (1990) says:

> The fundamental assumption of chaos theory, by contrast[to the Newtonian paradigm] is that the individual unit does not matter. What does matter are recursive symmetries between different levels of the

system. . . . The regularities of the system emerge not from knowing
about individual units but from understanding correspondence across
scales. (p. 170)

Translated into curriculum terms, this quotation says it is not the individual as an isolated entity which is important but the person within
the communal, experiential, and environmental frame. In fact, the concept of isolated or rugged individualism, sacred to so much of modern
(and American) thought, is a fiction. To use John Donne's (1624/1955)
phrase, "No man is an Iland; intire of It selfe" (p. 538). What is important, epistemologically and pedagogically, is a comparison of the patterns an individual develops operating in a number of different situations—this is an ecological, holistic, systemic, interrelated view. Within
this view, lie patterns otherwise unseen.

Graphs made from Cartesian grids—*x* and *y* axes—are usually
used to show the relationship between two variables, one plotted on
each axis. In phase space graphing (often three dimensional) the variables are coordinated together in one point so the graph shows the system as a whole as it moves over time. Time is not one of the axes but
occurs as one moves along the lines of the figure itself, as in the Lorenz
attractor, or the "owl's eyes," shown in Figure 4.1.

What is important here is that instead of looking at the relationship
of parts or variables to each other, one sees the system related to itself
over time. In this manner it is possible to see patterns not apparent in
the usual Cartesian grid; in chaotic systems, or systems which have
reached chaos (that is, the wildly fluctuating pendulum), these patterns
can be dramatically beautiful, as much of the "chaos art" generated by
computers shows.

The illustrations in Figure 4.2 show what differences can be
achieved by phase space diagramming. All the phase space diagrams
have been transferred to two-dimensional representations for purposes
of economy.

Illustrations 1a and 1b show a system converging to a steady state.
Both illustrate this, but the phase space graph shows the system being
"attracted" to a fixed point much more dramatically than does the traditional graph. Illustrations 2a and 2b illustrate periodicity, with the
sense of alteration coming forth clearer in 2a and the sense of closure
coming forth clearer in 2b. Both show repetition, although 2a probably
dramatizes this better than 2b. Illustrations 3a and 3b show a complex
and inverted waltz rhythm with the long beat on the third step. The
period "three" is illustrated differently in 3a and 3b. Illustrations 4a and
4b represent a system in chaos, with 4b a two-dimensional representa-

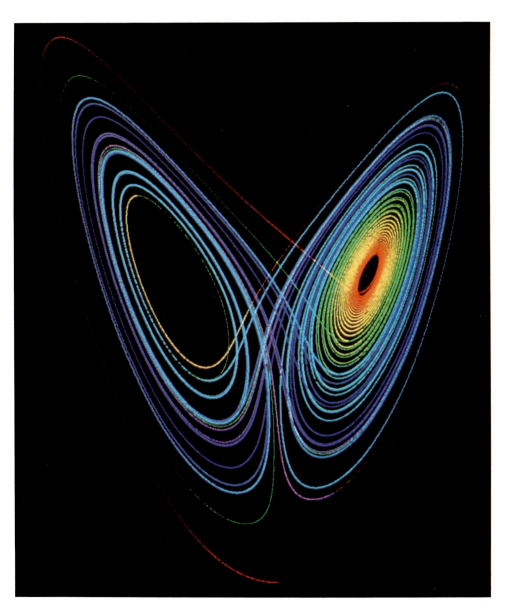

Figure 4.1 The Lorenz attractor *(see legend on reverse)*

The figure on the other side of this page is a "phase space" diagram of a nonlinear system. It has become a common symbol for "chaos" and is often called the Lorenz attractor, after Edward Lorenz who first used this type of graph to show a systems view of weather patterns (Gleick, 1987, pp. 21–31). Sometimes the design is referred to as "owl's eyes" or "butterfly wings"—both visual metaphors.

A phase space diagram or graph is akin to, but not the same as, bar and coordinate graphs. These more common graphs compare two variables as they relate to each other—velocity and distance, rate and time, etc. Figure 4.2 shows the different types of designs a coordinate (4.2a) and phase space graph (4.2b) make. A coordinate graph always deals with the relations between two variables; a phase space graph shows a *system,* with all the coordinates *collapsed to* one point, relating to itself moment by moment, or time-phase to time-phase. Imagine a point moving along any of the swirling trajectories in the Lorenz attractor—never repeating itself, yet always bounded. Such a point is the mathematical construct of a system's variables coordinated at a given moment of time. The trajectories are a series of a "snapshots" of these point-coordinations, moment after moment after moment. Thus, the trajectories are really pictures of the system relating to itself (as a whole system) over time. The overall diagram shows how the system (qua system) changes from time-phase to time-phase.

At least three features stand out in the particular diagram shown. One, the "chaos" described is not a wild, random abandon. Far from it; the pattern is quite orderly but complex. Chaos refers to this complex ordering. It is not possible to predict with complete accuracy where the next point on the trajectory will be (no two trajectories ever repeat exactly) but neither do the points fly beyond the bounds of the diagram. Two, the trajectories have both "bounds" and a center "attractor" area. Neither of these are precisely defined, but as the trajectories fly out from the center area they are attracted back, only to fly out again. The system, in its dynamic tension between moving out and back, has an overall coherence. Three, on occasion, any given point on the trajectory will "flip over" from one "owl's eye" or "butterfly wing" to the other. These "flip over" events are certain to happen over time but unpredictable for any given moment. One cannot say when such flipping will occur, only that it will. The pattern is random, but it is a pattern.

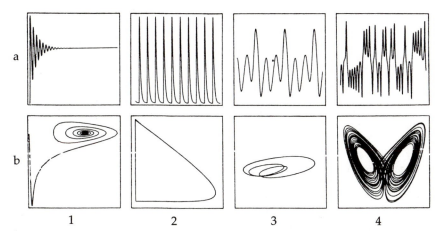

Figure 4.2 Traditional time series *(row a)* and trajectories in phase space *(row b)* are two ways of displaying the same data and gaining a picture of a system's long-term behavior. (From Gleick, 1987, p. 50, by permission.)

tion of the commonly found "owl's eyes." Note that in 4b the sense of chaos having "bounds" to it as well as a central attractor area is evident.

It is this concept of chaos bound inextricably to order, as is the yin to the yang in Eastern thought, that Katherine Hayles (1990) makes so much of in her book, *Chaos Bound.* Hayles is one of a number who argues that not only does chaos perform its magic within bounds or limits, but that deep within chaos itself there is a universal structure. One aspect of this deeper structure is that the "pathway" taken when a system moves from simple to complex order is always the same, no matter what the subject. Thus, the "pathway" of a pendulum moving to chaos is the same as that of an insect colony moving to chaos (through a dramatic increase in the birthrate). Both exhibit "period doubling" as they move from simple to complex and chaotic order.

To explain period doubling (Figure 4.3, and especially Figure 4.4)—the attractors increasing by powers of two in a 2–4–8–16–32–64 pattern—it might be advantageous first to discuss how increases and decreases in variables, such as food supply and population, birthrate and deathrate, or pendulum swings by natural freefall and those induced by mechanical "kicks," relate to each other. Again, a story seems appropriate: Joseph's biblical interpretation of the Pharaoh's dream that Egypt would experience seven years of feast (seven fat cows) followed by seven years of famine (seven lean and gaunt cows) can be related to the

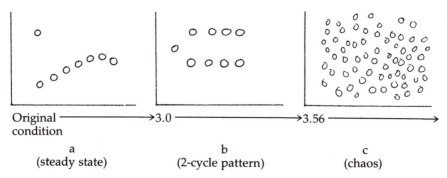

Original ——————————→3.0 ——————————→3.56 —————————→
condition

      a   b   c
(steady state)   (2-cycle pattern)   (chaos)

Figure 4.3   Movement from a steady state pattern to a chaotic pattern of change in the size of a population of gypsy moths. Population is shown as a function of the birthrate/deathrate ratio. (Adapted from Davies, 1988, p. 40, and from Briggs & Peat, 1989, p.60, by permission.)

fact that populations, under certain conditions, swing back and forth between two numbers. Here these numbers might be considered as positive and negative seven, themselves related to zero, a position of neither growth nor decline. The numbers seven form the boundaries or limits of this oscillation. The Reverend Thomas Malthus, whose substantial influence on Charles Darwin's theories was discussed in Chapter Three, was aware that populations depended on food supplies. However, his dire predictions of a modernist chaos was based on the assumption the ratio of people to food would increase in a linear manner, ending in a literal "dog-eat-dog" stage. Linear thinking was not part of Joseph's pre-modern culture, thus allowing him the possibility of describing the ratio of population to food in cyclic, recursive terms. While the down part of the cycle—Egypt's seven lean years—did bring misery, suffering, even death, the pattern cycled itself; it did not go on unidirectionally as Malthus assumed.[4] When the total population shrank below the food supply, feasting replaced famine. The magic of the number seven was certainly a part of the author's Hebrew culture. Its significance, though, may lie more in the culture's numerology than in its existence as an empirical fact.

    Feasts will not always follow famine, pestilence can destroy a population, and it is possible for the human race to extinguish itself. However, feasts will follow when the population–food system oscillates in a two-stage cycle. Such oscillation (frequent to a host of occurrences in our world) is shown in Illustration b of Figure 4.3.

Part a of Figure 4.3 shows a total population (here of gypsy moths) slowly rising, over time, to a steady state, one of equilibrium where the moth population remains steady from year to year. This occurs when the annual birthrate is about 1.5 times the deathrate, food and other variables remaining constant. But, if the birthrate increases to 3.0 times the deathrate (as in part b), then the total population fluctuates around two numbers—the Joseph effect. Finally, in part c, the birthrate increases to 3.56 and the oscillations become unstable. As Figure 4.4 shows, the pathway to chaos—done by period doublings—prepares to enter chaos at 3.56 and actually does so at 3.56999, where the dark lines begin. Here the number of "attractors" to which the overall population is drawn increases from 1 to 2 to 4 to 8 to 16 to 32 to 64 and so on. This doubling pattern happens no matter what is being increased: electric circuits, optical systems, business cycles, populations, pendulum swings. It is a deep structure lying within the broad concept of chaos or complexity theory—indeed, within nature itself. Further, if the proportional increase continues beyond the 3.56999 ratio, going deeper and deeper into chaos where there is neither predictability to the oscillations nor a hint of attractors, an even more interesting pattern emerges.

Figure 4.5 shows this pattern—what happens when the birthrate/deathrate ratio is increased from 3.5 to 4.0. Notice that at 3.56999 the doublings break into chaos with the darker, more densely packed areas, showing more varied responses to increases in the birthrate–deathrate ratio. Notice, too, that during the chaos from 3.6 to 4.0 there are three

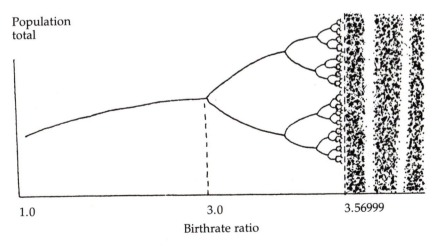

Figure 4.4 A continuous view of the function displayed in Figure 4.3, emphasizing the bifurcation points. (Drawing by Ashley Robertson.)

Population
total

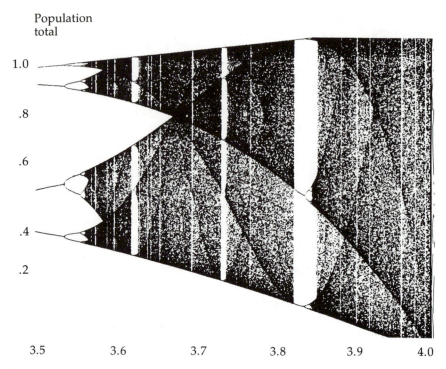

Figure 4.5 A magnification of the area of chaos shown in Figures 4.3 and 4.4.

white bands, areas of strong predictability in a sea of nonpredictability. Here, order of the simplest and most stable sort exists within a sea of chaos. This shows that chaotic order is not an oxymoronic, self-contradictory term; rather, it describes a complex order wherein the nonpredictability and nonlinearity of chaos is embedded within the predictability and linearity of simple order, or what Briggs and Peat (1989) call "familiar order" (p. 77).

In terms of curriculum, chaos-complexity theory and the study of turbulence have a variety of applications. At the curriculum design level it means that school physics and mathematics courses need to move the study of turbulence and nonlinearity from the later (optional) sections of texts into the main body of these works. Certainly the *Fractals for the Classroom* workbooks that Heinz-Otto Peitgen and his colleagues (1991) are developing are a major step in this direction. Along with this might well go the study of what happens when an equation is iterated, particularly the parabolic equation of $y = 4\lambda x (1 - x)$. Exploring this equation iteratively—that is, feeding the answer to y back into the equation as the new value of x—can be done using a simple hand-held calculator. The actual mathematics is quite simple. What is new is the change of focus: from producing discrete answers in linear algebraic equations to observing and comparing patterns of nonlinear relations as the iterations proceed many, many times[5] and as the original x "seed" is changed by as little as one ten-thousandth.

This shift in focus from the discrete to the relational has tremendous implications for the humanities as well as the sciences. The principal theme in Katherine Hayles' (1984, 1990) works is that in a given culture, there is a general *episteme* which underlies and guides both scientific models and literary theory. This cross-disciplinary and ecological approach is brought forth in the writings of the post-structuralists, such as Michel Serres, whom Hayles cites so often. She calls Serres "a theorist who locates himself at the crossroads of disciplines" (1990, p. 177). In a number of his works Serres interweaves ancient history, literature, philosophy, religion, science, mathematics, and myth. I have already cited Serres' delightful essay on geometry and Cartesian reason, which he embeds in LaFontaine's fable about the fox and the sheep (*Hermes: Literature, Science, Philosophy*, 1983, Ch. 2). To emphasize the relational rather than the discrete is one of the links between postmodernism and post-structuralism. Indeed, the subtitle of Hayles' (1990) book is "Orderly Disorder in Contemporary Literature and Science."

At the instructional level, the implications of chaos theory deal mostly with the concept of recursion (iteration) in which the individual looks back on him- or herself, and through this self-referential experience a sense of self and value emerges. Here curriculum becomes strongly imbued with *currere*, more a process of experiential transformation and less one of a set product to be mastered, or "racecourse to be run." Personal reflections and communal (hence public) discussion of those reflections are key ingredients in this curriculum.

Overall, chaos-complexity theory leads us to see that we have arrived at a major turning point in our relations with the world, nature, and ourselves. We are embarked on constructing a new paradigm, one based on a new sense of order. As one contemporary scientist (Cvitanović, 1984) has said:

> Junk your old equations and look for guidance in clouds' repeating patterns. . . . The key concepts of phase-space trajectories, Poincaré maps, bifurcations and local universality are common to all non-linear, dynamical systems. The essence of this subject is incommunicable in

print; intuition is developed by computing [by playing with the pat-
terns]. (p. 4)

We might go further and say what we really have now is not only a new
way of dealing with nature but the beginning of a new cosmology—one
scientific and spiritual, metaphorical and mystical, playful and serious.

Nothing is more central to this new beginning than the concept and
practice of iteration. In its simplest form iteration is an operation repeating itself over and over again—mathematically a function such as
$y = 3x$ repeated in the sequence 3, 9, 27, 81, with each solved y becoming a new x. Some linear iterations, such as this one, do not produce
anything unusual—the line just goes on. However, with an iteration
that comes from an equation with a "hump" in it—⌐_ for instance, the parabolic function of $y = 4 \lambda x (1 - x)$—a whole new, magical world appears. When $\lambda = $ approximately .7 and x lies between 0
and 1, a two-cycle iterative pattern emerges, as shown in Figure 4.6.
Here the y solution flips back and forth between two attractors.[6] Again,
the Joseph effect.

All the beauty of fractals, the complexities of the Mandlebrot set,
the infinite regressions of the Koch curve or the Sierpinski triangle come
from iterations, many of them done with imaginary numbers (the is)
and almost all done via computers with a thousand or so repetitions
likely.[7] There is much to study in this new field: how patterns hold
across changing scales; how very small, even minute changes—say, a
.0001 difference in the original (seed) x—will grow into major transformations over time: how the world of computer simulations relates to
the world of nature. And most important, especially for curriculum,
how self-organization (here in the form of chaos mathematics with its
spontaneous and strange attractors) becomes the pivotal focus around
which open systems work. Without self-organization chaos mathematics would not exist; chaos would be, as Alexander Pope (1728/1830) said,
an "uncreating void." But with self-organizating attractors it becomes
the source of creation itself.

ILYA PRIGOGINE, SELF-ORGANIZATION, AND DISSIPATIVE
STRUCTURES

The law that entropy always increases—the Second Law of Thermodynamics—holds, I think, the supreme position among the Laws of
Nature. If someone points out to you that your pet theory of the universe is in disagreement with Maxwell's equations—then so much the

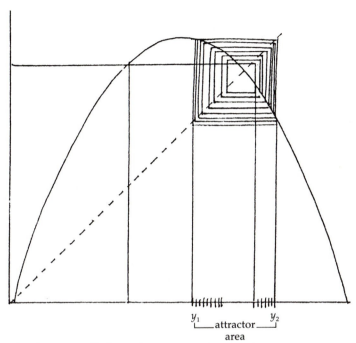

y_1 y_2
attractor
area

Figure 4.6 A two-cycle iterative pattern generating an attractor area, for the equation $y = 4 \lambda x (1 - x)$

worse for Maxwell's equations. If it is found to be contradicted by observation—well, these experimentalists do bungle things sometimes. But if your theory is found to be against the Second Law of Thermodynamics I can give you no hope; there is nothing for it but to collapse in deepest humiliation.
—Eddington, *The Nature of the Physical World*, 1928, p. 74

In 1865 when Rudolf Clausius formulated the Second Law of Thermodynamics, the modernist mind-set was firmly established. The statement that entropy (in the form of dissipated energy) will always increase (or "strive towards the maximum") is reminiscent of Thomas Malthus' prediction that human populations would eventually and inexorably outstrip the food supply. Both statements assume linear progressions, stable states, and closed systems. The closedness of the system is shown in Clausius' First Law of Thermodynamics, that the total energy in the universe is constant (*Die Energie der Welt is Konstant*). It is this first law that made the second law in any way acceptable to the Newtonians: The dissipated energy was not really "lost"; it was merely dispersed over a broader framework, the entire universe, even the cosmos itself. As James Joule (1887/1963) expresses it:

> Thus it is that order is maintained in the universe—nothing is deranged, nothing ever lost . . . everything may appear complicated and involved in the apparent confusion . . . yet is the most perfect regularity preserved—the whole being governed by the sovereign will of God. (p. 273)

The preservation of this perfect regularity comes at the expense of Life itself, for in the dissipation of heat energy into the vastness of the cosmos, Life (like the Sun's energy) will eventually run down. So the magnificent order God created, called Nature, is doomed to die in the equilibrium of its own being. The irony of this argument was not lost on the pessimistic philosophers Søren Kierkegaard (1843/1941) and Friederick Nietzsche (c1888–1895/1968), who asked the existential questions: Why would God have created this universe in the first place? Just what sort of God is it who would create only to destroy? Finally, how does evolution—the other *E* of the nineteenth century, with its belief in the perfectability and perfection of humankind—fit into the pessimistic picture entropy describes?

Today these two *E*s remain in sharp, diametrical contrast. As Paul Davies (1980) phrases it, many, indeed most, believe the unpalatable truth to be

> That the inexorable disintegration of the universe as we know it seems assured, the organization which sustains all ordered activities . . . is slowly but inevitably running down. (pp. 197–98)

On the other hand, a few, like Freeman Dyson (1971), believe

> Life may have a larger role to play than we have yet imagined. Life may succeed against all the odds in molding the universe to its own purpose. (p. 51)

It is to this latter and growing group that Prigogine, Piaget, and other organismic biologists and theorists belong. This group proposes that nature is inherently creative; that there is a "predisposition in nature" to be creative (Davies, 1988, p. 202).[8] This creative urge is found in the self-organizational features of all the sciences, but especially in biology, chemistry, and chaos mathematics. Whether the metaphysics and cosmology this new paradigm proposes will hold up and sustain the paradigm over time is an open question. But it does seem certain that the Newtonian, modernist paradigm has collapsed. No longer do we envision the universe as composed of "hard, massy, impenetrable particles," static on their own, and moving only through external force. Nor do we see a universe created by an external God, *ex nihilo*. Rather, we see creation *in continuo*, an ongoing, inherent process of nature, one where new and more complex structures and processes bubble up spontaneously and self-generatively from prior interactions. In a creative universe, order is not pre-set and then forced to disintegrate over time; rather, order arises continuously from formlessness; higher levels of complexity arise from lower levels; *time works magic.*

For some it may be possible to read the foregoing statements in a nineteenth-century, modernist, dichotomous mode—that is, as preaching a non-God, pro-vitalist doctrine. But as Davies (1988), Griffin (1989), Peacocke (1986), and other process thinkers and theologians point out, this need not be *the interpretation*. Moving from a cosmology that posits a pre-set, stable universe, created *ex nihilo*—where order is stable—to one emerging, unstable, and *in continuo*—where order is continually coming into being—changes but does not deny the concept of a deity. Atheism is not the only alternative to a modernist theology; process theology is just as viable and far more exciting. It maintains a God-oriented frame while, at the same time, changing our understanding of the nature and being of God. God is itself (or himself/herself) part of the creative cosmos. Nor is a vitalist frame with its belief in a pre-set and deterministic vital force—an eschatalogical teleology as it were—either needed or desired from a process viewpoint. Self-organization demonstrates that complexity can arise from unformed mass. New and higher levels of order arise spontaneously from simple elements. According to this view evolution and the creation of life are not miracles, "swimming upstream" against the flow of entropy; rather, they are anticipated but not predictable outcomes of a creative cosmos.

A creative paradigm has major implications for education and curriculum. First, the teaching–learning frame switches from a cause–effect one where learning is either a direct result of teaching or teaching is at least in a superior–inferior relationship with learning. The switch is to a mode where teaching becomes ancillary to learning, with learning dominant, due to the individual's self-organizational abilities. Further, in this mode teaching changes its *modus operandi*, from the didactic to the dialogic. Here recent work on questioning—not for the purpose of achieving an efficient production of correct answers but for digging deeper into the nature of the problematic—becomes important (Doyle, 1992). It is through such questioning that recursion—itself a reflective looking back on where we have been and what we have done—operates to allow (indeed encourage) us to develop a sense of who and what we are. It is through our actions, reflected upon, that such understanding and depth develop. The teaching act can, and indeed we may now say should, "seed" this process. But the process is not dependent on teaching as the only seed, and once begun the process builds its own parameters. The teaching role, here, is ancillary not causative. This is not to lessen teaching's role but to change it. Indeed, it is to bring to consciousness what I suspect self-reflecting teachers already know, at least tacitly: that through their interaction they fertilize certain ideas, but the development of these ideas is internal, via the reflective process.

Finally, curriculum materials can be organized to encourage such reflection if they are approached iteratively and recursively, not linearly. It is almost sacrilegious to consider the organization of content material in a manner other than sequential. But Jerome Bruner's (1960) "spiral curriculum" is worth looking at again and reframing in light of recursion theory. In one sense it is worth constructing a curriculum where students revisit with more insight and depth what they have done. In another sense curriculum—as a total package with content and instruction entwined—becomes exciting and engaging as it spirals off into the unknown. The world's knowledge is not fixed waiting to be discovered; it is continually expanding, generated by our reflective actions.[9]

How, when, where, and under what conditions self-organization takes place is a question Ilya Prigogine and his Brussels (now also Texas) colleagues have been working on for two decades. It is an issue that drew Piaget, in the later years of his life, to Prigogine. Piaget (1971a) is one of those who saw evolution with its emphasis on creation "swimming upstream" against the entropic flow. As he says:

> Cognitive schemata imply no absolute beginning [*no ex nihilo*] but are built-up [*in continuo*] by a progression of equilibrations and autoregulations. . . . [As such they are part] of vast regulator systems by means of which the organism as a whole preserves its autonomy and, at the same time, resists entropic decay. (p. 13)

However, the best Piaget could do regarding how such a schemata or system develops, as in the movement from one stage to another, was to assert that such development could not be rushed (always the "American question"), that development happens via internal mechanisms of action (phenocopy), and that when such development does occur it happens in a sudden *tout ensemble* manner, with disequilibrium acting as a positive force.

Prigogine agrees with all Piaget has to say here and goes further in his theory of *dissipative structures*. The essence of Prigogine's argument is that transformative change, involving basic restructuring, does not happen in a system at-or-near equilibrium. A system at-or-near equilibrium is a stable and closed system; indeed, it is one worn out in terms of energy–matter exchange. The very stability of such a system is a forerunner to its own demise, as in our death or the solar system's death. In metaphorical terms, such a system is characterized by a beat that "marches not dances."[10] In advocating a post-modern perspective for curriculum, I am suggesting we develop a "dancing curriculum," one where the steps are patterned but unique, the result of interactions between two partners: teacher and text, teacher and student, student and text.

A number of examples could be taken for transformative self-organization occurring in far-from-equilibrium situations. The creation of life itself is one such example. However, Prigogine has two favorites: the action of Acrasiales amoebae (slime molds) in biology and the Belousov-Zhabatinski reaction in chemistry. The slime mold amoebae generally live off the environment as single-cell units. However, when the food supply becomes low, they "undergo a spectacular transformation" (Briggs & Peat, 1989, pp. 138–139, Prigogine & Stengers, 1984, pp. 156–159). The amoebae send out a chemical pulse attracting other amoebae, which gather randomly to form an aggregate mass. As a mass, the amoebae move to another location where they form a stalk or "foot" from their aggregate clump. This stalk, rich in cellulose, breaks off from the main mass and sprouts new spores, which themselves separate into individual new cell units. As Prigogine and Stengers (1984) say:

> This is a spectacular example of adaptation to the environment. The population lives in one region until it has exhausted the available resources. It then goes through a metamorphosis by means of which it acquires the ability to invade other environments. (p. 159)

Another of Prigogine's featured examples is the Belousov-Zhabatinski reaction (1984, pp. 151–152; see also Briggs & Peat, 1989 pp. 140–141; Hayles, 1990 pp. 196–197), named after the two Russian chemists who first analyzed its features in the 1960s. These consist of a mixture of chemicals (malconic acid, potassium bromate, cerium ions) and a gentle stirring. (Alchemists of old, working more from feel than analysis, used to ruffle their beards over the mixture to create the stirring.) From the homogeneous mass a colored circle suddenly appears, spreading from the center. Soon the whole solution appears "red," but with a slight jiggle a new "blue" circle appears. The mixture then automatically flashes "red," "blue," "red," "blue" by itself at regular intervals. Further, at certain oscillations (as in chaos mathematics) the circles spiral crossways so that turbulence occurs both horizontally and vertically. The process is autocatalytic and iterative; it feeds on itself, creating its own changes, needing only slight periodic jiggles to continue. For alchemists this reaction was magic indeed. Today it is seen as but one example of nature's many self-organizing actions, an integral part of nature's complex and chaotic order.

Prigogine labels these self-organizing patterns "dissipative." In part, the label is meant to be ironic, to challenge the modernist concept of dissipation always leading to entropy. In part, though, the label calls attention to the fact that in open systems a great deal of dissipation *must be* developed if transformation is to take place, if the system itself is to survive. An open system depends on great amounts of dissipation; photosynthesis—the process by which life exists on this planet—could not occur if the sun did not dissipate enormous amounts of energy. Dissipation, then, is a necessity if transformation is to take place. However, dissipation is not itself sufficient. In biology, there is a sense of will, purpose, desire based on "communication"—even down to the male sperm traveling in the Fallopian tubes. Recently medical researchers have been talking of the female egg "communicating" with male sperm, of the two "exchanging information before fertilization," leading to a selective number of sperm then having a "desire" to swim toward the female egg in order to fertilize it (Ralt, et al. 1991).

In physics and chemistry this sense of desire or purpose is harder to ascertain. We "see" such qualities in animated forms but not in inanimate ones. However, *en masse* self-organization does exist in all the sciences, even in physics, with crystals and magnets self-organizing under certain conditions. Furthermore, the dichotomous breaking of disciplines into animate biology and inanimate physics with its Comtean structural hierarchy "misses the whole problem," as Howard Pattee has said (1973, p. 67). The problem is not to look at an assemblage reductively but cooperatively, systemically; that is, to see how any system works as a whole, coherently, collectively.[11] Field theory, rather than mechanistic reductionism, may be of help here (Davies, 1988, pp. 105–106; Hayles, 1984), for fields deal with organized complexities as complexities, not as aggregate simples.

However the issues of communication, desire, and purpose are ultimately worked out at the metaphysical level, it does seem obvious, after looking at the work of Prigogine and chaos mathematicians, that self-organization is an actual reality in all scientific fields and in the social sciences as well (Dyke, 1985, 1988). What seems characteristic of all self-organizing patterns is that they occur when "a critical threshold is reached," whereupon atoms, cells, or other entities "suddenly organize themselves on a global scale and execute cooperative behavior" (Davies, 1988, p. 82). Such a statement has powerful curricular as well as cosmological implications. One curriculum implication is that if cooperative, purposeful behavior (which leads to higher levels of organization) suddenly appears at critical threshold points, then teachers need to work toward finding these junctions in their own group interactions. And if autocatalysm and iteration take over at some point, so that a given class generates its own order and methods of development, then finding these junctions might well be one of the most important tasks a teacher has. In this frame, John Dewey's sense of community is placed in a new light. More than being merely a pleasant frame in which to work or in keeping with our democratic beliefs, community—with its sense of both cooperation and critical judgment—may be essential to meaningful, deep learning. It may well be also that individualism—again see Dewey (1929/1962)—which has formed the backbone of our American culture and is one of the factors that separates our schools from those in European and Asian cultures, will need to be reassessed. Indeed, the new post-modern paradigm is asking us to make just such a reassessment in fields as diverse as architecture, biology, chemistry, mathematics, and theology. It may be time to make such a reassessment in the fields of education and curriculum.

While it seems a truism that curriculum organizers and theorists such as Madeline Hunter, Roger Mager, James Popham, and Ralph Tyler would applaud Dewey's sense of community—and indeed have—it is also true that this sense of community is not part of the scientific-efficiency movement whose assumptions underlie these thinkers' curricular recommendations. In fact, as was shown in Chapter Two, the scientific-efficiency movement, which has spawned the behavioral objectives movement, the competency-based movement, and the effective schools movement, sees the teacher as a manager who directs the students as followers. The students' role here is not dissimilar from that of Schmidt, who as a "first class" man was to take orders and give no "back talk." In such a frame, words like self-organization, recursion, and iteration have no grounding. They work only in holistic, systemic, ecological frames, where the patterns are relational and interrelational, not individual and unidirectional.

In his work with self-organization, Prigogine goes beyond his field of technical expertise—far-from-equilibrium thermodynamics, for which he won the 1977 Nobel Prize in Chemistry—to create a whole cosmological perspective. It is this that makes his work so exciting and so dubious, as his critics point out (Pagels, 1985, pp. 97–99; Hayles, 1990, Ch. 4). The heart of Prigogine's cosmological argument is not only that dissipative structures are sources of orderly creation, "order through fluctuation" is the phrase he uses, but that by their openness they are indeterminate. Thus, the future direction of any far-from-equilibrium system cannot be predicted. These systems may well drive through into erratic and self-destructive behavior or they may organize themselves into new, more comprehensive and complex forms. Which occurs depends on the interactions within the system itself and between the system and its environment. Since the system develops *in continuo*, not from the unfolding of a pre-set plan, there is no way to predict in advance the particular results of these interactions. And since slight variations grow over time into major changes within a nonlinear framework, even probability theory is of little help—the success of prediction is *inversely related* to the length of time for which the prediction is made. This is why Edward Lorenz has concluded that long-range weather predictions are impossible. It is this fact that Prigogine uses to question Clausius' long-range prediction of the universe's heat death through entropy. Local self-organization systems may create a negative entropy within a total entropic process—"negentropy" to use a term coined by Erwin Schrödinger (1945) and developed by Jeffrey Wicken (1987)—so that our specific universe will increase and grow while the cosmos still runs down. On the other hand, the self-organization of our local system may well itself become generic, so that—as Freeman Dyson (1971) says—"life may succeed against all odds in molding the universe to its own purpose" (p. 51). It is this optimistic view which is Prigogine's personal hope.[12]

NOTES

1. Padraic Colum's "Babylonian Creation Story" is a retelling of the myth *Enuma Elish* but not in its usual form. A translation of this myth can be found in O'Brien and Major's book, *In the Beginning: Creation Myths* (1982).

2. It is interesting to note that Einstein, in developing relativity theory, was not emphasizing relativity but unity. He saw his theory as a method of preserving unity given the differences in astronomical measurement between relative positions in the universe. Before settling on the word relativity, he had considered the name "Theory of Invariance" (Hayles, 1990, p. 99).

3. A fine illustration of how a phase space graph is developed is shown in Gleick (1987, p. 28). Good written descriptions of phase space diagrams exist in Hayles (1990, pp. 146–149) and in Briggs and Peat (1989, Ch. 1).

4. For a graphic representation of the difference between Malthus' linear as-

sumptions and the nonlinear ones of chaos theory, see James Gleick's (1987) graphs on p. 176 of *Chaos*.

5. Obviously the advent of the computer with its ability to iterate many thousands of times was key to developing chaos theory. However, beginning work in this area can be done by any high school or even junior high student with a simple hand-held calculator. Iteration, of course, provides a tangible need for calculators in the classroom—a need presently not realized.

6. For more on the attractors in this parabolic pattern, see Douglas Hofstadter, "Mathematical Chaos and Strange Attractors" (pp. 364–395) in his book *Metamagical Themas* (1985).

7. For more on these issues and particularly the application of chaos mathematics to school curricula, see the work of Heinz-Otto Peitgen and his colleagues, notably *The Beauty of Fractals* (1986) and *Fractals for the Classroom* (1991).

8. Such a predisposition may be in evidence from the recent findings of the Hubble space telescope. Certainly, observation here support Prigogine's assertion that the "night sky" is filled with a complexity Newton would have considered impossible—supermassive black holes, newly formed globular clusters, double-quasar mirages, unexplained intergalactic hydrogen clouds, and other "remarkable goings-on." It may well be that the universe is infinite, expanding forever, and filled with a "dark matter" of some yet unknown type.

As scientists scramble to rethink their cosmologies, it may be that Davies' proposal of a self-organizing or "continuously creating" universe, one without beginning or end, will seem more acceptable. After all, a universe created *ex nihilio* has as many conceptual problems as one created *in continuo*; the former "seems" more natural only because it is part of our intellectual history. See articles by Chaisson, 1992; Fienberg, 1992; Maran, 1992; and Paul Davies' book, *The Mind of God*, 1992.

9. At a practical level my own course syllabi (for high school, college, and university students) no longer are "complete" by matching works studied and weeks in the term. Instead I plant seeds by outlining approximately half the course and then proposing directions the students may take to finish the course. Such "finishing" always includes their reflections on what has gone before as well as their sharing and comparing their pathways (chreods) of development with those others have taken.

10. In "Chaos, not Stability, Sign of a Healthy Heart" (Brown, 1989); see also "Nonlinear Dynamics of the Heartbeat" (Goldberger et al., 1985).

11. Stephen Jay Gould, in an interesting article on the Russian school of evolutionary theory, points out that it is possible—from Darwin's own writings—to interpret the "struggle for existence" as something other than personal, competitive struggle. As Gould (1988) says:

> A second form of struggle . . . pits organism against the harshness of surrounding physical environments. . . . These forms of struggle . . . are best waged by cooperation by members of the same species—by mutual aid. (p. 18)

Gould goes on to state that personal, competitive struggle is as much a part of the British social character, passed on intellectually "from Hobbes through Adam Smith to Malthus," as cooperative struggle is of the Russian social character. Again, scientific facts are interpreted in particular social-historical frameworks. See Gould's article, "Kropotkin Was No Crackpot," *Natural History,* August 1988, pp. 12–21.

12. The best interpretive description of Prigogine's views on entropy that I have found exists in Arthur Peacocke's Appendix, "Thermodynamics and Life," in his *God and the New Biology,* 1986, pp. 133–160. This article was originally published in *Zygon,* Vol. 19, No. 4, December 1984, where a number of other articles, including ones by Ilya Prigogine and Jeffrey Wicken, are devoted to issues surrounding the concept of entropy; for a mathematical treatment of the subject, see Edgard Gonzig, Jules Gehenian, & Ilya Prigogine, "Entropy and Cosmology," *Nature,* December 1987, *330.* Prigogine's own comments on the cosmological importance of entropy and his personal hope regarding the future of the universe can be found in his "The Rediscovery of Time," Chapter 8 in Richard Kitchener's *The World View of Contemporary Physics* (1988).

CHAPTER 5

The Cognitive Revolution, Bruner, A New Epistemology

CONCEPTS OF COGNITION

Is not mind that which calls things by their names, and is not mind the beautiful? And are not the works of intelligence and mind worthy of praise?

—Plato, *Cratylus*, 416 d

I rightly conclude. . . . I am composed of a body and a mind.

—Descartes, "Sixth Meditation," 81

Mind is primarily a verb. It denotes all the ways in which we deal consciously and expressly with the situations in which we find ourselves.

—Dewey, *Art as Experience*, 1934/1980, p. 263

As these quotations—one from each of the pre-modern, modern, and post-modern eras or modes—show the concept of mind has been part of Western intellectual thought since the time of the ancient Greeks. By now the concept is firmly woven into the fabric of our culture, affecting theories of cognition and curriculum through epistemology, learning theories, linguistics, and metaphysics. The present issue, arising from the new fields of artificial intelligence, computers, and cognitive science (Gardner, 1985; Winograd & Flores, 1987) is whether mind can best be thought of in substantive terms, as a "thing," or, instead, in abstract terms, as an idea. That is, whether mind and the logic it generates can best be considered in mechanical, linear terms or in metaphorical, non-linear, but heuristically generative terms. This difference is connected with the broader issue of either extending the modernist paradigm—with its strong emphasis on Descartes' (1664a/1985) notion of the human body as a machine and with mind as the immaterial substance which moves that machine (its "ghost")—or devising a new paradigm, where mind is a metaphor for the unique, self-conscious, self-organizing, and often unpredictable qualities displayed by functioning and reflecting humans. Devising such a paradigm would break with the now long-held Lockean tradition of mind as a blank tablet, a *tabula rasa*, on which ideas are written or imposed. This view has underlain virtually all our curriculum thought during the past century and has dominated our theories of learning and epistemology as well.

In one sense, mind has always been a metaphor: Plato's troika, Descartes' "etherial substance," Locke's *tabula rasa*, the nineteenth century's "muscle," Chomsky's "black box" are all metaphors. But rarely have we recognized mind as a metaphor. Since Descartes we have tended to think of mind as a place where reality itself is represented; hence mind has tacitly been considered an actual "thing." Only recently, with our acceptance of the strangeness of quantum thought, have we begun to question and rethink this representational realism so embedded in the modernist tradition. With this acceptance we see that we not only use metaphors to describe mind, but that mind itself is a metaphor. It is our "invention," to use Richard Rorty's (1980) term, for conceptualizing and labeling human powers of organization, reflection, creativity, and communication. In the modernist mode the assumption has been that mind, if not actually a tablet or muscle, is akin to such; it has been that which "mirrors" reality, albeit in a cloudy way. Only in the past few decades have we been able to see mind itself as a metaphor, a creation devised for organizational and communicative purposes. This movement beyond representational realism to abstract symbolism, itself an indicator of the human mind's power, has freed metaphor from the confines of representational reality. It has allowed metaphor to become more whimsical and insightful—the "charm" of quarks, the mystery of the mind's "black box." This more liberated use of metaphor, of course, is one of the key features of post-modernism; it represents the "deceit" of which Charles Jencks speaks (1987, p. 19).

In such a post-modern frame we can move beyond the confines of modernist realism to conceive of education and curriculum in more open terms—in the nonanalytic modes Oliver and Gershman (1989) mention, in the "narrative" mode Bruner (1986) describes. Further, the thrust of the move encourages us to find a new epistemology, which goes beyond the task of assessing how accurately our ideas and facts mirror reality. Instead, we wish to develop an epistemology which is more generative than representational, that "endows our lived experiences" with meaning. Such an epistemology will deal not merely with truth but with playfulness, paradox, complexity, and indeterminacy—

to name but a few aspects of what makes our lived experiences meaningful. This will be a hermeneutical, not a positivist, epistemology.

The Ancient Greeks: An Artful Balance

For the ancient Greeks, especially Plato and Aristotle, mind or *nous* referred to that part of the soul in which reason resided; it was but one part of the soul, albeit a part with special powers. In Book III of the *Republic*, Plato describes the soul as divided into three sections—reason, spirit, appetite—akin to the tripartite division he used later in the "Myth of Er" to divide the city-state's inhabitants into philosophers, soldiers, artisans. As philosophers possessed a "gold metal" in their character fitting them to be the rulers, so the soul's rational powers were to govern its other parts. As soldiers possessed a "silver metal" in their character, fitting them to be guardians, so the soul's spirited powers gave it courage. And as artisans possessed a "bronze metal" in their character, fitting them to be workers and producers, so the soul's appetitive powers gave it desires for the fullness of living and doing. Harmony or justice occurred both in the state and the soul when each part performed its own function in coordination with other parts doing their function. This concept of balance became the Greek ideal of the Good; analogously, knowledge was equated with wisdom, not with the accumulation of facts.

In Plato's theory of the soul, mind or reason is that part able to connect with and appreciate the Ideas, those external Forms existing beyond the control of human actions. Spirit or Will represents the personal qualities of determination, courage, honor, passion, and pride. Appetite is the natural desire for life's sensual pleasures—food, drink, intercourse (physical, social, verbal). When this tripart arrangement is well balanced, with reason (*nous*) as the leader among equals ("prima interpares"), the soul exudes a new concept, that of goodness or justice—a concept not found in any of the parts by themselves.

Developing cognition, in this model, means training each soul to its appropriate (indeed preordained) level: gold, silver, bronze. However, to limit this development to training only is to miss the essential quality of balance so important to the Greeks. Thus cognition, *per se*, moves well beyond the concept of acquiring particular skills into the areas of tempered experience, wisdom, and lives well lived. Here reason is broader than the solving of problems or achieving of right answers; it is making good judgments. Factual knowledge, needed for good judgments, is considered only remembrance. Through proper dialogue, as in the *Meno*, this knowledge is recollected by questioning. While the educational program in Plato's *Republic* is devoted to acquiring this art of questioning and factual knowing, the methodology of knowing itself is always encased within the broader frame of judgments. Judgments balance the appetitive and the willful, using experience to produce a just and harmonious life. The rulers of the state, as the *Republic* depicts them, are allowed to govern only after long years of training in music and mathematics, both harmony-oriented subjects, and after 15 years of practical apprenticeship. Thus, while the Greeks devoted time to the methodology of knowledge acquisition, they encased this methodology in ethical dimensions. Obviously, it is impossible to have virtue without knowledge (such virtue would lack meaning), but for the Greeks, at least in terms of Socrates and Plato, it is just as meaningless to consider knowledge without virtue. Life for the Greeks is of one piece; to fragment it is to destroy it. The modernist view of knowledge, independent of virtue, scientific in ethos, objective in nature, comes from the technical rationality spawned by the Enlightenment. From the seventeenth century on, this knowledge has been increasingly defined in mechanistic and mathematical terms.

While Aristotle, who studied at Plato's academy, did not accept all of Plato's doctrines, especially the more mystical aspects of factual knowledge as remembrance and a universal Oversoul existing beyond the world, he did accept the general thesis of reason (*nous*) connected with harmony and of harmony connected with virtue. In *De Anima* Aristotle talks of the soul's imperishable quality (Book I) and of its having various levels, with reasoning power the highest of all levels (Book II). Unlike Plato, he does not see this as a power inherent in the soul's nature; it is developed through use—technically a potential power is inherent, which use actualizes or brings into being (Book III). Here the extremes of Plato's mysticism are moderated by Aristotle's more commonsense approach.

The power of reason, as wisdom and judgment not as factual knowledge and correct answers, helps individuals aim at the mean or the moderate. In Book II of the *Nicomachean Ethics* Aristotle talks of virtue as adhering to the mean in life; avoiding excesses and deficits, the virtuous (and reasonable) person "seeks and chooses" the mean. Virtue as a mean lies between the extremes of excess and deficit. The virtuous person needs knowledge "to hit" the mean, and the wise or knowledgeable person becomes virtuous through the act of aiming at this mean. There is a process at work here whereby the two qualities of knowledge and virtue develop one another, producing a just and wise person.

Enlightenment Views of Knowledge: The Birth of Mechanistic Measurement

A different view of knowledge, the modernist one wherein knowledge is acquired, came into Western sensibility with the Scientific Revolution of the seventeenth century and the Industrial Revolution that followed. Both of these revolutions depended on mechanical measurement. As Carolyn Merchant (1983) has pointed out, the development of micro-measurement allowed science to proceed on its own, apart from the metaphysics of Greek mysticism. Even Aristotle, the naturalist, believed objects fell to earth because it was "in their nature." However, the birth of mechanistic measurement, with its new realm of micro-precision, brought with it the "death of nature" as a holistic, interconnected, living environment. Cosmologies changed. Knowledge became a separate, isolated quantity, removed from the experiences and wisdom of life. The cognitive emphasis shifted from making good judgments to making accurate predictions. The metaphor of mind shifted from being an abstract quality of the soul to being a "thing" in the body. What was spiritual became mundane.

The individual who contributed the most to this transformation was René Descartes. First, he categorically separated mind from body in a manner that placed each in dichotomous realms. Second, he set out his rationalist rules of reason whereby the mind could achieve certitude through introspection and geometric deduction. His most important contribution to the modernist concept of mind-as-organ, however, came from equating the body with a machine. As the centuries progressed, modern thought more and more adopted a mechanist and positivist perspective. Except for a few followers of Kant, mind now became associated with a particular part of the body, usually the brain. Ironically, Descartes' dichotomous separation of mind from body resulted in mind becoming another bodily organ. The 1828 Yale Report, which greatly influenced curriculum thought during the nineteenth century, implied the metaphor of a "muscle" in describing mind. This muscle needed "daily and vigorous exercise" (p. 300): Humanists advocated Latin and Greek; scientists advocated mathematics and the physical sciences; grammar school teachers advocated memorization and recitation.

Descartes' fascination with the concept of mechanization showed itself early in his youth. While living in the village of St. Germain, away from the Paris he found so distracting, he became intrigued by the mechanical statues Louis XIII's engineers had set in grottoes along the Seine. Walking the river bank, as he often did in his meditations, Descartes was able to peer into these grottoes and see mechanical figures automated by hydraulic pressure. One such figure, the goddess Diana, was especially appealing: She was taking a bath. However, the closer one approached the more the modest Diana retreated—hidden plates in the path activated a mechanical, hydraulic system. Finally, if a voyeur approached too closely, Neptune himself appeared waving his trident. While these statues were designed by the King's fountaineers strictly for the Queen's amusement, they suggested to the young Descartes that "*real* animal bodies could be understood as hydraulically operated automata" (Fancher, 1979, p. 9). He developed this concept extensively and with great consequences in his *Treatise on Man* (1664/1985d). Here, Descartes places the human functions of digestion, circulation, growth, respiration, sleeping and waking, sensation, imagination, and memory—all except reason—within a mechanistic frame. Indeed, he places them within a hydraulic frame, believing nerve fibers to be hollow tubes through which passes a fluid he calls "animal spirits" (p. 100ff). As Fancher (1979) says, with this treatise Descartes laid the "cornerstone" of American psychology's behaviorist movement, especially its mechanistic stimulus-response theory and its close alignment with neurophysiology's linear chains of communication (p. 40).

Descartes' interest in mechanism, though, went beyond the physiological or hydraulic; for him there was a deeper, metaphysical aspect to mechanism: It was *the method* "of rightly conducting reason for seeking truth." In one of his first (but never finished) works, *Rules for the Direction of the Mind* (1701/1985c), Descartes lists 22 rules. A reading of these makes Descartes' commitment to deductive reasoning quite evident. As Joachim (1957) notes:

> Descartes always tends to conceive of reasoning as a chain of links or sequence of states—a moment of thought along a chain of truths, each link being self-evident [or logically deducible from the first self-evident truth]. (p. 44).

This chain-link method of reasoning, geometric in origin, underlies Descartes' commitment to mechanism. He saw mechanism as an extension of his faith in mathematics, producing the certainty he sought. There are in Descartes' thought connections with both Plato and Aristotle, but the Greek concept of balance, integration, and harmony has vanished. It has been replaced by the measured and mathematical logic of certainty. Instead of searching for essences, as Socrates does for virtue in the *Meno*, Descartes "proves" his deeply held convictions, those he sees "clearly and distinctly" via the one method he believes will lead to right reason and truth. Such a mechanistic methodology permeates modernist epistemology and is evident at both subtle and overt levels in contemporary curriculum instruction. Classroom pedagogy does not question assumptions, beliefs, and paradoxes, as Socrates did; rather, it begins with what is self-evident or given and moves in linear links to reinforce, establish, or prove that already set and valued.

This mechanistic model lies at the heart of the Tyler rationale, a system closed, not open, in its methodology. Frederick Taylor's time-and-motion studies, the foundation of curriculum theory and planning from Bobbitt to Tyler, are based on such mechanistic assumptions. The same can be said of the artificial intelligence community's recent attempts at simulating human intelligence. The issue here, as Hilary Putnam (1988) points out, is whether we can devise a "reckoning machine" that "duplicates the achievements of what we intuitively recognize as intelligence" (pp. 269–270). One way to do this, of course—in fact the only way Putnam believes it can be done—is to limit intelligence to what the reckoning machine can do; that is, solve problems in a linear fashion. But if we define intelligence in terms of intuitive leaps, heuristic insights, or acts of volition based on feeling—as Putnam believes we should—then we move beyond mechanism, no matter how fast the gears spin or the electrical circuits race.

Historically, Descartes' division of the human into two mutually exclusive parts—*res cognitans* (the mental) and *res extensa* (the physical)—has led to two different views of mind. One view, following *res cognitans*, has seen mind as an immaterial but nonetheless controlling object or force. Immanuel Kant, Sigmund Freud, Jean Piaget, and Noam Chomsky have, in different ways, contributed to this view. The other view, following *res extensa*, has seen mind either as a physical, material object, usually the "grey matter" of brain, or as so subsumed by bodily actions that it is indistinguishable from the body. The British empiricists, the phrenologists, the associationists, the behaviorists, the psychometricians, and the neurophysiologists have, again in varying ways, contributed to this view. The "mind-as-muscle" metaphor, so popular in shaping nineteenth-century curriculum, collapsed when, in a series of experiments in the early 1900s, E. L. Thorndike was able to show that exercise in the hard, classical subjects had no carryover to the practical, industrial-oriented subjects of English, spelling, and arithmetical computation (Cremin, 1961, p. 113). While the metaphor of the mind-as-muscle disappeared from the literature, the concept of teaching in a mechanized, linear fashion did not; it was simply transferred from classical subjects to vernacular ones. Joseph Mayer Rice in his *Public School System of the United States* (1893/1969) gives a number of illustrations of such teaching in the elementary grades.

Having both the mentalists and the behaviorists take their concepts of mind from the same source means that antagonists such as Noam Chomsky and B. F. Skinner (pro- and anti-mind) have had their debates framed by the very problem that bothered Descartes—the relation between mind and body. On the one hand, Descartes wanted the mind to remain pure, isolated from the body. As he says in the "Sixth Meditation":

> Body . . . is only an extended being which does not think, [while] "I," that is to say my soul by virtue of which I am what I am, is entirely and truly distinct from my body and can exist or be without it. (1641/ 1951, p. 70)

On the other hand, Descartes wanted the mind to have some "union" with the body, lest he, as pure mind, not be a full person. Thus, he chose the pineal gland—not as the place where the mind was housed, but as the place where the mind performed its "functions":

> Although the soul [mind] is joined to the whole body, nevertheless there is a certain part where it exercises its functions . . . a certain very small gland.
> —*The Passions of the Soul,* Part I, 1649/1985, p. 340

To avoid this dualism that forces a choice between mind and body, we may well need to conceive of these two in a new, non-coequal way—as complementary categories each reinforcing the other, not as dichotomous and competing realms. Gilbert Ryle (1949) suggests the mind-body dualism is a category mistake, one comparing things like rocks with "Wednesdays" (p. 23). Each exists but on different conceptual levels; one is a thing, the other is an abstraction. Following Ryle's lead, Paul Davies (1988), a theoretical physicist, suggests we conceive of mind at two levels—as a thing at the brain level, and as an abstraction or a metaphor at the conceptual level. At the brain level, mind can be considered in terms of brain cells that work mechanistically and obey the basic laws of physics. At the self-conscious, mental level, mind can be regarded as a metaphor for the activities of the brain, as "a fantastically complex *network* around which electrical *patterns* meander" (p. 183). This higher, mental level, where "patterns think," is filled with nonlinear, spontaneous, chaotic activity. It has its own "laws and principles," which, while different from the "neural events of which they are composed," in no way violate the basic physical laws on which the neural events are based (p. 191).

In Davies' view mind and body refer to different categories.[1] Adopting a computer metaphor, he calls mind the "software," which the body as "hardware" uses. While the body uses the mind, mind is not reducible to body; each category is a separate, albeit interdependent entity; together they complement one another and act harmoniously in their integration. Davies carries this concept of hierarchical levels further, into the cultural realms of art, literature, social and scientific theories, and religion. Davies (1988) says these abstract, social entities "transcend the mental experiences of individuals and represent the collective achievements of human society as a whole" (p. 194). Again, it is important to recognize that these social organizations carry their "own irreducible laws and principles," apart from the mental events and bodily substances that spawned them.

This triad of entities—(1) material objects, (2) mental events, (3) social organizations—is organized hierarchically: Each level is more complex than the preceding one, more systemic. Thus, due to the increasing complexity and systemic character of the levels, no one level is reducible to a prior level. Rather, higher levels "grow" out of former, simpler ones. This concept of transformative, qualitative growth is based on two assumptions fundamental to post-modern science. One is the concept of self-organization; the other is the concept of transformation. Both have important implications for curriculum. Self-organization is essential for the biological concepts of adaptation and evolution, for Piaget's theory of equilibration, and for Prigogine's concept of order arising from fluctuations or chaos. It is not, though, part of the behaviorist movement, based as this is on a stimulus-response theory of external causation working in a mechanistic fashion. As Davies (1988) sees it, self-organization is an expression of one of the universe's most fundamental and deeply mysterious properties—*its inherent creative power*, a power which allows nature "to produce a progressively richer variety of complex forms and structures" (p. 5). Like Prigogine and Waddington, Davies believes that at certain points in the chaotic, active milieu that is nature, thresholds are reached whereby new and more complex organizational structures spontaneously develop. Such a threshold was reached when the energy in nature coalesced to form matter via the "Big Bang."

Educationally, we may derive from Davies' insights our new metaphor for curriculum organization, that based on spontaneous generation. Again, such a curriculum would allow the human power of creative organization and reorganization to be operative. Here the art of curriculum construction is that of helping students develop their own creative and organizing powers. This cannot be done by overdirection or by underdirection: Creative organization requires a tension between set practices and infinite possibilities, between our need to find closure and our desire to explore. Obviously, what we call the facts or basics of a field are needed; but we also need to play with these facts, to rearrange them in imaginative ways. Facts take on the colors of the contexts in which they are placed and at times are transformed by their interactions with and within these contexts.

Transformation over time is another concept Davies draws on for his view of mind as an abstraction from neuronal activity. While each organizational level in the triad of material objects, mental events, and social organization has its own "laws and principles," it is also true the more advanced levels emerge from the previous ones. Complex organization is actually generated from simple combinations. As was described in Chapter Four, mathematical chaos theory shows that development over time often produces bifurcation points—in insect populations, in swinging pendula, in long-range weather forecasts—where past patterns are qualitatively transformed into new and different patterns. In the active creativity of nature, with its self-generating processes, complex patterns are actually produced from simple beginnings. We see this in such diverse fields as human or animal reproduction and mathematical iteration.

Educationally, this means we need to consider development as more than external imposition, as more than linear accumulations: Self-organization and qualitative, nonlinear transformations are natural and key parts of the developmental process. Such organization and transformation can be helped to occur by our reflection on what we have done. A paper written or a test taken can serve as an opportunity for a new level of analysis, an internal analysis of our intentions and purposes. As Dewey argued so many times, reflection on what we have done is a key tool for our own transformation. Primary, doing experiences need not stand alone; they can serve as the basis for secondary, reflective, indeed self-organizing experiences. Every completed action can serve as a new beginning, as the springboard for new and open "ends-in-view."

BRUNER

I am convinced that we shall do better to conceive of growth as an empowering of the individual by multiple means for representing his world, multiple means that often conflict and create the dilemmas that stimulate growth.

—Bruner, *Beyond the Information Given*, 1973a, p. 323

This quotation, from one of Bruner's essays, "The Growth of Representational Processes in Childhood," summarizes much of what he believes mind to be, as well as his views on how mind can be developed. Growth, as the title of the essay indicates, refers to an individual's personal ability to represent the world, its reality and culture. The *power of representation*, especially in its higher, more symbolic forms—the symbolic is higher than the iconic, itself higher than the enactive—is what Bruner means by mind. It is a power either unique to humans or at least more fully developed in them than in other species. It is a power that allows humans to have control over their destiny; and it is a power that can be developed, especially through "social reciprocity," or learning from others. This point, Bruner says, is recognized by Lev Vygotsky but not by Noam Chomsky, Jean Piaget, or B. F. Skinner. For these theorists, the learner, especially the child, lives alone, separate from others, in a calm and logical world, "detached from the hurly burly of the human condition." Only Vygotsky's theory of learning posits social interaction as an essential ingredient (Bruner, 1983, pp. 138–139; 1986, Ch. 5).

Bruner (1983) calls mind "an idea we construct" to frame the remarkable powers humans have "to go beyond the information given" (p. 201). As such, it is not a thing but a concept. Any sense of mind as a particular *place* to house ideas is metaphorical, not material. The powers of mind represent the whole person, emotional as well as intellectual, in both reflective and social interaction with the environment.

This concept of social interaction, a reciprocity with others that leads to ideas of both self and community, has significant importance for learning. One aspect, neglected by the behaviorists, is that we learn through, by, and with others—learning is not an isolated, programmed activity. The behaviorists have generally missed this point, due to their experimentation [almost exclusively with animals]. As James Watson (1936) the father of behaviorism, said in his autobiographical reflections:

> I never wanted to use human subjects. I hated to serve as a subject. . . . With animals I was at home. I felt that, in studying them, I was keeping close to biology with my feet on the ground. More and more the thought presented itself: Can't I find out by watching this behavior everything that other students are finding out by using "O's" [human subjects]? (p. 276)

The answer, of course, is No! Humans are able to learn from one another, to transmit knowledge to one another. Animals cannot do this, at least not in as sophisticated a form. Thus, Bruner argues, educators, psychologists, even philosophers need to pay far more attention to this most important and unique human ability—learning from others. As

Bruner sees it, we need to develop curricular plans and instructional strategies that utilize student-student and student-teacher dialogic interactions. Further, we need to realize that much of human learning comes from this interaction—via the conflicts that create the dilemmas which generate growth. If we have, as Chomsky argues, an innate propensity to learn (a language)—if we are born with a Language Acquisition Device (LAD)—then the performance of this propensity or competence is developed by and within a Language Acquisition Support System (LASS). Bruner's point here is that whatever innate, genetic powers we have are dependent for their development on the culture in which they exist. As he and Bornstein (1989) say:

> LAD and LASS between them assure the . . . rapid acquisition of language by the young child—an acquisition that is more rapid than could be accounted for by either induction or by imitation.

This concept of interaction, which Bruner sees as key to human development, was first proposed by John Dewey in his 1896 essay, "Reflex Arc Concept in Psychology." Here he argues that the notion of a conditioned reflex arc, prominent at the time and instrumental in behaviorism's rise, was too unidimensional, a "patchwork of disjointed parts, a mechanical conjunction of unallied processes" (1896/1972, p. 97). For Dewey, the reflex arc is a reflex *circuit,* really a whole, integrated network. He says that reflexes are not merely mechanistic responses to the external pressures of environment but are the results of an overall "coordination," which takes into account *the active and searching nature* of the individual as well as "the motor responses of psychical existence" (p. 99). In short, the circuit is part of a larger network, one that is continually undergoing change as we intentionally interact with the world around us.

The "new psychologists," though, those of the behaviorist school founded at the turn of the century, paid no attention to Dewey. Watson (1936), who studied with Dewey at Chicago, confessed in later years that he "never knew what Dewey was talking about" (p. 274). For Watson behaviorism offered a new vision, where the natural but inefficient connection between unconditioned stimuli and unconditioned responses could be raised to a higher, more efficient level. *Conditioned stimuli* would be connected to *conditioned responses,* and the unilateralness of this connection would lead to efficiency, predictability, control. The potential power of this vision to shape human behavior, to carry out the Enlightenment project, to make a better society through scientific management and technical rationality was too great to brook any alternative conceptions. The movement had to run its course before we could consider the wisdom of Dewey's remarks.

The first American psychologist, after Dewey, to challenge the behaviorist position was Karl Lashley, a former student of J. B. Watson. At the Hixon Symposium in 1948, taken by many to be the beginning of the current cognitive movement, he voiced his conviction that behaviorism's simplistic linear view of "A evokes B" was theoretically incapable of explaining *complex* human behaviors. Simple associated chains of stimulus–response arranged in a linear fashion cannot account for the integrated, multilevel network demonstrated by human thought—thought patterns happen too quickly and change too frequently; nor do such chains account for anticipatory behavior, such as speaking errors which anticipate words yet to come. For Lashley, as for Dewey, the nervous system is not a reflex arc but an interactive, organized network, with internal control. As Lashley (1951) says:

> Attempts to express cerebral functions in terms of the concepts of the reflex arc, or of associated chains of neurons, seem to me doomed to failure because they start with the assumption of a static nervous system. Every bit of evidence available indicates a dynamic, constantly active system, or, rather, a composite of many interacting systems. (p. 135)

This statement depicts mind not merely as a network of physical or chemical interactions, as most neuropsychologists argue, but as more—a network influenced by interacting with other, more ephemeral, networks: those of purpose, planning, intention, and will as well as those of history and culture. This multiplicity of networks moves the concept of mind beyond that of brain. In its full breadth, Lashley's statement not only challenges behaviorism's particular tenets of stimulus-response and the reflex arc but also encourages questioning of empiricism's scientific method and of modernism's assumptions of a stable universe and a spectator theory of knowledge.

Noam Chomsky, an avowed Cartesian but of the mentalist not the materialist strand, raised again the questions of mind and human actions in his 1960s and 1970s work on language and mind. In the 1950s, B. F. Skinner unwittingly sang behaviorism's "swan song" in his book *Verbal Behavior* (1957). Chomsky's (1959/1984) devastating critique of the book attacked not only Skinner's view of how language is acquired, but the empirical base of his epistemology as well. This critique signaled, many say, the death knell of behaviorism and showed what Howard Gardner (1985) has called the "theoretical bankruptcy" of the behaviorist position (p. 193). To this day, neither Skinner nor any other behaviorist has publicly answered Chomsky's (1959/1984) criticism: that the behaviorist position empirically "fails to account for [certain important] facts of verbal behavior"—notably, recognizing new, unseen sentences, distinguishing nonsentences from sentences, detecting ambiguities in language, and generating an infinite variety of sentence strings from a few rules (p. 565ff). In short, says Chomsky, native speakers, even as young children, seem to be carrying out "a remarkable type of theory construction" (p. 577).

While Bruner does not see children or beginning learners in such exalted terms, he does see all learners as constructors whose constructions improve through tool use, social interaction, and recursive thought. Analogously, a curriculum based on (1) experience with symbol manipulation (especially language), (2) public dialogue, and (3) private reflection can, Bruner believes, transform the learner from a copier of others' patterns to a generator of one's own.

Bruner accepts Piaget's notion that meaningful learning—learning that allows one to be generative with the material at hand, thus going beyond that presented—is dependent on an individual's particular way of representing the world. Bruner does not, though, accept Piaget's view of a genetic, stage framework for representing these ways of thought, perception, and action; nor does he believe there is little or nothing the teacher can do to aid the growth of these forms of representation. Drawing on Vygotsky's "zones of proximal development," Bruner (1986) believes there are areas just beyond an individual's generative competence (hence proximal) where the learner can follow another's activities and thoughts without being able to construct these personally (p. 73ff). In these zones, the learner is able to use hints from others, to take advantage of others' help in organization; in effect, to "borrow" another's consciousness or reflection. Through the interaction between one's own reflective understanding and that of another (teacher or tutor), an individual is able to transform and heighten personal consciousness. The teaching art here, of course, is to help the learner transform personal consciousness without merely copying that of another. This is why Bruner & Bornstein, (1989) pay so much attention to interaction as the way to overcome the dilemma of choosing between empirical, external experience and rational, internal maturation. The issue is not either-or but how externality and imitation are integrated with internality and maturation. As was said in Chapter Three, the issue is not the relative merits of nature or nurture but how "nature is nurtured."

In developing a LASS, Bruner (1986) uses the example of a mother "cooing" with her child. This playful act has its cognitive aspects: In doing this the mother "remains forever on the growing edge of the child's competence" (p. 77), leading the child into areas not yet, but soon to be, mastered by him- or herself. The mother's actions are in the "zone of proximal development." As the child's experiences develop, mind develops, with the powers of representation and reflection increasing. Representation moves from being purely enactive to enactive-iconic and finally to enactive-iconic-symbolic. This latter, tripartite mode not only has the power of the symbolic (especially as developed in language), it also has the power of the symbolic integrated with the iconic and the enactive. Maturing individuals now have multiple means for representing their worlds; and, in turn, their own growth is influenced by multiple perspectives. Bruner believes education should take advantage of these multiple means and not confine curriculum to the logical and analytic. The artistic and metaphorical are just as important tools of expression and thought as are what Piaget calls the logico-mathematical. Bruner (1986, Chs. 2 & 9) encourages curricularists to use and develop a culture's artistic, metaphorical, and intuitive modes in conjunction with the more dominant analytic (paradigmatic) mode.

The concept of challenging or pushing personal structures so they are transformed to higher, more comprehensive levels of organization is a point Bruner shares with Piaget. But where Piaget abstracts these structures and builds them around forms of logical organization, Bruner particularizes them to *an* individual within *a* culture. Where Piaget is universal, Bruner is local. Thus, there is far more emphasis on self and self-reflection in Bruner's frame. This is shown in his social studies curriculum, "Man: A Course of Study" (1966). In more recent writings he talks of recursion theory, from the Latin *recurrere* (to "run back"). Again, in mathematics, recursion refers to the iterative process where in an x/y equation ($y = 4x + 1$), the derived value of y becomes the new value of x. Thus, in an x/y series the former y becomes the next x. In a broader sense, "running back" means that each statement or proposition is re-examined in terms of re-looking at its original foundational assumptions. This "looping back" is different from that found in cybernetic systems—these are more interested in a goals-results "fit" than in questioning and exploring original assumptions and procedures, as one steps back or "distances one's self" from one's creation. A hermeneutic reflection where "the mind turns around on itself," creating both a "summary of its capacities" and a "sense of 'self'" (1986, p. 97), is one where new possibilities emerge, where transcendence occurs. This reflective process plays for Bruner, as it did for Dewey and Piaget, a key role in the concept of mental growth.

For Bruner, the curriculum, in terms of courses of study, should also turn around on itself. This is Bruner's famous "spiral curriculum," where school subjects are studied developmentally over a number of years with increasing levels of complexity. The teacher's art is in translating the structures of whatever subject is being studied into the learner's "way of viewing things" and then operating in the zone of development just beyond the learner's sense of comfort. When this process of translation is done well, Bruner (1960) believes, it is quite possible to teach any subject "effectively in some intellectually honest form to any child at any stage of development" (p. 33). When the translation process is not well done, chaos of the disruptive (nongenerative) sort emerges.

Bruner does not see teachers teaching the formalisms of calculus or the paradoxes of quantum physics to first graders; but he does see teachers in the elementary grades introducing notions of changing limits and irregular (maybe even indeterminate) patterns into their dialogue with students. Further, these introductions should be done in such a way (often through play and intellectual challenges) that students gradually increase their zones of development, their own ways of effective representation. This growth process, interactive and personal by nature, will not proceed in a linear, sequential, accumulative, and stable manner; rather, it will occur sporadically and spontaneously as each individual builds a rich matrix of representations, utilizing multiple perspectives, consciousness presuppositions, and personal subjectifications. These three are features of literary or historical discourse, not of philosophical analysis—of hermeneutics, not of logic. For Bruner (1986, Ch. 2) *multiple perspectives, presuppositions, and subjectifications* form the "other" mode of knowing, the narrative, humanistic mode, which draws its meanings from the heuristics of metaphor not from the validity of logic. Here, meaning is personally created and historically generated, not just empirically discovered and validly proved. The two modes, the narrative and the analytical, different as they are, complement one another. Bruner believes they should be integrated, producing a curriculum that utilizes both the methods of hermeneutics and the canons of logic.[2] Such a curriculum would encourage us to think of knowledge in a new light.

A NEW EPISTEMOLOGY

If we did not believe in causality, there would be no science.
    —Reichenbach, *The Rise of Scientific Philosophy,* 1951, p. 42

If we are to use the methods of science in the field of human affairs, we must assume that behavior is lawful and determined. We must

expect to discover that what a man does is the result of specifiable
conditions and that once these conditions have been discovered we
can anticipate and to some extent determine his actions.
                        —Skinner, *Science and Human Behavior*, 1953, p. 6

As Jacob Bronowski (1978) has pointed out, the nature of scientific
predictability expressed in these quotations—where causes and effects
are inextricably bound, so much so that when one "sees an effect one
looks for its cause" (p. 25)—appears so pervasive that "no other method
is conceivable"; it has become "our natural way of looking at all problems" (p. 59), the central tenet of modernist science. Newton used this
cause-effect principle to predict the orbit of his friend Edmund Halley's
comet; Kant used it for the development of his *synthetic a priori* philosophy; and Skinner along with other behaviorists used it not only for his
theory of conditioned responses but also for a broader view of a scientific approach to the social sciences. In this view lies the positivist conception of knowledge—one that transcends the observer and the observed, residing in a realm removed from the "hurly burly" experiences
of life. This epistemology falsely separates the knower from the known
in its desire to create a transcendent "objective." And in this view of
knowledge, to which we are mere spectators, lies the view of curriculum
formalized in Ralph Tyler's rationale.

Six years before Skinner made his modernist pronouncement, relating human affairs to physical science, Hans Reichenbach (a propo-
nent of the "new" positivist science) criticized such a view as assuming
a causality, prediction, and certainty which do not exist. The absolutist
view, he says, "has nothing to say to us who are witnesses of the physics
of Einstein and Bohr" (1951, p. 44). Foreshadowing Bronowski, Reichenbach labels this view "speculative," based as it is on metaphysical,
philosophical assumptions, not on the methods of science. In its place
he proposes a "new and truer" scientific philosophy, one that actually
continues the tradition it criticizes. This new "scientific philosophy"
emphasizes group processes, empirical validation, and logical induction. It does not pander after *absolute* certainty but is willing to accept
probable certainty (statistical probability) in its place. Empirical verification remains a central tenet, though; there is, according to Reichenbach
(1951), a "verifiability criterion of meaning" (p. 258).

Obviously, verification—empirical, positivist, and lying at the very
heart of our traditional, modernist concept of epistemology—does not
endow an individual's personal experiences with meaning; a verifica-
tionist epistemology neither looks for nor honors multiple perspectives,
conscious presuppositions, or personal subjectifications.[3] As Reichenbach (1951) says, "The empiricist theory of meaning does not supply a

description of a person's subjective meanings" (p. 258). But it is just these subjective meanings which form the heart of personal experience, and in the process of transformation give us an experiential epistemology. This new theory of knowledge—interactive and dialogic—is one that emphasizes knowledge creation not discovery, negotiation not verification. In an epistemology of verification, the knowing subject is peripheral to that known, an external object. Paradoxically, in another sense the object so overwhelms the subject that the subject is lost or embedded within the object. These two foci—an external, controlling object and a lost subject—allow the Tyler rationale to legitimate the pre-setting of goals and objectives, the pre-determination of student experiences, and the definition of individual meaning and learning in terms of how closely the chosen experiences match the pre-selected objectives. Here the individual is both subordinate to and embedded within the objectives. The closure of this system—always working toward pre-determined ends—makes it an ideal one to measure. And the concept of curriculum it generates, the "measured curriculum," is that of pre-selected courses of study reinforced with tightly written lesson plans and lecture notes. All this stays close to the task-at-hand, with little opportunity for new or divergent ideas—those near the "border" of a frame—to spiral off into the unknown, as in those beautiful iterations of complex numbers found on the edge of the Mandlebrot sets.

In contrast, an epistemology of experience shifts the focus of study to the back-and-forth interplay between that known and the local knower. The subject of study is both the knower and the known; really, it is the interactive (or transactive) discourse between these two. Bruner (1990), drawing on a quotation from Michelle Rosaldo, says that notions of self "grow not from 'inner' essence relatively independent of the social world, but from experience in a world of meanings, images, and social bonds" (p. 42). The self now becomes primary not peripheral—but, as the quotation shows, primary within a dialogic, dual-focused process, not in an exclusive or isolated frame. The self is not the be-all and end-all the existential movement made it, but is a key ingredient in the knower–known transaction. Consciousness, particularly reflective consciousness—which turns both inward to the self and outward to society—is an intellectual tool humans use to effect this transaction.

Such recursion, whereby "the mind turns around on itself" is, for Bruner, the central concept in any definition of mind which considers development as one of the primary purposes of education. The concept of curriculum this epistemological view generates emphasizes *currere*, the active verb form of "the course to be run." Mind as a verb representing our human power to organize can also be considered a noun (a gerund) representing the cultural development of that organization. A curriculum that emphasizes culture and its role in our building of organizing frames, incorporates private and public reflection on what we do, why we do, and who we are. At the practical level, journal writing and story telling can play important roles in such a curriculum. However, too often such personal activity is seen only as an adjunct to a verification-oriented curriculum, something added on, peripheral. A *currere*-oriented curriculum would make self-reflection, imaging, and public discourse central, the essence of transformation. Even school tests could be designed to serve the purpose not just of verifying what has been learned but of understanding better the why's of choices made and procedures followed, as well as of contrasts and alternatives that could have been taken. In this frame, changes occur in evaluation and teacher–student relationships. Evaluation becomes generative, not just summative; the emphasis is on what the student can do with the knowledge acquired not on how well the knowledge acquired matches a frame set by others. Teacher–student relations take on the personal quality of dialogic interaction—bilateral and transactive, not merely unilateral and informative. Such changes require teachers to be good listeners and interactors, not merely good expositors, although good exposition is certainly a desired quality—one of many desired qualities.

Richard Rorty (1980, 1982, 1989) carries forward the concept of dialogic interaction and links it to that part of the hermeneutic tradition represented by Hans-Georg Gadamer's (1975) concept of "open" conversation. Such conversation is ongoing, never ending. Assumptions, prejudices, historical interpretations are continually re-interpreted. For this type of conversation the objective–subjective split of modernist philosophy is transcended; the objective and subjective become entwined in one another and lose their categorical distinctiveness. From this perspective, Rorty (1982, Ch. 12) critiques Reichenbach's attempt to found a "new" scientific philosophy. Rorty points out that Reichenbach's philosophy continues to assume all the positivist doctrines—verification, induction, predictability—inherent in the model it attempted to replace. In short, under the label of "newness" Reichenbach tried to shore up the old paradigm, not develop a new one.

The charge Rorty leveled against Reichenbach, Eric Bredo (1989) has more recently leveled against Dennis Phillips (1987) and his attempt to provide yet *another* " 'new' philosophy of science," one now willing to reject the validity of verification, along with induction and the neutrality of facts. Instead, Phillips tries to maintain the positivist paradigm by "liberalizing" the empiricist doctrine through adherence to Karl Popper's (1968) falsification and deductionist concepts. The essence of this argument is that while verification in terms of truth can no longer be maintained in any time-independent way (universals no longer holding), there is still a need for positing hypotheses and making testable deductions. While such a need does and will always exist, Phillips' difficulty (as well as that of Popper) is in assuming all knowledge to be based on this empirical model. As Bredo (1989) says, "This formalistic view" with its "undue emphasis on formal logic . . . gives a misleading picture of actual reasoning" (p. 404). This positivistic approach leaves out other modes of knowing, particularly those Bruner classifies as narrative. Further, this view assumes we can "escape from our history"— an assumption pragmatists and hermeneuticians reject.

We appear to be, then, in Kuhn's crisis stage of paradigm change: The modernist paradigm with its deification of science, its assumption of an objective methodology, and its positing or inventing of a mechanistic "mind" has broken down. A post-modernist paradigm is still in the early stages of formation. No coherent theory has yet emerged to unite the disparate trends—constructive and deconstructive—inherent in the paradigm. Nor will such coherence emerge easily, for a post-modern paradigm wishes to utilize, not negate nor overcome, these disparate trends. Utilizing disparate trends—paradoxes, anomalies, indeterminacies—is one of the greatest hurdles traditional educators and curricularists have in accepting an eclectic and diverse post-modern pedagogical frame. If such acceptance can be accomplished, though, the pedagogic possibilities inherent in a post-modern frame are unlimited and immensely exciting, for both teachers and students.

In his *Acts of Meaning* (1990), Bruner starts us toward the development of such a post-modern pedagogical frame. He takes cognition and its revolution out of the scientific, behaviorist, and computer-oriented mode into which it slipped in the 1960s, back to its original beginnings of human meaning-making through acts laden with and embedded in culture, language, intentionality, and subjectivity. This act of meaning-making Bruner believes is innate but not restricted to humans, although the development of language and self-conscious reflection gives humans a qualitative ability other animals do not possess. He puts forth the *radical thesis* that there is in all humans a "push to organize experience." The radicalness of this thesis, though, is that we do this "narratively" not logically (p. 79). The logical, in the mode of Piaget and the positivists, he sees as coming after the narrative. Following A. R. Luria (1961) and Margaret Donaldson (1978), he writes that "logical propositions are most easily comprehended by the child when they are embedded in an ongoing story;" and, disagreeing with Noam Chomsky about the nature of innateness, further states that "we have an 'innate' and primitive predisposition to narrative organization," not to linguistic competence (p. 80). Such competence, he argues, arises "through use," via "assistance from and interaction with caregivers," and appears to be based on a "prelinguistic 'readiness for meaning.' " To give a fuller quotation: "There are certain classes of meaning to which human beings are innately tuned and for which they actively search" (p. 72).

This search is narrational, not logical, for the narrative is more natural and less formal. While logical analysis "proves" an idea or concept to be right or wrong, narrative negotiates passages between what we understand and what we do not understand but to which we are attracted. In short, narrative—living as it does on the border "between the real and the imaginary" (p. 55)—is a chief vehicle for helping people grow, expand their horizons or zones, and come in meaningful contact with the noncanonical.

In regard to contemporary philosophy, the issue is whether the present analytic and scientific bents should be continued, with the probability of "warranted assertions" replacing the (now lost) certainty of verification, or whether philosophy should seek radically new, although in some cases historically old, directions (Nielson, 1991). Another way to phrase this is to ask whether philosophy should remain in the modernist mode or turn elsewhere, away from "mirroring" nature via a positivist epistemology, to "edifying" human problems. Such a turn, hermeneutic in nature, would be Janus-faced—combining an indeterminate post-modern future with a re-interpreted, historical, pre-modern past. The accomplishments of technology and precision would not be lost in this new framework, but they would be placed within an experientially oriented frame. For some, the answer is clear: Philosophy should abandon its search for epistemology. For Rorty (1980), traditional epistemology is "a desire to find foundations [outside oneself] to which one might cling" (p. 315). Rorty (1986) wishes us to abandon this clinging and accept the temporality of our condition, the indeterminateness of knowledge, and the contingency of selfhood. To so accept means we give up the search for certainty and universality; we deal with the particulars of situations as particulars, not as anything more. We accept the "contingent character of starting points," the fact that there is no set beginning, no set end. Conversation with "our fellow humans . . . [is] our only source of guidance" (1982, p. 166). Rorty (1982) thus asks philosophy to turn its bias from an epistemological-verifiable one to a hermeneutical-historical one, to consider knowledge in terms of coping with, not copying, reality, and to develop a "vocabulary of practice rather than of theory" (p. 202). Such a move is not to find a new epistemology, or even to find a new methodology for seeking truth; rather,

Rorty turns to hermeneutics as a vehicle to "keep the conversation going." Conversation with our fellow humans is our only source of guidance; it is the "ultimate context within which knowledge is to be understood" (1980, p. 389). Such conversation has no set beginning or set end; its very framework is contingent on us and our language. As Elaine Atkins (1988) says, here "dialogue is not a disguised form of inquiry" into truth; it is the "activity that enables participants to make reasoned choices" (p. 79). The making of reasoned choices is what Bronowski calls the real "common sense of science." The hermeneuticians, neo-pragmatists, and meaning-making cognitivists have brought to our awareness how personal, historical, situation-bound, and system-framed are these reasoned choices.

It is through experience that we make reasoned choices; not the experience of just doing but of reflecting on what we do; experience that is analyzed through the lenses of culture, language, and personal bias. The role these lenses play in cognition is what brings the neo-pragmatic philosophers Richard Bernstein and Richard Rorty to the hermeneutical philosophy of Hans-Georg Gadamer (1975)—a philosophy which has also attracted the computer scientists Terry Winograd and Fernando Flores (1987) and is now attracting the psychologist Jerome Bruner (1986, 1990). Bruner (1986) shows his kinship to hermeneutic thought when he says:

> It is far more important, for appreciating the human condition, to understand the ways human beings construct their worlds than it is to establish the ontological status of the products of these processes. (p. 46)

It appears to me that in this move from asserting the validity of the beingness of products to affirming the importance of process, especially process embedded in cultural, linguistic, interpretive norms—a move from the ontological to the historical—lie the beginnings of a new epistemology. In saying that " 'hermeneutics' is not the name for a discipline, nor for a method," Rorty (1980, p. 315) declines to recognize the validity of either epistemology or methodology, believing both to be directly connected with that transcendent Enlightenment rationality he inveighs against so strongly. However, I agree with Richard Bernstein (1986, Ch. 2) that Rorty means more by hermeneutics than merely "keeping the conversation going;" that he does indeed propose a new epistemology, a hermeneutic epistemology, one akin or at least aligned with the current popular concept of a socially constructivist epistemology,[4] one I prefer to call an experiential epistemology. Further, I agree with Elaine Atkins that in Rorty's hermeneutically oriented neo-pragmatism lie the seeds of a new concept of curriculum, a "currere," process curriculum. While not unsupportive of this interpretation, Rorty (1990) is dubious as to whether such a curriculum reconceptualization can occur within our current frames of philosophy, social thought, and education. But he wishes such a reconceptualization to occur.

In all this, there is, I believe, a "hope" supporting and encompassing the dictum about conversation being our "ultimate context" and "only source of guidance." That hope, social in nature, resides in our developing for ourselves a sense of community. As we begin to give up the "false metaphysical comfort" Western philosophy and theology have provided us, we see that it is community which binds us together in and against the "dark night of existence." It is conversation which fuels this sense of community, that allows us through imagination and play (more than through rational or scientific analysis) to bring some light to our search.

This hermeneutic view where we engage ourselves in conversation with our histories provides us with a concept where curriculum is not just a vehicle for transmitting knowledge, but is a vehicle for creating and re-creating ourselves and our culture. Again, as Dewey said, mind is a verb, an active verb; an active, seeking verb; an active, seeking, self-organizing verb. It should not be wasted.

NOTES

1. Davies' view of mind has overtones of behaviorism, as do the views of Ryle and Pagels, on whom he draws. I reject these overtones. Like Bruner and Dewey, I see mind as a metaphor to describe the active organization of an individual's whole being encased within a culture. To limit mind to overt behavior or to neuronal activity in the brain is to limit the power of being human. It neglects human purposiveness, creativity, and social being.

2. Practical development of the narrative mode, following from Bruner's assertion that we see in the drama and metaphor of good stories significant ways of understanding human experience, can be found in Carol Witherell and Nel Noddings' *Stories Lives Tell: Narrative and Dialogue in Education* (1991).

3. For a discussion of the subjectivist issue in epistemology see Imre Lakatos and Alan Musgrave's *Criticism and the Growth of Knowledge* (1970). With articles by both Karl Popper and Thomas Kuhn, this book summarizes well the debate

about subjectivity in the sciences. Paul Feyerabend (1988), of course, takes the debate even further with his railing against all prescriptive methods.

4. For more on the constructivist debate in curriculum, particularly science and math curricula, see the *Journal for Research in Mathematics Education*, Monograph No. 4 (1990). See also Paul Ernest, *The Philosophy of Mathematics Education* (1991); and R. Good, J. Wandersee, and J. St. Julien, "Cautionary Notes on the Appeal of the New 'Ism' (Constructivism) in Science Education" (1992).

CHAPTER 6

Dewey, Whitehead, and Process Thought

TRADITIONS OF PERMANENCE, CHANGE, AND INTERPRETATION

Nor is [it] divisible, since [it] all alike is;
Nor is [it] somewhat more here, which would keep it
    from holding together;
Nor is [it] somewhat less, but [it] is all full of what-is.
Therefore [it] is all continuous.
                    —Parmenides, "Fragment 8," verses 22–25

As they step into the same rivers, different and (still)
different waters flow upon them.
                    —Heraclitus, "Fragment 12"

It is not possible to step twice into the same river.
                    —Heraclitus, "Fragment 91"

These quotations on the nature of reality—flux or permanence—represent contrasting metaphysical alternatives to the question of reality's composition. Written in the pre-Socratic era, before Plato provided a synthesis to the permanence–change issue, these are sharply dichotomous views. Plato, drawing on Socrates' cosmology, combined both views, "seeing" reality at one level as existing in the permanence of the abstract Forms and at another level as existing in the flux of contemporary life. However, he assigned a greater value to the Forms—permanent, good, and virtuous in their being—than to the concrete objects of everyday lived experience, which he saw as but "copies" of the Forms (*Republic*, Book VI). Thus, permanence acquired a privileged position in Western thought; Aristotlean, Ptolemic, and Christian philosophies and theologies reinforced this view. Science and theology, in the pre-modern and early modern eras, also reinforced one another, with God considered stable, permanent, and the center of a well-ordered universe. Mind was considered the "eye of the soul," while mathematics with its own sense of permanence "mirrored" the calm reality to be found in God or the Forms. Descartes carried this view of reality-as-permanence even further by attributing to the reflective mind the power of self-being: "Cogito ergo sum." Drawing heavily on Cartesian, Newtonian, and Enlightenment thought, modernism still assumes permanence superior to flux, providing a "home" for reality. Like Johannes Kepler, scientific modernists believe that mathematics is the vehicle by which we discover that reality. To quote Kepler:

> The chief aim of all investigations of the external world should be to discover the rational order and harmony which has been imposed on it by God and which He revealed to us in the language of mathematics.
> —Cited in Kline, *Mathematics: The Loss of Certainty,* 1980, p. 31

Contrary to this essentialist tradition, heavy on rational order and harmony, has been that emanating from Heraclitus, insisting that life is a continual flux. Here life is compared to a stream, always moving— one cannot enter the same stream twice for the stream itself is always changing. This flux tradition has existed as a shadow of the permanence tradition. It has appeared in the Gnostic gospels, in alchemy, in Romanticism, in the *élan vital* movement, in organicism, in progressivism— always emphasizing process, movement, temporality. As a shadow tradition, it has had a certain dark side—the notion of the Fates mysteriously spinning out the yarn of life appears in both Greek drama and the Victorian writings of Charles Dickens (*A Tale of Two Cities,* 1859/1962). This sense of fate, whether exemplified in the spinning of life's web, the reading of cards and tea leaves, or the romantic idealism of unfettered nature (a powerful metaphor for the progressive education movement), has always been plagued by a sense of *teleology*—an exorable movement toward a final, pre-set end. In its own way, the reality-as-flux movement has seen process in more deterministic than dialogic terms. Douglas Browning (1965), among others, places both Dewey and Whitehead in this Heraclitean tradition. However, to do so is to assume there are only two traditions and by elimination to place those in the one which do not fit in the other.

I believe both these thinkers can be interpreted better in a third tradition, that of hermeneutics, which only recently has received serious attention (Bernstein, 1983, 1986; Rorty, 1980, 1989; Soltis, 1990; Wachterhauser, 1986). Hermeneutics, the study of interpretation (particularly biblical and literary interpretation), originated with the Greek god Hermes and the Greek verb *herméneuein* meaning "to interpret." As the messenger-god, Hermes not only had to deliver messages from the gods to humans; he also had to interpret these messages into a form "human intelligence could grasp" (Palmer, 1969, p. 13). Analogously, the resident priest at the Delphic oracle was called a *hermeios*, one who interpreted or translated the oracle's sayings.

This issue of interpretation became paramount for Protestant ministers in the seventeenth century. Without the aid of Rome's Curia and its ecclesiastical councils to pass on canonical interpretation of sacred scripture, with each minister his own interpreter, it became imperative to develop a theory or set of rules for interpretation, to have a hermeneutics. In more modern times, F. D. E. Schleiermacher and Wilhelm Dilthey expanded hermeneutics to the general science of understanding all texts—literary and biblical. Both realized that texts are human expressions, so to comprehend a text it is necessary to comprehend the author and the author's time, place, and mental state. This tradition, often a psychological assessment of "the mental processes of the author" (Pannenberg, 1967/1986, p. 117), is one major branch of contemporary hermeneutics, of which E. D. Hirsch, Jr. (1987), an ardent critic of the American curriculum, is a leading theoretician. For Hirsch, as for Dilthey and Schleiermacher, the object of hermeneutics—the very reason we enter into "the mental processes of the author"—is to objectify the author's meaning. The focus is not on us and our interpretive interactions with the text; it is on validating and objectifying the text through empathy with the author and the author's circumstances—both cultural and psychological.[1]

The other major branch of contemporary hermeneutics is that derived from the writings of Martin Heidegger, Hans-Georg Gadamer, and Paul Ricoeur. Here, the "reader, observer, or interpreter" is placed "as the actual center of the hermeneutical theme" (Pannenberg, 1967/1986, p. 125). Understanding our time, place, and culture is essential if we are to have a conversation or dialogue with the text. All being exists in time; we do, the author does. Meaning is not extracted from the text; it is created by our dialogue with the text. Thus, the difference between the author's historical situation and our own is a necessary and productive difference. This branch of hermeneutics, cultural and existential—based on Heidegger's *Dasein* (literally "there-being" or, more colloquially, being which is there)—goes beyond the issue of texts to deal with the ontological nature of *being* and the epistemological one of *knowing*. As "beings-in-the-world" we can never escape our cultural situations; we are caught in the "hermeneutic circle" of having our culture and language define us just as we define our culture and its language.[2] Epistemologically, we can push against the boundaries of this circle and we can even expand the circle but we can never break outside it. Knowledge is that which we create—interactively, dialogically, conversationally—always within our culture and its language.

Pedagogically, a hermeneutic framework focuses our curricular attention on the interactions—or, to borrow a phrase from John Dewey, on the transactions—between the text and ourselves. This frame transcends (or bypasses) the objectivist–subjectivist split by arguing that meaning is created by personal and public dialogic transactions: with ourselves, confreres, texts, histories. To create *transformative transactions*—where we change as do the transactions—it is imperative we question the assumptions and prejudgments we hold so dear, particularly those supporting our own historical situations. Goals and ends, those beacons that guide so many of our curricular actions, do not just appear; they are personal decisions made by cultural beings at historical moments. We need to understand the beings and the moments in order to create the curriculum. By dialoguing with texts, their creators, and ourselves we come to a deeper, fuller understanding not only of issues but of ourselves, as personal and cultural beings.

Such a hermeneutic frame, while certainly not one expressly used by John Dewey or Alfred North Whitehead, does, I believe, provide a better background for understanding the particulars of their curricular thought than either a Parmenidean or Heraclitean one. As Jonas Soltis (1990) points out, Dewey's concept of aims as continual, ongoing human activities—making intelligent choices within a cultural frame—is indeed hermeneutic. The same may be said of his method for transforming experience. In fact, both Richard Bernstein (1983, 1986) and Richard Rorty (1980, 1989) have begun to negotiate passages between Dewey's pragmatic thought and what might be called "discourse" hermeneutics, generally based on Martin Heidegger's *Being and Time* (1926/1962) but particularly based on Hans-Georg Gadamer's *Truth and Method* (1975), especially Jürgen Habermas' critical review of the book (1977) and the "debate" which followed (Mendelson, 1979; Ricoeur, 1981).

Discourse hermeneutics is usually not associated with Alfred North Whitehead's work; and for good reason—what with the scientific bent of his philosophy (1925/1967b), the complexity of his cosmology and the mathematical mode of his writing (1929/1978). Nonetheless, Whitehead's sense of process, based on a post-Newtonian contingency of space and time, and his emphasis on prehension and on the creativity inherent in process—itself an ongoing continuum of becoming and decaying, one where being is becoming—do connect with the hermeneutic tradition. Against this background his curricular comments are worth revisiting for they represent an early attempt to base curricular thought on relations, not on particularized entities. For Whitehead, entities are not atomistic particles but are congregations or intersections of relations—*concresences* he calls them (1929/1978, p. 21).

Curricularly, the challenge process-hermeneutic thought gives us is to devise a frame for teaching and learning that accepts the contingency and relatedness of being, language, and understanding. Drawing on post-modern thought, particularly in the areas of hermeneutics, self-organization, chaos mathematics, process theology, and dissipative structures, helps us frame a curriculum matrix designed for the "making-of-meaning."

JOHN DEWEY AND THE CONCEPT OF PROCESS

Actual thinking is a process . . . it is in continual change as long as a person thinks.

The real problem of intellectual education is the *transformation* of natural powers into expert, tested powers: the transformation of more or less casual curiosity and sporadic suggestion into attitudes of alert, cautious, and thorough inquiry.
—Dewey, *How We Think*, 1933/1971, pp. 72, 84

These two quotations, first written in 1910 and rewritten in 1933, are one way of expressing Dewey's curricular philosophy. Together, they show a sense of change and movement toward a goal—becoming a mature, intelligent adult. But, concentrating on the first quotation only—itself removed from the second by twelve pages of text—and adding Dewey's further elaboration of the categorical separateness of psychological process from logical product, it is easy to place Dewey within Heraclitus' view. Within this frame, process, the epitome of change, is easily seen not only as separated from but also as superior to product. Progressive educators often made this hierarchical mistake, the remnants of which occur today in the phrase "it is the process which counts."

While Dewey railed against dichotomies, he nevertheless dichotomized many of the categories he used, albeit adding the word "and" to draw together that which he separated—that is, child *and* curriculum, process *and* product, idealism *and* realism. In these pairs, Dewey was often portrayed as favoring the former: the child, process, idealism. Certainly progressive education took this tack. In favoring the child, process, and a romantic idealism, progressive education did not place these within a larger network but saw each as a valuable factor in its own right. Process for progressive education was often a mindless (nonreflective) activity, a hands-on doing that became its own end. And the doing was often seen as more important than what was done—a frame open education put on Piagetian thought. Such a dichotomous, limited, linear, and nonreflective approach, Dewey called "really stupid" (1926/1964, p. 153). Nonetheless, his progressive views were saddled with the belief that physical activity (hands-on manipulation) constituted, if not the whole, then the major part of learning.

Process for Dewey, however, was never meant to be separated from product, any more than ends were to be separated from means. In this latter combination, Dewey was able to develop an ends-in-view intermediary, turning each end into a new means. Oddly, such an intermediary was not developed within the process–product frame. Reflection, of course, was to play this role. In *How We Think*, Dewey (1933/1971) states that in the course of reflection:

> Partial conclusions emerge. . . . [These products] are temporary stopping places, landings of past thought that are also stations of departure for subsequent thought. (p. 75)

But such an interactive frame between process and product was somehow neither seen nor developed. Thus, as Dewey himself says, "The internal and necessary connection between the actual process of thinking and its intellectual product is overlooked" (p. 79). The problem of *transformation*, which Dewey marks as "the real problem of intellectual education" (p. 84), was not dealt with by either his theoretically or practically oriented advocates. While many Deweyan ideas have found their way into curriculum literature and practice—albeit too often in forms Dewey would not recognize—the concept of transformation via reflection is missing, either as an interpreted or misinterpreted part of that literature.[3]

"Reflective thinking"—the vehicle by which transformation occurs—is the rubric under which Dewey (1933/1971) places his famous five steps of thinking or problem solving: (1) the *feeling* of a problem, (2) *definition* of the problem, (3) *hypothesis* for solution of the problem, (4) *logical reasoning* about the problem and methods of solution, (5) *testing* the hypothesis developed by action (p. 102ff.; emphasis added). While he labels these the "five phases of reflective thought," they have come down to us as either the five steps in scientific thinking or the pragmatic method of problem solving. Reflection as the intermediary that binds the primacy of hands-on experience with the secondary experience of "continued and regulated reflective inquiry" (1925/1958, p. 4), or as the broad rubric under which process and product are entwined, is often not seen by interpreters of Dewey. Without an understanding of the role reflection plays, however, the concept of how "casual curiosity" is transformed into "thorough inquiry" is missed. Further, Dewey's notion of transforming "ises" into "oughts"—heretical in modernist terms—seems fallacious. In fact, the whole notion of transformation is mystical, part of the romantic aura that pervaded both the progressive and open education movements. Finally, without a feeling for reflection and its transformative power, Dewey's metaphor of mind as "primarily a verb" takes on no richness of meaning.

In his reflections on the history of Western thought (*The Quest for Certainty*, 1929/1960; *Reconstruction in Philosophy*, 1948/1957), Dewey states that mainstream philosophy has "bequeathed to generations of thinkers as an unquestioned axiom [self-evident to both Euclid and Descartes] the idea that knowledge is intrinsically a mere beholding or viewing of reality" (1948/1957, p. 112). This is Dewey's famous "spectator theory of knowledge," based as he says on what was "supposed to take place in the act of vision." Namely,

> The object refracts light to the eye and is seen; it makes a difference to the eye and to the person having an optical apparatus, but none to the thing seen. (1929/1960, p. 23)

Analogously, knowledge remains aloof from and untouched by our thinking, unaffected by our "spectating." Epistemologically, this view leads to the concept of mind-as-a-mirror whereby we are able, under Descartes' right circumstances, to view an "out there" reality but not to interact with it. Pedagogically, a "spectator theory of knowledge" leads to a concept of curriculum that sets out the *a priori* in clear and concise terms, and to a concept of instruction whereby the teacher (as knower) shows and transmits the *a priori* to the student. The teacher's success (as well as the student's) depends on the size of the deficit between the ideal reality "out there" and the existential reality the student possesses. It is feasible to call this curriculum a "measured deficit curriculum," with grades designed to measure the size of the deficit: The higher the grade the lower the deficit. Here the student is a spectator to *a priori* knowledge, a receiver of what teacher and texts transmit, active only in the narrow sense of keeping "on task." The "spectator theory of knowledge" helps us understand that Frederick Taylor's time-and-motion studies, foundational for much of curriculum design, including Ralph Tyler's rationale, have metaphysical origins deeper than mere scientific-efficiency. They are the expression of an epistemology dominating Western thought for thousands of years, going back to Plato's cosmological beliefs.

Stephen Toulmin, in the chapter "Death of the Spectator" in his book *The Return to Cosmology* (1982), gives a history of the spectator concept and its relation to theoretical knowledge in both pre-modern and modern times, as well as its "death" in post-modern times. In ancient Greece, the word *theoros*, the root of our theory or theorist, referred to one who went to the Olympic games as a spectator, not as a participant. Originally *theoros* was an official representative of a city-state, but eventually the word referred to any spectator. Aristotle used the word to represent the philosopher's contemplation removed from practical, daily-life affairs (*praxis*). A theorist, then, for the Greeks—and for the Romans who used the Latin *contemplatio* for the same role—was one *who did not participate*, one who had "the detached intellectual posture . . . associated with the philosopher's study, observation, and reflection about the world" (Toulmin, 1982, p. 239).

The concept of philosophy as the prime way to develop theory, and the concept of mind as that special device used to "see" into nature's reality (or as that which "mirrors" this reality), received strong reinforcement and considerable development from Descartes' bifurcation of reality into *res cogitans* and *res extensia*. Philosophy and theory both became categorically separated from life's temporal, ongoing, practical activities—with the latter controlled by and inferior to the former. The ideal of a rational, objective knowledge of which we could be certain underlay this *theoros* concept.

The "death" of the concept came with the advent of relativity theory and quantum thought. Using these frames, it now becomes obvious we are all participators in reality, none of us is a spectator; and, as Rorty (1980) has pointed out, no one discipline can act as a foundation for all learning. Nor is there one special methodology—scientific or otherwise—in which learning can be packaged. Curriculum in a post-modern frame is not a package; it is a process—dialogic and transformative, based on the inter- or transactions peculiar to local situations.

Dewey's concept of experience, with its emphasis on reflection, interaction, and transaction, was his effort at founding a new, practice-oriented epistemology—an experiential epistemology.[4] Key to this epistemology, what makes it transformative, is the concept of reflection. Reflection is for Dewey the vehicle for bridging the gap past philosophies established between theoretical and practical thought: the former

practiced only by those formally trained in the special methods of philosophy; the latter done by ordinary people in the daily living of human
experience. Reflection is taking experience and looking at it critically,
variously, publicly: that is, connecting our experiences with others' experiences, building a network of experiences wherein past, present, and
future are interrelated. Reflection steps back and examines past experiences in the light of other connections and alternatives. It is a reconstruction of actions taken; it is a re-look at meanings made. "Thinking,"
says Dewey (1948/1957) "is a method of reconstructing experience" (p.
141); it is a method of reflecting on experience; it is a uniquely human
activity and is our only reliable guide to further action. It is crucial such
reflection be recursive: that once accomplished it acts as a guide to further practice, itself the occasion for further reflection. In this ongoing
process, the past and present provide a basis for the future without
limiting or tightly controlling the future. Here the future is unique, not
a repetition of the past, but continuity exists. It is this sense of continuity which Dewey (1938/1963) prized highly, calling it one of the two
criteria of the quality of experience. As he says:

> The principle of continuity of experience means that every experience
> both takes up something from those which have gone before and
> modifies in some way the quality of those which come after. (p. 35)

Through recursion such a "hermeneutic" modification takes place.

Recursive reflection whereby individuals are transformed by the
process itself is a quality I believe schools can provide. Here curriculum's role is not to pre-set experiences but to transform the experiences
had. Toward this end, Dewey organized his own school around hands-
on or activity experiences, which he had the students carry out *but only
to a point.* He did not wish students to become technically expert in their
manual skills, only to develop those skills as a base for broader, more
reflective, and transformative experiences. Transformative experience,
he believed, could be done by common people sharing their insights
and thoughts in a critical yet cooperative manner. As he says, "Common
experience is capable of developing from within itself methods which
will secure direction for itself and will create inherent standards of judgment and value" (1925/1958, p. 38). Here Dewey presages a thought
Prigogine makes a half-century later: that under certain conditions communal activity operates in a self-organizing manner providing both direction and standards.

In such a reflective and transformative frame, a student's present
experiences are seen in terms both of themselves and of future possibil-

ities. These possibilities will emerge only if the process of reflection is *critical, public,* and *communal.* These three attributes cannot be overemphasized; they act not only as attributes defining (reflective) process, but also as ideal characteristics for classroom curricula. Dewey believed classrooms could be communal, places where "had" experiences could be openly analyzed and transformed; not a competitive environment where right is pitted against wrong, but one where, through mutual cooperation, students and teachers explore alternatives, consequences, assumptions. This communal and public exploration is done in a critical and rigorous yet sympathetic manner. Ideas are put forward for the purpose of exploration, to be part of the recursive process. The curricular challenge is to put this process into *practical operation.* Undoubtedly such will require a new concept of what it means to be a student as well as to be a teacher.

ALFRED NORTH WHITEHEAD AND THE CONCEPT OF PROCESS

> Do not teach too many subjects. . . . What you do teach, teach thoroughly. . . . Let the main ideas which are introduced to a child's education be few and important, and let them be thrown into every combination possible.
>
> —Whitehead, *The Aims of Education,* 1929/1967a, p. 2

> That *how* an actual entity *becomes* constitutes *what* that actual entity *is;* so that the two descriptions of an actual entity are not independent. Its "being " is constituted by its "becoming." This is the "principle of process."
>
> —Whitehead, *Process and Reality: An Essay in Cosmology,*
> 1929/1978, p. 23

When curricularists read Whitehead, it is usually the first set of quotations to which they pay attention. Few venture beyond his *Aims of Education,* and even fewer venture into *Process and Reality.* Yet without such venturing the power inherent in his curricular comments is lost— the first set of quotations remains intriguing but trivial.

Whitehead was anything but trivial. He was a fine mathematician—writing both *A Treatise on Universal Algebra* (1898) and, with Bertrand Russell, his student, *Principia Mathematica* (1910–1913); a provocative philosopher—providing the base for both process philosophy and process theology; and the originator of a cosmology that transcends the modernist one based on Newtonian physics and metaphysics. As a young student at Trinity College, Cambridge, Whitehead did much of his work in applied mathematics, particularly on the mathematics needed for understanding Clerk Maxwell's seminal work on electromagnetism, the subject of Whitehead's undergraduate thesis. Thus began his interest in the philosophy of physics, natural for anyone with a bent toward mathematics and philosophy studying at Isaac Newton's alma mater. It was as a philosopher of physics that Whitehead came to Harvard University in 1924, and his first American book, the foundation for his later philosophic thought, was *Science and the Modern World* (1925/1967b).

Looking back on his years at both Cambridge and Harvard, Whitehead, in conversation, stated that the most original piece of work to which he could lay claim was his 1906 piece for the Royal Society of London, "On Mathematical Concepts of the Material World" (Lowe, 1985, p. 296). What is interesting about this piece, really a memoir, is that here he begins to look at the material world, the "stuff in space," to use his phrase, in terms of relations. As Lowe says: In this piece Whitehead takes "relation as a foundational idea"; indeed, he "views the material world as a set of relations" (p. 297). Here is the break with Newton's view of the world's ultimate reality made up of "hard, massy, impenetrable objects"; and here, too, is the beginning of his own process or relational view that reality is ultimately an ongoing process: of becoming, of perishing.

The development of Whitehead's process thought came after he left Cambridge, beginning in his middle-aged years at the University of London and continuing into his final years at Harvard (the "other" Cambridge). Whitehead left the English Cambridge in 1910, partly because he felt himself to be "in a groove"—really a rut—partly because he was displeased with some personal actions by Trinity College's governing Council, and partly because he felt he needed the more dynamic stimulation a large city provided for the ideas forming in his mind. In his last years at Cambridge—years in which Ernest Mach, Max Planck, and Albert Einstein were exploring the universe and the nature of reality in new ways—Whitehead became aware that it was impossible to measure motion in any but a relational way (*The Axioms of Projective Geometry*, 1906/1971, Ch. 1). The universe was not the static or stably ordered one Newton posited; it was a changing universe, and the only way harmony could be assessed (as Einstein saw so clearly) was through a relational frame—by comparing one object with another through their relative motions. But such a relational frame, with its attendant metaphysics and cosmology, had not been proposed. Whitehead was anxious to do just that.

In his first public lecture as a Harvard professor—to which he came to avoid the University of London's badgering him about retirement (he was 63 when he accepted Harvard's offer)—Whitehead put forth a "new philosophy of nature." The eight Lowell Lectures were quickly turned into his seminal book, *Science and the Modern World* (1925/1967b).

Whitehead had two purposes in presenting this work; that is, two beside the overtly stated one of studying the effect (modernist) science had on Western culture in the seventeenth through nineteenth centuries. (The original title of his Lowell Lectures was "Three Centuries of Natural Philosophy.") One of these purposes was to present his *new philosophy of science*, while the other was to introduce the new metaphysics or cosmology he believed the new philosophy required. In Chapter One he states that throughout the centuries in question there has been a "fixed scientific cosmology which presupposes the ultimate fact of an irreducible brute matter, or material, spread throughout space" (1925/1967b, p. 17). This matter, of course, refers to Newton's atoms, which formed the basis for his physics and metaphysics (see Burtt, 1932/1955, Ch. VII). The assumption that such irreducible matter exists as the primordial basis for all other existence Whitehead labels "scientific materialism," an assumption he sets out to challenge.

As a mathematician, interested in relations and committed to logical abstractions (presaging Piaget, Whitehead reserves special praise for the individual who first noticed a numerical connection between *seven* fishes and *seven* days—1925/1967b, p. 20), Whitehead believed Nature's ultimate composition to be not solid particles but "a structure of evolving processes" (p. 72). Here is Whitehead's famous "philosophy of organism," allied obviously with biology but also coming from quantum physics and his own reflections on mathematics. Quantum physics was teaching that "an electron does not continuously traverse its path in space" but "appears at a series of discrete positions in space which it occupies for successive durations of time" (p. 34). In short, Newton's linked continuum among the atoms, his ether, mechanistic frame, and stable order are at the very least questionable. There is no inherent, logical reason to stay with these hypotheses.

As a mathematician, Whitehead was enamored of abstraction; it not only had beauty and order but gave a sense of power not otherwise found. This last point is crucial, one on which Whitehead says "everyone misconstrues me" (in Lowe, 1990, p. 346). Whitehead believed mathematical abstraction—the greatest power "the human mind can

attain" (1925/1967b, p. 34)—to be historically (and mistakenly) associated with Universals apart from sense experience. The "sheer error"
(1929/1978, p. 79) of this Platonic view saw abstraction, particularly
mathematical abstraction, as giving insight into an *a priori*, set order—
an order to which we act only as spectators. Whitehead saw "things"
differently (note the modernist metaphor). For him, mathematical abstractions give the power to create, to bring into actual existence an in-
finitude of possibilities. Abstractions provide the frame and describe the
process for guiding entities as they come into being. Abstractions—extending beyond mere sense perceptions—are key factors in the becoming process, in the "concresence of prehensions," to use Whitehead's
language. Through abstraction experiences come into being, become
entities; without abstractions the multiple possibilities inherent in any
situation are limited. Reality is itself always in process—becoming and
perishing—it takes on its particular or local colorations, its status as
events, as we go through the process of experiencing, including that of
abstracting. This doctrine of creative abstraction (or "extended abstraction" as he sometimes calls it), the "ultimate principle" (p. 21) he elab-
orates in *Process and Reality*, is a difficult one to grasp: partly because of
its strangeness to our modernist constructs, partly due to the invented
language (*concresence, prehension, nexus*) Whitehead uses to express it.[5]
However, the general thrust is simple: Experience is not a vehicle to
help us understand a reality bifurcated from ourselves (as both Plato
and Descartes thought); experience is the reality of our being. More, it
is the reality of Reality itself; that which is "really real," to use his col-
orful phrase (1929/1978, p. 18).[6] The curricular implications of this view
are enormous.

Once we "see" a unity between ourselves and what we call reality,
once we see being in terms of becoming (and perishing), then curriculum does not represent an "aboriginal reality out there" (to use Bruner's
phrase), it represents our own acts of experiencing. For this reason it is
not only good we, as teacher and students, throw "ideas into every
combination possible"; it is *essential* we do so. For in this "throwness,"
meaning, experience, reality are created.

Three points stand out in Whitehead's comments on education.
One is his objection to the hollowness which accompanies a purely technical professionalism, what Schön labels "technical rationality." Another
is his sense of educational development moving in a rhythm or balance;
partly by skills being conjoined with interests and partly by the intellectual being blended with the aesthetic, leading to a fullness and richness
of experience. The third point is the transformative power Whitehead
posits as inherent in *the proper interplay* of his three stages of learning:

romance, precision, and generalization. This last point—the transformative power inherent in Whitehead's concept of curriculum—is often overlooked but holds, I believe, the greatest developmental potential of any of his curriculum ideas. All three of these points have overtones and connections with Dewey and Piaget. But they are also uniquely Whitehead's, blending as they do the precision of a specialized, well-mastered skill with the broader appreciation inherent in the aesthetic and intuitive modes. This blending, Whitehead says, "produces a full interplay of emergent values," an "interplay of diverse values" (1925/1967b, p. 198).

As a student, tutor, and finally examiner at Cambridge University, Whitehead dealt with the (in)famous *Tripos,* those three-part examinations all Cantabrigians had to pass in order to graduate, the scores of which determined a graduate's professional future—namely, whether one would be a university don or a village schoolmaster. In mathematics, the heart of the *Tripos* was speed and accuracy: the ability to solve quickly and without reflective thought extremely artificial problems. Whitehead said these examinations set back the development of mathematics in England by at least one hundred years. A carryover from these examinations can be found in our own elementary algebra books, in problems involving a rower moving upstream meeting another rower who, having entered the river at a different point and time, is traveling downstream. For reasons not easily explained, the algebra texts seem interested in knowing how long these rowers have been on the river and at what point they are about to meet, provided both row at steady rates of speed. This hardly is of interest to anyone but the algebra student (and of only tangential interest there) since neither rower A nor rower B know one another.[7]

From his earliest days as a Cambridge don, Whitehead objected to this "examination knowledge" being labeled mathematics or being considered the mark of education. He said it produced no more than "inert ideas" and led to the demise of "curiosity, of judgment, of the power of mastering a complicated tangle of circumstances" (1929/1967a, p. 5). Such learning led to mathematics being considered as no more than a "mechanical discipline."

Technical proficiency alone, Whitehead believed, would lead only to mediocrity and dullness. He commented that one could "understand all about the sun and all about the atmosphere and all about the rotation of the earth" and "still miss the radiance of the sunset" (1925/1967b, p. 199). What was wanted, therefore, was "an appreciation of the infinite variety of vivid values achieved by an organism in its proper environment." It is this sense of vivid values—of intellectual variety that moves beyond the technically rational to introduce the artistic, the narrative, the intuitive, and the metaphoric—that so attracts Oliver and Gershman to Whitehead's cosmology as a basis for curricular thought. Developing these vivid and diverse values into an integrative and relational frame is what makes Whitehead's curricular thought so post-modern.

Whitehead, in pace with both Dewey and Piaget, believed that "the pupil's mind is a growing organism" and that "the only avenue towards wisdom is by freedom in the presence of knowledge" (1929/1967a, p. 30). The latter part of this quote represents a key element in Whitehead's thought; namely, that growth and wisdom occur when there is a balance between the creative opportunity freedom can give and the knowledge we acquire from discipline. Thus, freedom should live its existence in "the presence of knowledge." To balance and integrate these, Whitehead developed his "rhythm of education"—romance (play), precision (mastery), and generalization (abstraction). While believing that these three should be integrated continually instead of ordered sequentially, Whitehead also believed that life's natural, developmental rhythms favored a predominance of romance or play of ideas in the elementary and lower high school grades, with the development of precision or mastery starting in the high school years, and abstraction or generalization being the focus in the university years. To break away from this general plan, particularly to push precision and mastery before the student is psychologically ready for them, is to go against life's natural rhythm; it is to render the educational experience barren and boring. Here is denial of self-development and the opportunity for each individual to make "ideas one's own."

Ideas do not emerge full-blown nor are they logically integrated into a well-defined system; they are "created piecemeal ad hoc" from "unexplored connexions," from "possibilities half-disclosed" and "half-concealed" (1929/1967a, p. 17ff.). In this "ferment" lie the possibilities to be actualized, to be created. The process of education like the process of life must work to order this ferment, not to impose a pre-set and nonmeaningful pattern on it. To do the latter is to render the process barren. As he says:

> Education must essentially be a setting in order of a ferment already stirring in the mind. . . . In our conception of education we tend to confine it to the second stage of the cycle; namely, to the stage of precision. But *we cannot so limit our task without misconceiving the whole problem.* We are concerned alike with the ferment, with the acquirement of precision, and with the subsequent fruition. (1929/1967a, p. 18; *emphasis added*)

I believe the Tyler rationale, Frederick Taylor's scientific-efficiency movement on which the rationale is based, and the behavioral curriculum movement both have spawned, have all "misconceived the problem." And from this misconception of what education is about and how development occurs, we have adopted an inappropriate concept of curriculum—one firmly rooted in modernism. The Tyler, Taylor, and behavioral movements have not dealt with the ferment, but rather have denied, bypassed, or overlooked it. However, in this *ferment*, or in Schön's *messes*, Prigogine's *chaos*, Dewey's *problems*, Piaget's *disequilibrium*, or Kuhn's *anomalies* lie the seeds not only of development and transformation but of life itself. To deal with curriculum as a transformative process means to utilize the ferment to develop both precision (discipline) and generalization (abstraction). How we will handle this issue of creative development is by no means clear; it is a *problematic* we will need to live with for generations. Only through the intimate contact of *living with* this idea, though, will we be able to frame the issues. As we worked for centuries developing the modernist paradigm, so will we need (at least) generations to develop a post-modern paradigm. However, I agree with Whitehead that the beginning lies in recognizing "the radically untidy, ill-adjusted character" of actual experience. "To grasp this fundamental truth"—the nerve center of Whitehead's epistemology, the keystone of his cosmology, and the central tenet of his sense of process—"is the first step in wisdom" (1933, pp. 157–158). From this it follows, I believe, that an essential criterion in the examination of a post-modern curriculum is the *richness of its quality*, not the precision with which its goals are stated or met.

PROCESS THOUGHT BEYOND DEWEY AND WHITEHEAD

In both ordinary and philosophical usage, Dasein, man's Being, is defined . . . as that living thing whose Being is essentially determined by the potentiality for discourse.
—Heidegger, *Being and Time*, 1926/1962, p. 47

To argue, as I am doing, that within a frame of post-modern thought it is possible, even desirable, to connect Dewey and Whitehead with hermeneutics, it is necessary first to connect Dewey and Whitehead (via process) and then to connect process to contemporary hermeneutics (via the "making of connections"). I have presented Dewey's view, on transforming experience, and Whitehead's view, on reality as an ongoing connection of relations, as complementary aspects of process. While I consider this Dewey–Whitehead connection essential in developing a new, experience-based epistemology and curriculum methodology—one that moves beyond the stasis of "spectatorship"—I do not want to minimize the differences between Dewey and Whitehead or the difficulty inherent in equating Whitehead with post-modern thought.

Process—particularly self-organizing process—is, I believe, the essential ingredient in a post-modern, transformative pedagogy. Dewey's notion of immature, ill-formed experiences transformed into mature, well-formed experiences and Whitehead's notion of ideas thrown into every combination possible are key elements in making this pedagogy operable; in moving the pedagogy from the level of platitudinous generalizations to practical, teaching activities. However, only a few educational theorists—individuals such as Brian Hendley, Bob Gowin, Donald Oliver—have thought seriously of connecting Dewey and Whitehead in a process frame. Generally, Dewey advocates and Whitehead advocates have remained apart, the former calling themselves pragmatists, the latter calling themselves process thinkers or process theologians.[8]

Dewey's reflective comments on Whitehead's philosophy, written over a half-century ago, help us understand why this bifurcation has occurred. Dewey says that any serious reader of Whitehead has a sense of uncertainty as to "just what course is followed by Mr. Whitehead" (1941, p. 659). On the one hand, in a book like *Science and the Modern World*, Whitehead's union of the physical with the human, using events as the ultimate unit of all reality, creates new ways to conceive of experience and its transformations. Here, Dewey says, Whitehead has "opened an immensely fruitful new path for subsequent philosophy to follow" (p. 659). On the other hand, Whitehead's more "formal statements," particularly those found in *Process and Reality*, "often lean . . . [to an] ontological idealism," even to a "spiritualism . . . [which] the history of thought demonstrates to be the fatal weakness of the whole [philosophical] movement initiated by Plato and Aristotle" (p. 661). Further, Whitehead himself states at the beginning of *Process and Reality* that his intent is to produce a "general scheme" for the interpretation of all our "enjoyed, perceived, willed, or thought" experiences. This "general scheme" is

> To frame a coherent, logical, necessary system of general ideas in terms of which every element of our experience can be interpreted. (1929/1978, p. 3)

Such a grand cosmological frame makes Whitehead a candidate for modernism, not post-modernism, especially if we accept Francois Lyotard's (1984) definition of the post-modern as possessing "incredulity toward metanarratives," and modernism as that which "legitimates itself with . . . explicit appeal to some grand narrative" (pp. xxiii, xxiv).

However, Whitehead's grand scheme is not metanarrational or transcendental in the usual (historical) sense; it aims not at stasis but at a continual, dynamic emergence of the newly created. It is this creative, emergent quality of Whitehead's system which attracts Prigogine, leading him (with Stengers—1984) to say that in *Process and Reality* Whitehead goes "beyond the identification of Being with timelessness" to a conception of Being as continual Becoming, hence bonding the two together (p. 310). Here lies the connection between process and hermeneutic thought: Both believe that being is best defined in its connection with becoming. Heidegger, of course, is the theoretician who has done the most with the concept of Being, particularly with our "being-in-the-world."

Heidegger does not use the term *becoming*, but his sense of Being has within it not only the temporality of the present but also a consciousness of the historical past (which has helped shape the present) and the possibility inherent in a yet-to-be-determined future. Our being-in-the-world, our condition as historical humans, which he labels Dasein, has with it a potentiality permeated with possibility.

> Dasein *is* its possibility, and it "has" this possibility . . . [it is] in each case essentially its own possibility, it *can*, in its very Being, "choose" itself and win itself; [or] lose itself. (1926/1962, p. 68)

Being for Heidegger is not a static essence, as it was for Plato, the medieval Christians, Kant, and even for the psychometricians who—following Binet—rigidified the concept of IQ. Being for Heidegger is active immersion in the world; it is *existence* within a culture bounded by history and language, which shapes us as much as we shape it. Here lies a very real sense of process, an existential sense, where we are influenced, but not determined, by the past and whereby the future emerges from our active participation in the present. In such a frame, understanding and meaning, so important for curriculum, become new conceptions.

In the modernist paradigm, understanding and meaning are based on an assumed invariance and on our possessing the ability to "see" that which is, that which is invariant. Here the teacher takes her (or his) task as that of presenting what *is* clearly, and of admonishing the students to "look sharp"(ly). In fact, understanding is ascertained by asking whether the student "sees" what is being explained.

Meaning and understanding in a hermeneutic frame emerge from the process of making connections, from interpreting our being-in-the-world. Meaning, as Gadamer (1975) points out, is based on discourse, on having a discourse with others. This is why, as Rorty states, it is so important to "keep the conversation going." But our teacher-preparation programs do scant little to help teachers deal with conversation—to ask the sort of questions that elicit responses that can serve the recursive function of "keeping the conversation going." In conversation and discourse, questions are asked, issues posed, that go beyond the factual into the interpretive. Here, to use a common and I think apt post-structural phrase, "passages are negotiated"—between text and reader, between teacher and pupil, between experience and consciousness. Negotiating these passages—instead of laying out the truth of a proposition, term, or viewpoint—seems to me what curriculum is or should be. In "negotiating passages" each party *listens actively*—sympathetically and critically—to what *the other* is saying. The intent is not to prove (even to oneself) the correctness of a position but to find ways to connect varying viewpoints, to expand one's horizon through active engagement with another. This engagement is a process activity, which transforms both parties, be they text and reader or student and teacher. My own curriculum utopia would be to see this interactive, interpretative, iterative process proliferate endlessly. It would frame this process in an art born as "the echo of God's laughter," in an art that would create the "fascinating imaginative realm where no one owns the truth and everyone has the right to be understood" (Kundera, 1986/1988, pp. 158–159).[9]

In Chapter seven, the final one of the book, I will begin my own curriculum conversations within that "fascinating imaginative realm," which I identify with post-modernism.

NOTES

1. It may come as a surprise to some curricularists that Hirsch is a leading hermeneutic scholar, writing as he has the first full-dress treatise on this subject in the English language (1967). But knowing the conservative tone of his curriculum criticism, it should be no surprise to know he is an ardent advocate of the "objectivist" branch of hermeneutics.

2. In *Being and Time*, Heidegger (1926/1962) talks of what has come to be called the hermeneutic circle, in the following manner:

Any interpretation which is to contribute understanding, must already have understood what is to be interpreted. . . . But if interpretation must . . . already operate in that which is understood . . . how is it to bring any scientific results to maturity without moving in a circle? . . . It would admittedly be more ideal if the circle could be avoided and if there remained the hope of creating some time a historiology which would be as independent of the standpoint of the observer as our knowledge of Nature is supposed to be.

But if we see this circle as a vicious one and look out for ways of avoiding it . . . then the act of understanding has been misunderstood from the ground up. . . . What is decisive is not to get out of the circle but to come into it in the right way. . . . In the circle is hidden a positive possibility of the most primordial kind of knowing. (pp. 194–195)

3. Reflection, as a (Deweyan) concept has been brought to our attention by Donald Schön (1983, 1987, 1991). Indeed, it has become a buzzword in curriculum circles. However, his focus has been more on showing us the complexities of practice than on using reflection as a vehicle for transforming experience; more on describing practice than on developing it epistemologically. Schön quite rightly shows us that practice, especially as handled by those competent in their field, does not come from a *theoros* frame. Rather, it has elements of Michael Polanyi's (1966) *tacit dimension,* an artisan's *feel,* and a problem-solver's *intuition.* Schön calls this set of performative elements "reflections-in-action." However, Dewey wants more than a description of performance, no matter whether he would agree with Schön's description. Dewey wants to develop an epistemology in which performance, practice, and experience are transformed. And in his enthusiasm for science—part of the early twentieth century's ethos—he chose scientific method as a vehicle for this transformation. However, too easily did this method fit into progressivism's positivistic and behavioristic attitudes, thus becoming rigid, formula ridden, and rationalist. Dewey saw this, I believe, as time went on; but other than emphasizing the artistic and transactive aspects of experience, he was not able to develop his desired epistemology of experience.

The development of such an epistemology might yet be done by linking the American pragmatic tradition—Pierce, James, Dewey—as well as Whiteheadian process thought with the hermeneutics of Heidegger, Gadamer, and Ricoeur. Such would not deny Schön's performative reflections but it would go well beyond them. For more on Schön's "reflection-in-action," see Hugh Munby's "Reflection-in-Action and Reflection-on-Action" (1989), as well as Thomas Russell and Hugh Munby's "Reframing: The Role of Experience in Developing Teachers' Professional Knowledge" (1991).

4. With his interest in and commitment to "the scientific factor" (*Reconstruction in Philosophy,* Ch. III), Dewey probably would label this epistemology an "empirical epistemology." With my own interest in the hermeneutic, brought to general attention after Dewey's death, I'd stick with experiential—realizing full

well there is always the danger the experiential can become solipsistically existential, a danger Dewey warned us against.

Such a hermeneutic interpretation of Dewey is not, I believe, discordant with his own ideas. When he argues for his version of scientific knowledge (empirical *and* experimental) as "inspiring imagination," he also says that the "new ideas and methods should be made at home in social and moral life" (1948/1957, pp. 74–75). In fact, he argues here that twentieth-century philosophy's main "intellectual task" is to "take this last step." I would argue that this step of placing knowledge in a social and moral frame is a "hermeneutic" step. I think Dewey would agree.

5. In describing Whitehead's philosophy my interest is in getting a "feel" for his sense of process, particularly its relational underpinnings, and how together they translate into a theory of curriculum. I shall not delve into the intricacies of his cosmology. For those interested in this, I recommend Victor Lowe's two-volume biography, *Alfred North Whitehead: The Man and his Work* (1985, 1990), as well as his *Understanding Whitehead* (1962). I also recommend F. Bradford Wallack, *The Epochal Nature of Process in Whitehead's Metaphysics* (1980); George Lucas, *The Genesis of Modern Process Thought* (1983); and Lewis Ford, *The Emergence of Whitehead's Metaphysics, 1925–1929* (1984). Those interested in pursuing the nuances of Whitehead's theological thought will be rewarded by reading Charles Hartshorne, *Whitehead's View of Reality*, 1981; John Cobb, *A Christian Natural Theology* (1965); and David Griffin and John Cobb, *Process Theology: An Introductory Exposition* (1976). Among the works written on Whitehead's educational thought the following stand out: Robert Brumbaugh, *Whitehead, Process Philosophy, and Education,* (1982); Brian Hendley, *Philosophers as Educators: Dewey, Russell, Whitehead* (1986); and Donald Oliver and Kathleen Gershman, *Education, Modernity, and Fractured Meaning* (1989).

6. Obviously, there are strong pan-psychic attributes in this concept. Again, see Hartshorne (1964; 1981), Cobb (1965; 1982), and Griffin and Cobb (1976) for more on this.

7. Stephen Leacock, in his wonderful spoof on these algebra problems, argues that A and B (and C, too) do indeed know one another. A, he says, is "a full-blooded, blustering fellow, of energetic temperament, hotheaded and strong-willed." B, on the other hand, is "quite easygoing, afraid of A and bullied by him, but very gentle and brotherly to little C, the weakling." The three are always in motion—walking, horseback riding, bicycling, running, swimming, rowing, or racing locomotives. In their free time "they pump water into cisterns, two of which leak through holes in the bottom." A, of course, has the good one, as he has the best bicycle and locomotive, as he has the "right of swimming with the current." Hence, "A always wins." See Leacock's "Human Interest Put into Mathematics" (1929).

8. It is interesting to note that the Association for Process Philosophy of Education (APPE), a bastion of Whiteheadian thinking and long committed to dealing with Whitehead as *the only* process philosopher, is now seeking union with

"the work of other philosophers that represents a process perspective" ("Call for Papers," 1991).

9. The actual phrasing I use here is from the "Frontispiece" of Richard Rorty's *Contingency, irony, and solidarity* (1989). Rorty appears to have done his own translation of Kundera and in part to have elaborated on Kundera's text. While Kundera talks of the novel as this "fascinating, imaginative realm," Rorty uses these words to describe his vision of a liberal utopia, and I use them to describe my vision of post-modernism.

Part III

AN EDUCATIONAL VISION

My own educational vision centers around the Rorty–Kundera statement in Chapter Six: There does exist a "fascinating, imaginative realm
where no one owns the truth and everyone has the right to be understood." This is a frame for my (liberal ironist) vision of both a classroom and a society. Further, I believe that in our explorations of and
for knowledge, we are dealing not with a reality already set "out
there" for us to discover but with multiple ways of interpreting the
echo of God's laughter. This metaphoric phrase gives (to me) something more than a reality created entirely by ourselves or by chance. It
allows for the order we find not only at the commonsense level of ordinary experience but also at the deeper and more subtle level evident in
both quantum science and chaos mathematics; yet it sees that order as
complex, quirky, and both in- and codeterminate. Thus, we should
approach this order much as would Rorty's "liberal ironist": by making
a commitment to it, yet aware of the contingency of that commitment.
Morris Kline, the mathematics historian, has a story-metaphor which
illustrates this point. He likens those who work in science and mathematics to the farmer who, while clearing a piece of ground, "notices
wild beasts lurking in a wooded area surrounding the clearing":

> As the cleared area gets larger the beasts are compelled to move far-
> ther back and the farmer becomes more and more secure at least as
> long as he works in the interior of his cleared area. [But] the beasts are
> always there and one day they may surprise and destroy him. (1980,
> p. 318)

Within such a contingency frame, curriculum is a process—not of
transmitting what is (absolutely) known but of exploring what is unknown; and through exploration students and teachers "clear the
land" together, thereby transforming both the land and themselves.
This transformation is contingent on our willingness to work "where

the wild beasts lurk," and in our work not to look beyond ourselves for a *deus ex machina*, a "natural law," or a guiding eschatological teleology, but rather to look to ourselves, our community, and our ecology. When we approach these as liberal ironists, we are able to develop a sense of our own power and ability—a power and ability which can ultimately transform "ises" to "oughts," the immature into the mature, and the tentatively felt into the fully experienced. To cite Rorty (1985):

> One's sense of relation to a power beyond the community becomes less important as one becomes able to think of oneself as part of a body of public opinion, capable of making a difference to the public fate. (p. 169).

There is risk involved in this process view—as there is in all transformation—for it means we are willing to base our future on a present grounded on nothing but itself, its historical past, and our querulous faith in ourselves. This risk is intensified by the horrendous social, political, and human failures for which our century may come to be known: war, genocide, famine, poverty, enslavement, ecological devastation—all done under the aegis of rational thought and procedures, and in many cases with "good" intentions. However, it appears to me that these failures have all been based on *unquestioning faith* in a metaphysical reality that has separated us from a commitment to ourselves as humans, occupying a planet we did not create and do not yet understand. Where we have been successful we have been able to temper our faith with doubt; indeed, to base our faith on doubt, to develop the correct amount of tension between commitment and contingency. Developing the right amount of "essential tension" is the art I believe all curricularists, teachers, and learners need to develop—not to mention that special class: world and community leaders. This is an art born not of faith in the rightness of our ideologies but of our ability to be playful with serious commitments. Such a paradoxical blending becomes key, if we are to make our future age better, not poorer, than the one in which we now live.

In this frame, where curriculum becomes process, learning and understanding come through dialogue and reflection. Learning and understanding are made (not transmitted) as we dialogue with others and reflect on what we and they have said—as we "negotiate passages" between ourselves and others, between ourselves and our texts. Curriculum's role, as process, is to help us negotiate these passages; toward this end it should be *rich, recursive, relational, and rigorous.* These four R's I am proposing are decidedly different from the three

R's used in the late nineteenth and early twentieth century as a foundation for the elementary school curriculum, and different from the Tyler rationale we have used as a general curricular foundation for the past four or so decades. As we leave our present century and paradigm for another century and paradigm, we need to develop a new set of criteria as to what constitutes a *good* curriculum. This is a prime task contemporary curriculum theorists have before them.

One of the main themes of this book is that we are in the midst of radical intellectual, social, and political change. We are shifting paradigms (maybe even megaparadigms) from those of a modernist nature to those of a post-modernist nature: post-structural, post-philosophical, post-patriarchal, post-industrial, post-national. In disciplines from architecture to theology, foundations are being shattered. In fact, the concept of foundations, itself, is now challenged (Rorty, 1980; West, 1989). We are entering a new, eclectic, "post" era. In this era, the past will not disappear but will be reframed continually in the light of an ongoing, changing present. Whitehead left Cambridge, England, because it was too dominated by the past and came to Cambridge, Massachusetts, where he hoped to find more fertile soil for his emerging ideas about the nature of reality. He was looking for a place where new ideas could take root and grow. The same metaphor might be applied to a post-modern curriculum: It should be free of past domination but it does need the roots of history in order to grow and develop. For this reason the hyphen in post-modern is designed to connect the modern with the post-modern. In this way the post-modern transcends, really transforms, the modern rather than rejects it totally. Again, there is an "essential" and productive tension here between the past and present, between rejecting the old for the new and utilizing the old within the new. How this is worked out in specific, local curricula is a task for each teacher, school, and curriculum developer to decide.

Connecting and transforming modernism with "post" thinking will not be easy. Modernism is so well ensconced in our language and thought that its most basic assumptions seem self-evident. It is only "natural" to talk of imposing order, connecting effects with causes, transmitting ideas, and finding truth through scientific methodology. Many educators are probably more comfortable than disturbed by Skinner's (1953) well-known statement: In order "to use the methods of science in the field of human affairs, we must assume that behavior is lawful and determined"; further, once "specifiable conditions . . . have been discovered we can predict (at least to some extent) that person's actions" (p. 6). While this statement has a patina of obvious "common sense" to it, it also reflects a scientific cosmology more akin to Descartes, Newton, and Laplace than to Bohr, Heisenberg, and Prigogine. Concepts of self-organization, indeterminacy, stability across and through instability, order emerging spontaneously from chaos, and the creative making of meaning are not part of this statement, nor are they easily reconciled with it. Yet it is just these nonlinear concepts that become key as we work to develop both a new cosmology and a new set of curriculum criteria. Our current school curricula are not merely based on a scientific-efficiency model (Kliebard, 1986) but have their foundations in seventeenth- to nineteenth-century modernist thought. The "naturalness" of this thought needs to be questioned, for what is self-evident in one paradigm becomes absurd in another.

In the modern paradigm, stability, external control, an *a priori* aboriginal reality (with mind as the lens or mirror used to "see" that reality) were all considered self-evident—God, as Descartes pointed out, would not have willed it otherwise, for "He" neither deceives nor plays dice. However, in a post-modern paradigm, we are not only uncertain of God's gender, we also suspect the dice may be loaded. Contingency abounds. It is common to say that in post-modernism nothing is foundational, all is relational. But it does seem that at least one concept is foundational, a concept around which the whole paradigm revolves and without which it would not exist—self-organization. Katherine Hayles (1990) shows that self-organization exists in both science (Ch. 4) and literature (Ch. 5). Whether we are dealing with readers and texts, amoebae and algae, or bromate and cerium ions in an acidic medium, all display self-organization *under certain conditions*. If self-organization is to be valued and used, these certain conditions need study and elaboration.

The feature that I find most distinguishes the post-modern from the modern paradigm, and the one that also holds the most implications for curriculum, is self-organization. Piaget, of course, contends that self-organization is the essence of life itself, that which underlies the processes of assimilation and accommodation, especially as these interact to give life its harmonious and developmental qualities. Either process without the other leads to self-defeating and life-ending extremism. Through the inter- or transactions of assimilation and accommodation, growth, maturity, and development occur. In this book's Introduction I quote Stephen Toulmin (1982) as saying that post-modernism is still too new to define. When such defining does occur, I believe self-organization will be a major component, albeit at an assumed not explicit level. I also said in the Introduction that post-modern thought called into question "the rigid dichotomies" Cartesian thought had bequeathed to us. The unity or holism this suggests is not that of bland and entropic equilibrium, where everything meshes into everything else. Rather, it is the sort of transformative union that results (or can result) from differing qualities, substances, ideologies, selves combining in new and (thermo)dynamic ways. Underlying such transformative union is self-organization.

If we do not consider self-organization to be an essential (even defining) quality of process, then we are left—as Newton pointed out in his "First Law of Motion"—with the alternative assumption that all being changes from its present state only through external force. Whether we consider this external force in terms theological (God), metaphorical (fate, chance), or personal (the teacher), it—the external force—moves us at its will and in directions it chooses; we only respond and react. Our role is basically that of receiver and spectator. To a great degree this has been a dominating, though hidden, assumption framing American curriculum throughout this century.

Curriculum designed with self-organization as a basic assumption is qualitatively different from curriculum designed with the assumption the student is only a receiver. In the former, challenge and perturbation become the *raison d'être* for organization and reorganization (Piaget's "driving force" toward reequilibration); in the latter, challenge and perturbation become disruptive and inefficient, qualities to be removed, overcome, even stamped out as soon as possible. In systemic terms, open systems require disruptions in order to function, closed systems abhor disruptions—they threaten the very functioning of the system. Analogously, assuming a self-organizing, open system framework, teachers need student challenges in order to perform their role in the interactive process. In a nonself-organizing, closed system framework, student challenges threaten that role and the teacher's functioning. The question of teacher attitudes, then, reflecting fundamental world-view assumptions, is crucial. Often these assumptions are not evident, for they lie deep within our cosmological being and are known to us only in a tacit and murky manner. Bringing these private visions, these "ises" of our being-in-the-world, into the light of public scrutiny is an important act of both self-discovery and the development of communal "oughts." Here, now, on the following page, is my own pedagogic creed:

A PEDAGOGIC CREED

In a reflective relationship between teacher and student, the teacher does not ask the student to accept the teacher's authority; rather, the teacher asks the student *to suspend disbelief in that authority,* to join with the teacher in inquiry, into that which the student is experiencing. The teacher agrees to help the student understand the meaning of the advice given, to be readily confrontable by the student, and to work with the student in reflecting on the tacit understanding each has.

CHAPTER 7

Constructing a Curriculum Matrix

CURRICULUM CONCEPTS

The field of curriculum is moribund. It is unable, by its present methods and principles, to continue its work and contribute significantly to the advancement of education. It requires new principles . . . a new view . . . of its problems . . . [and] new methods appropriate to the . . . problems.

—Joseph Schwab, "The Practical: A Language for Curriculum,"
1970/1978a, p. 287

Today, the curriculum field is no longer moribund. A whole new part of the field has emerged in the decades since Schwab issued his pronouncement, that of curriculum theory. Within this part of the field, debates about the nature and purpose of curriculum are endemic, as are debates about how curriculum relates to issues of class, race, gender, process, ideology, individualism, self, hermeneutics, ecology, theology, cognition, and all the "isms" present in our "post" era, to give but a partial listing. While the emergence of these debates has not been caused by Schwab's pronouncement, their form and liveliness have certainly been shaped by it.

In this final chapter, I wish to put forth a number of curriculum concepts based on the new view, principles, problems, and methods post-modernism presents. These concepts will not be comprehensive for reframing the field but will, I hope, be sufficiently broad and provocative to provide a beginning for others interested in this task. One of the most needed practicalities in such a development is a new rationale to replace the one Ralph Tyler put forth almost a half-century ago. It may be that the four R's of *richness, recursion, relations, and rigor* can help us move in that direction.

I have chosen to call this chapter "Constructing a Curriculum Matrix" to emphasize both the constructive and nonlinear nature of a post-modern curriculum. From Piaget, Prigogine, Dewey, and Bruner come the ideas of construction—with all but Piaget, and he in part, favoring open-ended, nondeterminist construction. Hence, a constructive curriculum is one that emerges through the action and interaction of the participants; it is not one set in advance (except in broad and general terms). A matrix, of course, has no beginning or ending; it does have boundaries and it has points of intersection or foci. So, too, a curriculum modeled on a matrix is nonlinear and nonsequential but bounded and filled with intersecting foci and related webs of meaning. The richer the curriculum, the more the points of intersection, the more the connections constructed, and the deeper the meaning.

Considering curriculum in terms of constructing a matrix is in keeping with Dewey's idea of mind as a verb and with Bruner's (1986) idea of it "as an instrument of construction" (p. 97)—an instrument we use to make meaning.

Developing the Practical

After issuing his pronouncement about curriculum and moribundity, Schwab goes on to say: "The curriculum field has reached this unhappy state by inveterate, unexamined, and mistaken reliance on *theory*" (p. 287); theory that has been "adopted," "borrowed," misappropriated from other disciplines. Following Dewey, and preceding Schön and Rorty, Schwab asserts that "theoretical constructions are, in the main, ill-fitted and inappropriate to problems of actual teaching and learning" (p. 287). The problems of teaching and learning need to be handled from a *practical* rather than a *theoretical* perspective; that is, they need to be seen not as part of various competing theoretics but in terms of their own local "states of affairs." They need to be treated in a manner "concrete and particular . . . indefinitely susceptible to circumstance and therefore highly liable to unexpected change" (p. 289). They need to follow the nonlinear models quantum physics and chaos mathematics set up, not the universal, all-encompassing, grand designs so prevalent in modernism.

This shift in emphasis in the relationship between theory and practice, where theory no longer precedes practice and where practice is no longer the handmaiden to theory, is not to negate theory or to drive an inseparable wedge between the two. Nor is it to "practicalize" theory. Rather, it is to ground theory in and develop it from practice. It is to assume, as Dewey did, that "ises" can be transformed into "oughts." In fact, it is to use (see) the concept of transformation as central to curriculum—thereby transforming curriculum materials, processes, thoughts, and participants. This means, I believe, that teachers and students need be free, encouraged, *demanded* to develop their own curriculum in conjoint interaction with one another. General guidelines wherever they come from—textbooks, curriculum guides, state education departments, professional organizations, or past tradition—need to be just that: general, broad, indeterminate. Determinacy comes through the curriculum development process each local situation takes as the heart of its educational process. It is this curriculum development process via recursive reflection—taking the consequences of past actions as the problematic for future ones—that establishes the attitudes, values, and sense of community our society so desperately needs. If modernism considered "mind" as a metaphorical mirror for what *is*, postmodernism may consider it as a transitive verb for what *can be*. As Jerome Bruner says, we will use our actual minds to create our possible worlds.

Utilizing Self-Organization

If, as both Katherine Hayles (1990) and Stephen Toulmin (1990) say, the twentieth century is a century of turbulence, then it is also a century that has brought us an awareness of self-organization. For the order that (under certain conditions) emerges from turbulence is self-organizing order. Biologists have recognized this for decades, if not for centuries; it lies at the heart of Piaget's world-view and of his work with children, which is why he could never understand the "American" desire to speed-up transitions from one stage to the next. The more the transition is speeded-up, the less the chance for self-organization to work. However, it was not until chaos mathematics and Prigogine's work with oscillating (and hence autocatalytic and unstable) chemical reactions that self-organization began to acquire importance as a concept. If a postmodern pedagogy is to emerge, I predict it will center around the concept of self-organization.

How and when, then, does self-organization work? One requirement is perturbation. A system self-organizes only when there is a perturbation, problem, or disturbance—when the system is unsettled and needs to resettle, to continue functioning. As Piaget says, this unsettlement (disequilibrium) "provides the driving force" of redevelopment. However, as we well know from lived experience, not every perturbation leads to redevelopment; it is quite possible for a disequilibrated situation to lead to the sort of chaos that takes us not to a new and more complex level of order but to the abyss of destruction. The history of our present century has shown us the real potential of this possibility.

Under what conditions, then, does perturbation become a positive factor in the self-organizing process? The literature on this issue is not copious. In fact, I know of only two essays which address the question of the conditions necessary for self-organization to take place, and only one of these deals with perturbation directly. Further, neither essay is concerned with educational or curricular issues. Still, I find each essay useful in a heuristic way as I think about how to utilize the phenomenon of self-organization. One essay is by Stephen J. Gould, the other is by Jerome Bruner.

In his "An Earful of Jaw" (1990), Stephen Gould deals with the paleontological question of how fish gills evolved into reptilian jaws then into human ears—after all, fish have no ears, nor do snakes. As Gould says, "Really, how can jawbones become ear bones?" or How can fish gills become jawbones? (pp. 12–13). The answer, he says, lies in the *inefficient* way certain life forms were created. Bacteria are amazingly efficient cellular organisms; there is no waste or "slop" in their functioning with and within the environment. They have not, though, evolved from their original form for over 3.5 billion years and probably will remain as they are "until the sun explodes." However, the inefficient design of some fish provided enough "sloppiness" and "redundancy" (pp. 15, 18) that *multiple uses* could emerge from the same substance when fish needed gills both to breathe and as evolving jawbones. So, too, reptiles needed enough extra substance in the jawbones that these could serve the *multiple uses* of eating and evolving eardrums.

Now no one, certainly not I, would advocate that a curriculum be sloppy and redundant *per se*, nor should these be primary qualities a learner possesses. But, the learner in the curriculum course needs to know the material studied well enough and have enough personal confidence to be able *both* to solve, interpret, analyze, and perform the material presented *and* to play with that material in imaginative and quirky manners. The analogy to evolution's *multiple uses* is, I believe, curriculum's *multiple perspectives*. This requires a curriculum rich in diversity, problematics, and heuristics, as well as a classroom atmosphere that fosters exploration—itself a step beyond discovery. Perturbation will trigger self-organization only when the environment is rich enough and open enough for multiple uses, interpretations, and perspectives to come into play.

In "On the Perception of Incongruity: A Paradigm" (Bruner & Postman, 1949/1973)—an essay Thomas Kuhn (1970) says influenced his concept of paradigm and paradigm change—Jerome Bruner deals directly with the role *perturbation* plays in aiding *self-organization*. These are not words Bruner uses; he talks of perceptions depending on expectancy and anticipation, and of being interested in how perception is changed when the expectancy is not confirmed. For this, he inserted a "red" spade playing card into the more usual black spade expectancy frame. However, those able to overcome this anomaly did so through the process of self-organization, aided (not hindered) by the role perturbation played.

Bruner (and Leo Postman, his coauthor) conducted this experiment using playing cards because the expectancy of seeing hearts as red and spades as black is so universal. The experiment grouped the hearts or spades together in sets of five, with each set containing a mixture of regular and anomalous cards—that is, the spade groups would contain 4 black and 1 red spade, 3 black and 2 red, 2 red and 3 black, or 1 black and 4 red. The same 4: 1, 3: 2, 2: 3, and 1: 4 ratio of normal to anomalous was present in the heart groupings. The groupings were presented to college-age subjects on a tachistoscope at varying (and increasing) subliminal to liminal millisecond time exposures. The longest exposure was 1,000 milliseconds or one second, plenty of time for all to "see" what was on the screen.

The results were interesting, both in regard to questions of self-organization and by themselves. Almost all subjects (27 of 28) started out denying the presence of any anomalous cards. A "red" spade simply did not, could not, exist. Some subjects had difficulty leaving this *dominance* mode; a few even had extreme difficulty (50 exposures at one second apiece). The reaction modes that usually followed *dominance* were either *compromise* or *disruption*. In the compromise reaction subjects saw "brown" cards, "purple" ones, "reddish black ones," "blurred reddish," and so on. Most subjects adopting this mode as a principal way of dealing with the anomalous cards were not bothered by these reported sightings. They seemed to accept these new categories. On the other hand, in the disruptive reaction—sometimes following compromise, often not—the subjects became perceptually and conceptually confused, about both the anomalous and normal cards. As one subject reported (at about 300 milliseconds, the usual exposure time for recognition):

> I can't make the suit out, whatever it is. It didn't even look like a card that time. I don't know what color it is now or whether it is a spade or heart. I'm not even sure now what a spade looks like! My God!
> —Bruner & Postman, 1949/1973, p. 79

For this subject, the chaos of turbulence did not lead to reequilibration; it led (him) to the abyss of destruction.

The most interesting reaction, though—that dealing with perturbation and self-organization—was in the category Bruner and Postman called recognition. While all subjects eventually recognized the anomalous cards (as the exposure time increased), a small number (6 of 28) focused early on the "wrong" or anomalous cards. This "sense of wrongness" emerged well before recognition, was not personally bothersome to this group, was consistent whenever an anomalous card appeared, and often focused on peripheral attributes such as the pips. These are the pointed symbols in the extreme corners of the cards, and the direction of their "point" had not been changed to conform with the change of color.

Looking at this experiment in terms of self-organization, it does appear such was present. Virtually all participants had a sudden and seemingly spontaneous "ah ha!" or "shock of recognition" experience. To quote one subject: "Good Lord, what have I been saying? That's a *red* six of spades" (p. 82). Further, those who focused on the anomalous cards as perturbations, neither denying their existence (*dominance*) nor avoiding their importance (*compromise*) were the most successful in making transitions to a new order—sometimes they were the earliest, always they were the most consistent in redoing their frames once an anomalous card was recognized as such.

Extrapolating this to curriculum, as a heuristic, certainly not as a model, it seems plausible to posit that perturbations can work as a positive force when the atmosphere or frame in which they are perceived is comfortable enough that pressure is not produced to "succeed" quickly, when in this atmosphere the details of the anomaly can be studied (maybe even played with), and when time (as a developmental factor) is of sufficient duration to allow a new frame to emerge. While the emergence itself is spontaneous, a *gestalt switch*, the period of time before emergence seems to require almost a nurturing of the anomaly.

Nurturing anomalies, maybe even mistakes, means taking time (a factor the Newtonian frame disregards) to dialogue seriously with the students about *their* ideas as *their ideas*. Such a concept is not part of the Tyler rationale, nor was it part of the way Taylor believed Schmidt should be handled.

The Role of Authority

Probably no issue is more important to teachers, especially beginning teachers, than the one of who has authority, who is in control. While a group, class, or society out of control is a frightening thing to behold—as the present century so amply demonstrates—it is also true we have adopted a particular view about control, one that assumes control to be defined in terms of external imposition. Control in terms of self- or internal-control must always have the words self or internal as modifiers; otherwise, the assumption is that control means external intervention—bringing a *deus ex machina* into the situation. The roots of this view have many origins: a Calvinist frame for human nature (exemplified in contemporary literature by William Golding's *Lord of the Flies*, 1962); the seventeenth century's distrust of Nature (" 'tis all in peeces"); and a fascination with the anthropocentric perspective modernist science brought ("subject nature to the hand of man" [Francis Bacon, c. 1620/1852, p. 560]). All these have combined to create one of modernism's great myths: It is to the benefit of all, the common good, for nature to be controlled by science and civilization. The Industrial Revolution breathed life into this myth and Enlightenment thought deified it. We see this view of control in Frederick Taylor's time-and-motion studies and as one of the underlying assumptions common to the four ideologies Herbert Kliebard (1986) says dominated American curriculum thought in the early and mid-decades of the twentieth century: liberal humanism, developmentalism, social meliorism, and scientific-efficiency. Control as external imposition is firmly embedded in modernist thought. The educational aphorism, "Don't smile until Christmas," is not merely a piece of practical advice; it is a metaphysical metaphor.

Another, quite opposed, view of control is that found in self-organization, chaos mathematics, Dewey's naturalism, Whitehead's process cosmology, Bruner's narrative, Piaget's phenocopy, and Gadamer's hermeneutics. All of these assume authority to lie within (not outside) situational parameters. Further, all assume control to be the auto- or self-control that emerges from interactions within these situational parameters. This type of control has not been studied with much depth. Hence, too often teachers have (unwittingly and uncritically) assumed control to be of the *deus ex machina* type instead of the *prima interpares* type. It is this latter, "first among equals," which, I believe, defines the teacher's role in a transformative, post-modern curriculum. As the first among equals, the teacher's role is not abrogated; it is rather restructured and resituated from being external to the student's situation to being one with that situation. The authority, too, moves into the situation. Questions of procedure, methodology, and values are not decided in the abstract, away from the practicalities of life, but are always local decisions involving students, teachers, and local mores and traditions. Obviously, the teacher's role is crucial here, more so than in the *deus ex machina* frame where the teacher is an enforcer—at best, interpreter—

of others' values. In a situational frame, Schwab's "local states of affairs," the teacher is a leader from within, not a dictator (no matter how benevolent) from without. Developing this new role is a challenge teachers and teacher education programs need to face.

Obviously, a key ingredient in this situational frame is the establishment of community—making operable that "fascinating, imaginative realm where no one owns the truth and everyone has the right to be understood." Here lies the basis for dialogue, and it is through dialogue within a *caring and critical* community that methods, procedures, and values are developed from life experiences—that "ises" are transformed into "oughts."

Talking in these terms—*developing* authority and control instead of *imposing* them—sounds strange to our modernist ears. This is why my pedagogic creed, set forth earlier, may well appear unusual, even ludicrous, at first sight or hearing; it assumes control and authority to be developed internally not imposed externally. Such communal development of authority and control is imperative if the eclecticism and multivariate focus predominant in post-modernism are to be used generatively.

Metaphor and the Narrative Mode

As long as the spectator theory of knowledge holds sway—that reality is set apart from us to be *discovered* by certain methods—then logic and the analytic mode govern our epistemology and our pedagogy. In this frame, it is *clear explanations* that are needed. Thus, the Tyler rationale and its offshoots emphasize precision in the statement of goals and experiences, and in the design by which these goals and experiences are evaluated. While control and authority are important in this paradigm, at a deeper, metaphysical level the underlying concept is that precision in observation and in thought is the entrée into that realm which lies beyond our personal experiences, that realm believed to hold "true knowledge." Laplace dreamed of acquiring precisely all the data on the planets' celestial motions and then plotting their orbits for eternity—of discovering through science and mathematics the true order of nature God had devised. Taylor used stop-watch precision in working out the steps Schmidt was to take and the time he was to spend on each task. Teachers today encourage precision by admonishing students "to pay attention," to "listen carefully," to "be sharp in making observations." Underlying these admonitions is the assumption of a spectator (not constructivist) relationship between student and knowledge.

Knowledge is assumed to sit "out there" and the student, as a Schmidt-type, "first class" person, is to prepare to receive that knowledge as it is transmitted. How well the student has received this knowledge is mirrored in the grade received.

Lately, however, there have been strong criticisms of this view: Both Rorty and Toulmin have dramatically attacked the analytic-spectator tradition in philosophy; behaviorism seems a dead issue in psychology; and curriculum is at least flirting with concepts of construction and reflection. As Bruner (1986, Ch. 2) points out, there is another, complementary, mode of thought to the logical, analytic, scientific—this is the metaphorical, narrative, hermeneutical. The key difference between these two modes of thought is that the analytic is *explanatory* while the narrative is *interpretive*. In the former the teacher wishes to achieve precision in presentation; in the latter the teacher wishes "to keep the dialogue going." In this latter, the assumption is that meanings are made (constructed) through dialogue. Dialogue is the *sine qua non* of the whole process. Without dialogue there is no transformation; the eclecticism of post-modernism remains a pastiche.

Metaphors are more useful than logic in generating this dialogue. Metaphors *are* generative; they *help us see what we don't see*. Metaphors are open, heuristic, dialogue-engendering. Logic is definitional; it *helps us see more clearly that which we already see*. It aims for closure, for exclusion. In Serres' words, "it kills." We need, of course, both creative imagination and logical definition. We need generation and closure. Life is birth and death; and so, Whitehead said, is reality. It is through the interplay of metaphor and logic that life is lived, experienced, developed. As teachers, we need to bring this interplay into our curriculum constructions.

The narrative mode requires interpretation. A good story, a great story, enduces, encourages, challenges the reader to interpret, to enter into dialogue with the text. There is in the good story just enough *indeterminacy* to entice the reader to dialogue. As Wolfgang Iser (1978) says, "It is the element of indeterminacy that evokes the text to 'communicate' with the reader," and in turn that induces the reader "to participate" in the story (p. 24). As teachers, we need to present our lessons in enough narrative form to encourage our students to explore with us the possibilities that can be generated from dialogue with the text. It is this that Serres does so well and so rigorously in his Hermes stories—Hermes being, of course, the messenger, the trickster, the interpreter, the provocateur to Gods and humans.

Goals, Plans, Purposes

There is nothing more important to the human being than the set- ting, experiencing, and evaluating of goals, plans, and purposes. Here Tyler was right. Such purposive activity is what sets the human species apart from other species—in degree, if not in kind—and it is an activity that provides our species with the choice of *intentionally* creating or de- stroying. The ability to plan carries with it an awesome responsibility— to ourselves, to others, to the environment in which we live.

Underlying Dewey's concept of critical intelligence is, of course, this idea of the human as competent in purposive planning. The trans- formation Dewey wished to see occur was that of turning nascent or potential competence into mature ability and performance. Here is Dewey's dream of an enlightened electorate (West, 1989, Ch. 3). Dewey rightly saw that a curriculum which honored an individual's ability to form, plan, execute, and evaluate was one that needed to honor the individual's planning activities—that is, the individual's actual doing of planning. Such a curriculum had to be based on an interactive, not a spectator, pedagogy and epistemology. Unfortunately, the school curric- ulum of Dewey's day (and of our own day) is so mired in modernism it has misconceived goal-setting, meaning-making, and purposive plan- ning. Two misconceptions stand out as crucial. One is that we have assumed an individual best develops planning skills by being a passive receiver or copier of another's plans, rather than by being an active par- ticipant in the planning process—that is, a receiver or discoverer of knowledge, not a maker of meaning.

The second major misconception is that we have (tacitly) assumed a cosmology based on a universe stable in order. Quantum physics and Whitehead's philosophy, as well as the thermodynamic chemistry of dis- sipative structures and the philosophic thought of John Dewey and Richard Rorty have helped us see the inadequacy of this simplistic view of a stable universe. Complexity is the nature of Nature, and only in the past few decades have we begun a serious study of complexity (Dyke, 1988; Nicolis & Prigogine, 1989; Schieve & Allen, 1982). Anyone who has studied complexity realizes that it assumes concepts not recognized by modernism: Self-organization and transformation are two of these.

In a frame that recognizes self-organization and transformation, goals, plans, and purposes arise not purely prior to but also *from within action*. This is a key point with Dewey: Plans arise from action and are modified through actions. The two are interactive, each leading into the other and depending on the other. Curricularly, this translates into course syllabi or lesson plans written in a general, loose, somewhat indeterminate manner. As the course or lesson proceeds, specificity becomes more appropriate and is worked out conjointly—among teacher, students, text. Such conjoint planning not only allows for flexibility—utilizing the unexpected—but also allows for planners to understand themselves and their subject with a degree of depth not otherwise obtained. There are patterns to our planning, as Piaget, Vygotsky, Bruner have helped us realize; and the subject material (the text) we use in our planning has its own structure, history, and parameters. Inquiring into a subject's structure and history gives us insights beyond that found in textbooks. In Donald Oliver's (1990) phrase, we are acquiring here *"grounded* knowing," not just *"technical* knowing" (p. 64).

Conjoint, developmental planning takes advantage of the unexpected, leads to grounded knowing, and helps the student acquire (to use Rorty's phrase) "an expanding repertoire of alternative descriptions" (1989, p. 39). All these are important attributes in our attempts to develop competence in dealing with the world in which we exist.

An example of conjoint planning occurred a few years ago in a sixth-grade class I was assisting to find better ways to solve mathematics word-problems—a perennial difficulty for sixth-grade classes. All of us—the teacher, the students, myself—became frustrated at the students' (in)ability to set up the problems in a manner that facilitated solution. After much admonition to "pay attention to the wording," to "read carefully," to follow certain algorithmic procedures for decoding the word-problem or translating it into numerical structures, one of my colleagues[1] hit upon the idea of having the students plan their own problems. That is, we would provide a number of facts and certain operations, then groups of students would design a set of different word-problems from these facts and operations. Following Whitehead's dictum, we encouraged the students to put these facts and operations into "as many combinations as possible"—even to the extent of recommending that some problems not be solvable due to an insufficiency of facts, with other problems requiring a choice among the facts presented. Each group conjointly worked and reworked (recursively reflected) the various problems it designed and then presented its problems to another group. There was competition to see which group could solve the other group's problems first, but there was also generative discussion about the nature of the problems, their structures, and alternative ways of solving them. Competence in problem solving improved dramatically. After a short time creating their own problems, the students were able not only to solve standardized sixth-grade word-problems but also to take apart, easily, the structure of these problems. Standardized test scores ran high (Doll, 1989a), not by "teaching-for-the-test," as is often done, but by having the students construct their own tests. Dewey was right. Planning and executing are conjoint, integrated activities, not unilateral, sequential, serial ones.

Evaluation

To think of evaluation in post-modern terms is virtually impossible, for school evaluation is almost always associated with grades and both are based on assumptions so endemic to modernist thought that without this thought evaluation loses its meaning—at least its modernist meaning. The first of these assumptions is that our frame for teaching is based on a closed set; that is, our purpose as teachers is to have the students acquire a particular, set body of knowledge in a particular, set way—so they will deal with that knowledge in an "acceptable" manner. Obviously, this assumption is a corollary to the Cartesian-Newtonian paradigm; it assumes a stable epistemology and reality and a transmitive pedagogy. To say the set is closed is not to say that knowledge is constrained (it certainly is expanding all the time), but it is to say that the method for dealing with this expansion is done by experts in the field (Schön's technical rationalists) who follow an orderly, rational, linear, "scientific" procedure. Kuhn's suggestion of paradigm shifts following "gestalt switches" is suspect, while Feyerabend's anti-method is dismissed. Randomness, eclecticism, quantum leaps, self-organization are not part of this knowledge advancement process.

A second assumption is that evaluation in terms of grades is the assessment of how much of this canon and its method the student has acquired. Phrased differently, grades are a way of measuring the "deficit" between the canon presented and the canon acquired. In this form, evaluation becomes a way of measuring deficit, while curriculum may legitimately be labeled as both "deficit driven" and measurement oriented. That is, grades measure the deficit, and the curriculum is periodically revised to increase or decrease the deficit "gap," depending on the relationship desired between the ideal norm (the canon) and its actualization or reception (measured in terms of student performance). In the past this gap has been expressed in terms of a bell-shaped curve with the actualized norm (at grade C) a goodly way from the ideal. However, in recent decades there has been a move toward mastery, with the gap narrowing ("average" grades moving into the B range). This change has been more a change in the curriculum material presented and methods of evaluation than in increased learning ability or better pedagogy. But there has been no change in the assumption that a definite ideal norm exists; the canon does exist, even in second-grade reading and mathematics.

The difficulty with a post-modern, transformative curriculum is that there is no ideally set norm, no canon which can exist as a universal reference point. An open, transformative system is by nature always in flux, always in (thermo)dynamic inter- and transaction. Attractors do appear in this process but often dissipate as quickly as they emerge (as in a stream flowing or a cloud billowing). Further, the very process of transformation requires that the goals achieved be fed back (iterated) into the system so the process may continue. Finally, minute differences in the canon itself will lead over time to greater and greater internal discrepancies, with the canon eventually disintegrating. Ideal norms in any precise or stable sense then become meaningless—yet precision and stability are two qualities graded measurement assumes.

Instead, what does emerge in a self-generating, open system are parameters or limits (as in chaos swirls) and an infinity of relationships within those parameters. These relationships are among similar but slightly different patterns—as in the congruity diagrams which chaos mathematics can generate on a computer.[2] A curriculum based on infinite patterns within set parameters (as in the Sierpinski triangle with its triangles within triangles) is a curriculum richer and richer with more and more foci, networks, interrelations emerging and being generated. The simplicity that our present grading-evaluation system assumes— one norm for all to achieve and be measured against—becomes lost in a beautiful network of increasingly complex relations.

How then can we deal with evaluation in a post-modern, transformative frame? This raises another question—What is the purpose of evaluation? In a modernist frame, evaluation is basically used to separate winners from losers. This is what grades do and what state, national, and professional tests do—they separate. For this, a norm or specified level of performance is assumed. In the past few decades there has been some emphasis on having tests or papers returned to the authors as a means of feedback for improvement, but this emphasis is slight at best. Rarely do teachers—other than composition instructors— interact with students on their writing, and even more rarely do teachers iterate or use tests taken as a basis for future learning. National testing organizations are reluctant to give back the tests themselves, preferring to cite scores only. Almost universally, tests are used as demarcation points, not as the beginnings of dialogue. The same can be said of grades and evaluation in a modernist frame, although to a lesser degree. Generally, all three of these are used to separate those found to be acceptable from those deemed unacceptable.

In a post-modern frame evaluation could still serve this separation function if that was desired—probably by a variety of individuals doing the judging, as in doctoral committees, admissions committees, editorial reviews—but essentially evaluation would be a negotiary process within a communal setting for the purpose of transformation. Obviously, the teacher would play a central role in this process but would not be the exclusive evaluator; evaluation would be communal and interactive. It would be used as feedback, part of the iterative process of doing–critiquing–doing–critiquing. This recursive process of private doing and public critiquing—lying at the heart of Dewey's critical reflection or scientific method—is essential for the transformation of experience. For this to occur, dynamic social communities need to be established—communities whose function is to help the individual through constructive critiques. This is a role classrooms could adopt, I'd argue should adopt, although such a role would certainly change our present teacher-centered classroom. The focus would now be on a community dedicated to helping each individual, through critique and dialogue, to develop intellectual and social powers.[3]

THE FOUR R'S—AN ALTERNATIVE TO THE TYLER RATIONALE

The three R's of "Readin', 'Ritin', and 'Rithmetic" were late-nineteenth- and early twentieth-century creations, geared to the needs of a developing industrial society. Reading was the functional reading of sales slips and bills of lading, combined with the inspirational stories of Horatio Alger and the moral aphorisms of McGuffey. Writing was literally penmanship, with the Palmer method introducing a ledger-oriented style in the first grade. Such cursive training had to begin early, for by the fifth grade half of those who had entered as first graders had left. Arithmetic, not mathematics, was essentially column addition and subtraction, with algorithmic multiplication and division coming in the later elementary years. Again, the emphasis was on store clerk functionalism, keeping the sales slips and ledgers accurate and neat. Problem solving was introduced as early as the second grade, but it was heavily, if not exclusively, associated with buying in an urban store.

Born in the early 1930s, I had my early elementary school training in these three R's. My word-lists for reading and spelling prepared me for the urban, industrial society my parents and I inhabited. The Palmer method was begun in the first grade, with an itinerant teacher brought in weekly to instruct us in the big O's and C's so distinctive of its style—flowing but clear. From Miss Wiley, Miss James, and Miss Thatcher—the maiden ladies who taught grades one, two, and three—I learned to keep my ten's column digits out of my hundred's column or my unit's column, and *always* beginning with the right column to "bring down" a single digit and to "carry" into the next column any digits left over. Miss Newcomb in the fourth grade made a small modification to this "consonant" method—namely, that with decimals it was the decimal points which needed to form a vertical, unbroken phalanx. Zeros were added to the right of the decimal point to keep the right column, the hundredths (often considered as pennies), in line.

Mr. Bartlett, our corner grocer, was not as good as my triumvirate of maiden teachers at keeping his columns straight. Further, he began his addition with the left, not the right column. When questioned he stated that he wished to make no mistakes with the dollars or dimes and this method assured him greater accuracy with those important columns. Worse, he grouped digits together either in his head or with small notations in combinations equal to ten. This method intrigued me. I passed on my newfound wisdom to Miss Thatcher (married women were not allowed to teach school). She, however, dismissed Mr. Bartlett's methods as heresy. In retrospect, I think Mr. Bartlett was more industrially oriented than Miss Thatcher and maybe even a better pedagogue. In dealing with my own elementary school classes, I have found that much columnar addition—at least of any practical type—has a better "feel" when it is done left to right, thus allowing intuition and estimation to come into play. Further, doing simple columnar work by grouping numerals into combinations of ten not only produces more accurate and quicker answers but also encourages structural and situational thinking—for example, doing $101 - 49$ as $102 - 50$, or maybe as $100 - 50$ with two added on. Such "chaotic ordering" has been a hallmark of my students' *modus operandi* for many years now—before I read Whitehead or heard of post-modernism; it has generally served them well (Doll, 1977, 1989a).

At first glance one does not see a connection between the Tyler rationale and the three R's. However, a pre-set functionalism underlies both. While Tyler's frame expands and broadens industrial functionalism beyond the sales slips and ledgers of the three R's, the assumption of pre-set goals still exists. In this frame, *goals* do not emerge—as Cvitanović suggests they should—by "playing with" experiences; rather, goals are predetermined as are the *experiences* and *methods* for developing those experiences. All are firmly in place before any interaction with students occurs. *Evaluations* are designed to correlate the experiences only with the pre-set goals, not to explore what the students generate personally after reflecting on the experiences. In fact, as was pointed out earlier in the chapter, framing evaluation in terms of generation, reflection, transformation is virtually oxymoronic from a modernist perspective.

So what would serve as criteria for a curriculum designed to foster a post-modern view? What criteria might we use to evaluate the quality of a post-modern curriculum—a curriculum generated not predefined, indeterminate yet bounded, exploring the "fascinating imaginative realm born of God's laughter," and made up of an ever-increasing network of "local universalities"? I suggest the four R's of Richness, Recursion, Relations, and Rigor might serve this purpose.

Richness. This term refers to a curriculum's depth, to its layers of meaning, to its multiple possibilities or interpretations. In order for students and teachers to transform and be transformed, a curriculum needs to have the "right amount" of *indeterminacy, anomaly, inefficiency, chaos, disequilibrium, dissipation, lived experience*—to use words and phrases already described. Just what is the "right amount" for the curriculum to be provocatively generative without losing form or shape cannot be laid out in advance. This issue is one to be continually negotiated among students, teachers, and texts (the latter having long histories and basic assumptions that cannot be neglected). But the issue of the curriculum needing disturbing qualities is not to be negotiated; these qualities form the problematics of life itself and are the essence of a rich and transforming curriculum. Another way to state this is to say that the *problematics, perturbations, possibilities* inherent in a curriculum are what give the curriculum not only its richness but also its sense of being, its *dasein.*

The main academic disciplines taught in schools have their own historical contexts, fundamental concepts, and final vocabularies. Hence, each will interpret richness in its own way. Language—including reading, writing, literature, and oral communication—develops its richness by focusing heavily (but not exclusively) on the interpretation of metaphors, myths, narratives. Saying this places language within a hermeneutic frame; it is to see language as integrated with culture, as one of the determinants of culture.

Mathematics—a subject in which computational arithmetic plays but a small part—takes its form of richness from "playing with patterns." Obviously, this can be done *par excellence* with computers—tools that any mathematically rich curriculum should possess—but computers are not a *sine qua non.* Patterns may be seen, developed, played with in simple number combinations (as with the Fibonnaci series) or with geometry of both a Euclidean and fractal sort. Breaking a square into right triangles is an example of the former; the Sierpinski triangle is an example of the latter. At all levels, from kindergarten through graduate school, mathematics can be dealt with meaningfully as "playing with patterns."

Science—including the biological and the physical—can be seen as intuiting, developing, probing, "proving" hypotheses concerning the world in which we live. This moves science beyond the collection of "facts"—with the assumption these facts are objective bits of reality—into the realm of manipulating, creating, working with facts or information in an imaginative and (thermo)dynamic manner. This view of science is obviously more Whiteheadian than Newtonian, more oriented toward Prigogine than Laplace. The social sciences—those multiple disciplines of anthropology, economics, history, psychology, and sociology—take their concept of richness from dialoguing about, or negotiating passages between, various (often competing) interpretations of societal issues. Here, probably more than in any other discipline, assumptions are questioned. It is these assumed givens that form the foundations of society's mores, norms, standards; and in a democratic society it is imperative these givens be open to dialogue.

Obviously these disciplines, their languages, and histories are not mutually exclusive. The concept of developing richness through dialogue, interpretations, hypothesis generation and proving, and pattern playing can apply to all we do in curriculum. Again, such ideas sound strange to those imbued with a modernist perspective, which helps explain why we need to transcend this perspective to a post-modernist one.

Recursion. From recur, to happen again,[4] recursion usually is associated with the mathematical operation of iteration. In iteration a formula is "run" over and over, with the output of one equation being the input for the next. In $y = 3x + 1$, a y of 4 (if the $x = 1$) becomes the next x, and the new y of 13 becomes the next x, and so on. In such iterations, there is both stability and change; the formula stays the same, the variables change (in an orderly but often nonpredictable manner). As was explained in Chapter Four, some interesting complex patterns develop with particular formulae and particular x, y variables.

However, when Bruner (1986) states that "any formal theory of mind is helpless without recursion" (p. 97)—and asserts the importance of recursion for epistemology and pedagogy—he refers less to mathematics and more to the human capacity of having thoughts loop back on themselves. Such looping, thoughts on thoughts, distinguishes human consciousness; it is the way we make meaning. As Bruner says:

> Much of the process of education consists of being able to distance oneself in some way from what one knows by being able to reflect on one's own knowledge. (p. 127)

This is also the way one produces a sense of self, through reflective interaction with the environment, with others, with a culture. As I pointed out in Chapter Six, such "recursive reflection" lies at the heart of a transformative curriculum; it is *the process* which Dewey, Piaget, Whitehead all advocate. In the 1960s Bruner made a beginning at defining a recursive curriculum with his "spiral curriculum" (1960) and his elementary school social studies program, "Man: A Course of Study" (1966). However, in our then-modernist mode both of these were misseen, attaining only popular approval and notoriety. Their power never became evident; the former got lost in the question of calculus for first graders, the latter in the issue of Bruner's patriotism.

In a curriculum that honors, values, uses recursion, there is no fixed beginning or ending. As Dewey has pointed out, every ending is a new beginning, every beginning emerges from a prior ending. Curriculum segments, parts, sequences are arbitrary chunks that, instead of being seen as isolated units, are seen as opportunities for reflection. In such a frame, every test, paper, journal entry can be seen not merely as the completion of one project but also as the beginning of another—to explore, discuss, inquire into both ourselves as meaning makers and into the text in question. This curriculum will, of course, be open not closed; like post-modernism itself, it is Janus-faced, eclectic, interpretive.

Recursion and repetition differ in that neither one, in any way, reflects the other. Repetition, a strong element in the modernist mode, is designed to improve set performance. Its frame is closed. Recursion aims at developing competence—the ability to organize, combine, inquire, use something heuristically. Its frame is open. The functional difference between repetition and recursion lies in the role reflection plays in each. In repetition, reflection plays a negative role; it breaks the process. There is a certain automaticity to repetition that keeps the same process going—over and over and over, as in flash card arithmetic drills or in ball machine tennis drills. In recursion, reflection plays a positive role; for thoughts to leap back on themselves, as in Dewey's secondary experience reflecting back on primary experience, or in Piaget's reflexive intelligence reflecting back on practical intelligence, it is necessary, as Bruner has said, to step back from one's doings, to "distance oneself in some way" from one's own thoughts.[5] Thus, in recursion it is a necessity to have others—peers, teachers—look at, critique, respond to what one has done. Dialogue becomes the *sine qua non* of recursion: Without reflection—engendered by dialogue—recursion becomes shallow not transformative; it is not reflective recursion, it is only repetition.

Relations. The concept of relations is important to a post-modern, transformative curriculum in two ways: in a *pedagogical* way and in a *cultural* way. The former might, naturally, be called pedagogical relations, referring to those within the curriculum—the matrix or network which gives it richness. The latter might, just as naturally, be called cultural relations, referring to those cultural or cosmological relations which lie outside the curriculum but form a large matrix within which the curriculum is embedded. Both relations are important; each complements the other.

In focusing on *pedagogical relations*, one focuses on the connections within a curriculum's structure which give the curriculum its depth as this is developed by recursion. Here the twin processes of doing and reflecting-on-doing are important, and through these processes the curriculum becomes richer with the passage of time. As Prigogine is fond of saying, time in a Newtonian frame is *reversible and unimportant;* in the dissipative structure frames he studies, it is *irreversible and important* (1988; with Stengers, 1984, Ch. 7). If the universe is already set, time does no more than give one the chance to "see" more of that universe. "Mastery learning" assumes this frame—the student is to take the time necessary to master the material presented to a certain, predetermined level of repetitious proficiency (Torshen, 1977). In a universe of and in process, time takes on a different, qualitative dimension; it acquires a transformative aspect, since development of one sort or another is always occurring. Conditions, situations, relations are always changing; the present does not recreate the past (though it is certainly influenced by the past) nor does the present determine the future (though it is an influencer). So, too, the curriculum frame operating at the beginning of the course is unavoidably different from the curriculum frame operating at the end of the course. The issue is not difference but degree or quality of difference—whether the difference is a difference that makes a difference.

Recognizing the contingency of relations, and hoping that these relations will be positively and communally developed during the course of a semester, I organize my undergraduate and graduate university courses to enhance this development. Among the devices I use, one is to provide a syllabus that lists common readings for only two-thirds of the course; for the last third various groups choose their readings from a selected list. Class time is devoted not to summarizing these various readings but to interconnecting them to both the common readings and to each other. The quality of discussion improves as the semester *develops;* so, too, papers written early in the semester improve dramatically when rewritten and reframed after utilizing the insights gained. Sometimes the change is transformative.

In junior high classes, where I have often used a set text, I build time-oriented relationships by asking students to reframe the material presented, to choose from or reframe chapter questions, and to deal with the textual material on both a "what-if" (imaginary) basis and a "relate-it-to-yourself" (real) basis. In dealing with elementary school grades, I follow the same general procedures but use far more manipulative materials, story telling, projects, and dramatic presentations. The textbook, throughout all this, is seen as something to revise, not as something to follow. It is the base from which transformation occurs. Curriculum in a post-modern frame needs to be created (self-organized) by the classroom community, not by textbook authors.

It should be obvious in all these personal anecdotes that, in building a curriculum matrix with a rich set of relationships, I have been strongly influenced by Whitehead's (1929/1967a) dictum to "not teach too many subjects" but to "teach thoroughly" what I do teach, and to let the main ideas "be thrown into every combination possible" (p. 2).

The concept of *cultural relations* grows out of a hermeneutic cosmology—one which emphasizes narration and dialogue as key vehicles in interpretation. Narration brings forward the concepts of history (through story), language (through oral telling), and place (through a story's locality). Dialogue interrelates these three to provide us with a sense of culture that is local in origin but global in interconnections. Thus, all our interpretations relate to local culture and interconnect with other cultures and their interpretations via a global matrix. Discourse (narration and dialogue) operates, then, within such a double-tiered cultural frame; it does this far more so than within the foundationalist, abstract, and privileged frame modernism posited. Discourse now becomes what Jim Cheney (1989) calls "contextualist" (p. 123)—bound always by the localness of ourselves, our histories, our language, our place, but also expanding into an ever-broadening global and ecological network. It is this double-tiered or dual-focused nature that makes cultural relations so complex.

Recognizing the contextualist nature of discourse helps us realize that the constructs of those participating frame all conversations, all acts of teaching. As teachers we cannot, do not, transmit information directly; rather, we perform the teaching act when we help others negotiate passages between their constructs and ours, between ours and others'. This is why Dewey says teaching is an interactive process with learning a *by-product* of that interaction.

Modernism has not adopted such an interrelational view; it has taken as one of its hallmarks movement beyond the local and contextual to the universal and abstract. Instead of the narrational, it has aimed for, indeed created, the *meta*narrational, the *grand écrit* Lyotard attacks. Teachers, fitting unconsciously into this paradigm—as we all do—have unwittingly carried on their discourses with students by speaking *ex cathedra*. Too often, teacher explanations have resounded with the authority of God; too rarely have meaningful, interactive, participating dialogues been held.

C. A. Bowers (1987; with Flinders, 1990) has tied the concept of cultural relationships to the ecological crises we face today. In doing this he draws our attention to modernism's overly strong sense of individualism. Individualism has tended to pit humanity against nature (civilization is defined as society improving on nature) and to believe that progress occurs through competition, not cooperation. This is one of modernism's myths founded on beliefs like Bacon's that we should *subject Nature to the hand of man*. This statement would be abhorrent, even sacrilegious, to pre-modern or tribal cultures such as the North American Indian.

But this belief in competition and the virtue of controlling the natural is part of our present day pedagogy and cosmology. Bowers, Griffin, and Oliver (also Lydon, 1992) are among the few curricularists who encourage us to rethink our concept of relations, who see that *cultural relationships* extend beyond our personal selves to include the ecosystem—indeed the cosmos in which we live. Only now, in the past decade or so, are we beginning to develop a cosmic and interrelational consciousness. The challenge of such recognition is twofold: on the one hand, to honor the localness of our perceptions and, on the other hand, to realize that our local perspectives integrate into a larger cultural, ecological, cosmic matrix. Our progress and our existence—as individuals, as communities, as a race, as a species, as a life form—depend on our ability to bring these two perspectives into complementary harmony.

Rigor. In some ways the most important of the four criteria, rigor keeps a transformative curriculum from falling into either "rampant relativism" or sentimental solipsism. In presenting transformation as an alternative to our current measurement frame, it is easy to see transformation as no more than anti-measurement or nonmeasurement. Here, transformation becomes not a true alternative but yet another variation on the very thing it tries to replace. This certainly happened in the progressive and open education movements. Dewey wrestled with the problem in the progressive education movement and wrote "Need for a Philosophy of Education" to explain why progressive education needed to be more than anti-traditional, why progressive education had to have its own foundation and frame. In contrasting his view of progressive education—developmental and transformative—with either the received progressive view (which he considered too romantic) or the established traditional view (which he considered too rigid), he said:

> This alternative is not just a middle course or compromise between the two procedures. It is something radically different from either. Existing likes and powers are to be treated as possibilities. (1934/1964c, p. 8)

In such a transformative frame, with its emphasis on indeterminacy, shifting relationships, and spontaneous self-organization, rigor wears a very different set of clothes than it did in the modernist frame. Rigor began, at least in the scholastic sense, with the Jesuits' Q.E.D.— "Quod Est Demonstratum" (Thus it is demonstrated)—from the deductive power of their Aristotlean-based logic. Descartes objected to this logic, replacing it with his own "clear and distinct" ideas—those which no reasonable person could doubt, those he received from God, but also ones he "saw" with his mind's eye. Rigor thus moved from Aristotlean-Euclidean logic to deeply felt perceptions and conceptions. The English empiricists wanted to move rigor yet again, away from subjective states, no matter how personally appealing, to the objective and observable. Here rigor entered a world that could be measured and manipulated. Our present twentieth-century concept of rigor has elements of all these strains—scholastic logic, scientific observation, and mathematical precision.

To think of rigor without these qualities is to call for a virtual redefinition of the concept. Rigor in a post-modern frame requires just this. It draws on qualities foreign to a modernist frame—interpretation and indeterminacy, to mention but two. In dealing with indeterminacy, one can never be certain one "has it right"—not even to the 95th or 99th percentile of probability. One must continually be exploring, looking for new combinations, interpretations, patterns. This is why, in his scientific methodology, Dewey (1933/1971) listed the fourth stage as "the mental elaboration of an idea" (p. 107), "developing the relations of ideas to one another" (p. 113), and "playing with concepts" (p. 182). Here we find echoes and presagings of statements made by Whitehead, Kuhn, Bruner—not to close too early or finally on the rightness of an idea, to throw all ideas into various combinations. Here rigor means purposely looking for different alternatives, relations, connections. Michel Serres does this well, as shown in his wolf and sheep essay, drawing together LaFontaine's fable and Descartes' right method (see Chapter One).

In dealing with interpretation rigorously, one needs to be aware that all valuations depend on (often hidden) assumptions. As frames differ so do the problems, procedures, and valued results. Rigor here means the conscious attempt to ferret out these assumptions, ones we or others hold dear, as well as negotiating passages between these assumptions, so the dialogue may be meaningful and transformative. As Iser points out, dialogue between reader and text is a two-way process, each has a voice, and in this dialogue there is a combining of determinacy and indeterminacy. Indeterminacy here does not mean arbitrariness; rather, it "allows [for] a spectrum of actualization" (1978, p. 24)— better yet, it allows for a range of possibilities from which actualizations appear. Which actualization does appear for development depends on the interaction process itself, on mixing indeterminacy with determinacy.

So, too, rigor may be defined in terms of mixing—indeterminacy with interpretation. The quality of interpretation, its own richness, depends on how fully and well we develop the various alternatives indeterminacy presents. In this new frame for rigor—combining the complexity of indeterminacy with the hermeneutics of interpretation—it seems necessary to establish a community, one critical yet supportive. Such a community is, I believe, what Dewey thought a school should be.

NOTES

1. I am indebted to Samuel Crowell of the University of California–San Bernardino for this suggestion.

2. The relationships which are exact are those which move across dimensions of magnitude as when one magnifies (from one to a thousand to a million) the configurations at the edges of a Mandlebrot set. Exactitude in fractals exists then only in that which is self-referential, but the beauty of *proximate* symmetry, one of the features that makes computer graphics so outstanding, exists throughout their whole range. Analogously, the power and beauty of metaphor lie not in its exactitude but in its proximate symmetry.

3. This concept of evaluation, which might be labeled transformative negotiations, is akin to what Cornel West (1989) calls "cultural criticism" or "prophetic pragmatism" and underlies the social vision he has of American democracy. This vision, which he attributes to both Dewey and Rorty, began, he argues, with Ralph Waldo Emerson's notion of "creative democracy" (Ch. 6).

4. It is interesting to note that recursion (as well as recur) is derived from the Latin *recurrere* (to run back). In this way recursion is allied with *currere* (to run), the root word for curriculum.

5. As I've said already, it is this distancing of oneself from one's actions and thoughts that is missing in Schön's concept of reflection. See Chapter Six, note 3.

References

Aoki, T. T. (1983). Towards a dialectic between the conceptual world and the lived world: Transcending instrumentalism in curriculum orientation. *Journal of Curriculum Theorizing, 5*(4), 4–21.

APPE. (1991). Call for papers. Association for the Process Philosophy of Education. Bell Mead, NJ.

Aristotle. (1941a). *De anima* (J. A. Smith, Trans.). In R. McKeon (Ed.), *The basic works of Aristotle* (pp. 535–603). New York: Random House.

———. (1941b). *Metaphysics* (W. D. Ross, Trans.). In R. McKeon (Ed.), *The basic works of Aristotle* (pp. 689–926). New York: Random House.

———. (1941c). *Nicomachean ethics* (W. D. Ross, Trans.). In R. McKeon (Ed.), *The basic works of Aristotle* (pp. 935–1112). New York: Random House.

———. (1969). *Physics* (H. G. Apostle, Trans.). Bloomington: Indiana University Press.

Atkins, E. S. (1988). The relationship of metatheoretical principles in the philosophy of science of metatheoretical explorations in curriculum. *Journal of Curriculum Theorizing, 8*(4), 60–86.

Ayala, F. J., & Dobzhansky, T. (Eds.). (1974). *Studies in the philosophy of biology: Reduction and related problems.* Berkeley: University of California Press.

Bacon, F. (1852). The phenomena of the universe. In Basil Montague, ed. (original published c. 1620) *The works of Francis Bacon* vol II, 558–570. Philadelphia: Hart, Carey, & Hart.

Barber, B. (1963). Some problems in the sociology of the professions. *Daedalus, 92* (Fall), 668–688.

Beckner, M. (1959). *The biological way of thought.* New York: Columbia University Press.

Bell, D. (1973). *The coming of a post-industrial society: A venture in forecasting.* New York: Basic Books.

———. (1976). *Cultural contradictions of capitalism.* New York: Basic Books.

———. (1980). Beyond modernism, beyond self. In Daniel Bell (Ed.), *The winding passage: Essays and sociological journeys* (pp. 275–302). Cambridge, MA: Abt Books.

Bergson, H. (1911). *Creative evolution* (Arthur Mitchell, Trans.). New York: H. Holt and Co.

Berman, M. (1982). *All that is solid melts into air.* New York: Simon & Schuster.

Bernstein, J., & Feinberg, G. (1989). *Cosmological constants: Papers in modern cosmology.* New York: Columbia University Press.

Bernstein, R. J. (1983). *Beyond objectivism and relativism: science, hermeneutics, and praxis.* Philadelphia: University of Pennsylvania Press.

———. (Ed.). (1985). *Habermas and modernity.* Cambridge, MA: MIT Press.

———. (1986). *Philosophical profiles.* Philadelphia: University of Pennsylvania Press.

von Bertalanffy, L. (1933). *Modern theories of development.* Oxford: Oxford University Press.

Bettelheim, B., & Zelan, K. (1982). *On learning to read.* Chicago: University of Chicago Press.

Birch, C., & Cobb, J. B. (1981). *The liberation of life.* Cambridge: Cambridge University Press.

Bloom, A. (1987). *The closing of the American mind.* New York: Simon & Schuster.

Blake, W. (n.d.). The tiger. In *Songs of innocence and of experience.* San Marino, CA: The Huntington Library and Art Gallery. (Original work published 1794)

Bobbitt, J. F. (1912). The elimination of waste in education. *The Elementary School Teacher, 12,* 259–271.

———. (1918). *The curriculum.* Boston: Houghton Mifflin.

———. (1924). *How to make a curriculum.* Boston: Houghton Mifflin.

Bowers, C. A. (1987). *Elements of a post-liberal theory of education.* New York: Teachers College Press.

Bowers, C. A., & Flinders, D. (1990). *Responsive teaching.* New York: Teachers College Press.

Bredo, E. (1989, Fall). After positivism, what? *Educational Theory. 39,* 401–413.

Briggs, J. P., & Peat, F. D. (1984). *Looking glass universe: The emerging science of wholeness.* New York: Simon & Schuster.

———. (1989). *Turbulent mirror.* New York: Harper & Row.

Bringuier, J-C. (1980). *Conversations with Jean Piaget* (B. F. Gulatis, Trans.). Chicago: University of Chicago Press.

Bronowski, J. (1978). *The common sense of science.* Cambridge, MA: Harvard University Press.

Brooks, D. R., & Wiley, E. O. (1986). *Evolution as entropy: Toward a unified theory of biology.* Chicago: University of Chicago Press.

Brown, M. W. (1989). Chaos, not stability, sign of a healthy heart. *New York Times,* January 17, section C, p. 19.

Browning, D. (1965). *Philosophy of process.* New York: Random House.

Brumbaugh, R. (1982). *Whitehead, Process Philosophy, and Education.* Albany: SUNY Press.

Bruner, J. (1960). *The process of education.* Cambridge, MA: Harvard University Press.

———. (1966). Man: A course of study. In Jerome Bruner (Ed.), *Toward a theory of instruction* (pp. 73–101). Cambridge, MA: Harvard University Press.

—————. (1973a). *Beyond the information given.* J. Anglin (Ed.), New York: W. W. Norton.

—————. (1983). *In search of mind: Essays in autobiography.* New York: Harper & Row.

—————. (1986). *Actual minds, possible worlds.* Cambridge, MA: Harvard University Press.

—————. (1990). *Acts of meaning.* Cambridge, MA: Harvard University Press.

Bruner, J., & Bornstein, M. (1989). On interaction. In M. Bornstein & J. Bruner (Eds.), *Interaction in human development* (pp. 1–16). Hillsdale, NJ: Lawrence Erlbaum.

Bruner, J., Jolly, A., & Sylva, K. (Eds.). (1976). *Play: Its role in development and evolution.* New York: Basic Books.

Bruner, J., & Postman, L. J. (1973). On the perception of incongruity: A paradigm. In J. Anglin (Ed.), *Beyond the information given* (pp. 68–83). New York: W. W. Norton. (Original work published 1949)

Buffon, G. L. L. (1968). *Natural history, general and particular* (William Smellie, Trans.). (Original work published 1797–1807)

Burtt, E. A. (1955). *The metaphysical foundations of modern physical science.* New York: Doubleday, Anchor Books. (Original work published 1932)

Callahan, R. E. (1962). *Education and the cult of efficiency.* Chicago: University of Chicago Press.

Cassirer, E. (1955). *The philosophy of the Enlightenment.* Boston: Beacon Press. (Original work published 1932)

Charters, W. W. (1923). *Curriculum construction.* New York: Macmillan.

Charters, W. W., & Wapples, D. (1929). *The Commonwealth teacher-training study.* Chicago: University of Chicago Press.

Cheney, J. (1989). Postmodern environmental ethics: Ethics as bioregional narrative. *Environmental Ethics, 11* (Summer), 117–134.

Chaisson, E. J. (1992). Early results from the Hubble space telescope. *Scientific American,* June, 44–51.

Chomsky, N. (1971). Formal discussion. In U. Bellugi & R. Brown (Eds.), *The acquisition of language* (pp. 35–39) Chicago: University of Chicago Press.

—————. (1972). *Language and mind.* New York: Harcourt, Brace, Jovanovich.

—————. (1984). A review of B. F. Skinner's verbal behavior. In J. Fodor & J. Katz (Eds.), *The structure of language: Reading in the philosophy of language* (pp. 547–578). Englewood Cliffs, NJ: Prentice-Hall. (Original work published 1959 in *Language*).

Chubb, J. E., & Moe, T. M. (1990). *What price democracy?: Politics, markets and America's schools.* New York: Brookings Institute.

Clausius, R. (1865). Ueber verschiedene fur die anwendung bequeme formen der hauptgleichungen der mechanischen warmetheorie. *Annalen der Physik und Chemie, 125* (7), 353–400.

Cobb, J. (1965). *A Christian natural theology.* Philadelphia: Westminster Press.

—————. (1982). *Beyond dialogue.* Philadelphia: Fortress Press.

Colum, P. (1976). *Myths of the world.* New York: Grosset & Dunlap. (Original work published 1930)

Comte, A. (1974). General consideration on the hierarchy of the positive sciences. Lecture 2 of *Cours de philosophie positive* (M. Clarke, Trans.). In S. Audreski (Ed.), *The essential Comte* (pp. 42–64). London: Croom Helm. (Original work published 1830)

Copernicus, N. (1976). *On the revolutions of the heavenly spheres* (A. M. Duncan, Trans.). New York: Barnes & Noble. (Original work published 1543)

Cox, H. (1984). *Religion in the secular city.* New York: Simon & Schuster.

Cremin, L. (1961). *Transformation of the school.* New York: Vintage Books.

Cubberley, E. P. (1916). *Public school administration.* Boston: Houghton Mifflin.

Cvitanović, P. (1984). Introduction. In P. Cvitanović (Ed.), *Universality in chaos* (pp. 3–36). Bristol, England: Adam Hilger.

Darwin, C. (1894). *Descent of man and selection in relation to sex* (2nd ed.). London: John Murray.

———. (1959). *The autobiography of Charles Darwin.* (Includes all texts of 1887 publication plus excerpts not in 1st ed.) New York: Harcourt, Brace, and Company. (Original work published 1929)

———. (1964). *Origin of the species.* Cambridge, MA: Harvard University Press. (Original work published 1896) 1st ed. published 1859, 6th ed. published 1896.

———. (1990). *The correspondence of Charles Darwin: Vol. 6. 1856–57.* (Frederick Burkhardt & Sydney Smith, Eds.). Cambridge: Cambridge University Press. (Original work published 1856–1857)

Darwin, E. (1974). *Zoonomia.* New York: AMS Press. (Original work published 1794–1796)

Davies, P. (1980). *Other worlds.* New York: Simon & Schuster.

———. (1984). *God and the new physics.* New York: Simon & Schuster, Touchstone Books.

———. (1988). *The cosmic blueprint: New discoveries in nature's creative ability to order the universe.* New York: Simon & Schuster.

———. (1992). *The mind of God.* New York: Simon & Schuster.

Depew, D. J., & Weber, B. H. (1985). Innovation and tradition in evolutionary theory. In D. J. Depew & B. H. Weber (Eds.), *Evolution at a crossroads: The new biology and the new philosophy of science* (227–260). Cambridge, MA: MIT Press.

———. (1988). Consequences of nonequilibrium thermodynamics for the Darwinian tradition. In Bruce H. Weber, David J. Depew, & James D. Smith (Eds.), *Entropy, information, and evolution: New perspectives on physical and biological evolution* (317–354). Cambridge, MA: MIT Press.

Derrida, J. (1978). *La verité en peinture.* Paris: Flammarion.

Descartes, R. (1950) *Discourse on method* (L. J. LaFleur, Trans.). New York: Liberal Arts Press. (Original work published 1637)

———. (1951). *Meditations on first philosophy* (L. J. LaFleur, Trans.). New York: Liberal Arts Press. (Original work published 1641)

————. (1985a). Description of the human body (John Cottingham, Trans.). In *The philosophical writings of Descartes* (Vol. 1, pp. 314–324). London: Cambridge University Press. (Original work published 1664)

————. (1985b). *The passions of the soul* (Robert Stoothoof, Trans.). In *The philosophical writings of Descartes* (Vol. 1, pp. 328–404). London: Cambridge University Press. (Original work published 1649)

————. (1985c). *Rules for the direction of the mind* (Dugald Murdoch, Trans.). In *The philosophical writings of Descartes* (Vol. 1, pp. 9–76). London: Cambridge University Press, (Original work published 1701)

————. (1985d). *Treatise on man* (Robert Stoothoof, Trans.). In *The philosophical writings of Descartes* (Vol. 1, pp. 99–108). London: Cambridge University Press. (Original work published 1664)

Dewey, J. (1922). *Human nature and conduct: An introduction to social psychology.* New York: Modern Library.

————. (1938). *Logic: A theory of inquiry.* New York: H. Holt & Co.

————. (1941). The philosophy of Whitehead. In Paul A. Schilpp (Ed.), *The philosophy of Alfred North Whitehead* (pp. 643–661). Evanston, IL: Northwestern University.

————. (1956a). *The child and the curriculum.* Chicago: University of Chicago Press. (Original work published 1902)

————. (1956b). *The school and society* (rev. ed.). Chicago: University of Chicago Press. (Original work published 1915)

————. (1957). *Reconstruction in philosophy* (enlarged ed.). Boston: Beacon Press. (Original work published 1948)

————. (1958). *Experience and nature.* New York: Dover Publications. (Original work published 1925)

————. (1960). *The quest for certainty.* New York: G. P. Putnam. (Original work published 1929)

————. (1962). *Individualism old and new.* New York: Capricorn Books. (Original work published 1929)

————. (1963). *Experience and education.* New York: Collier Books. (Original work published 1938)

————. (1964a). The continuum of ends–means. In R. D. Archambault (Ed.), *John Dewey on education: Selected writings* (pp. 97–107). New York: Random House. (Original work published 1939)

————. (1964b). Individuality and experience. In R. D. Archambault, *John Dewey on education: Selected writings* (pp. 149–156). New York: Random House. (Original work published 1926)

————. (1964c). Need for a philosophy of education. In R. D. Archambault (Ed.), *John Dewey on education: Selected writings* (pp. 3–14). New York: Random House. (Original work published 1934)

————. (1966). *Democracy and education.* New York: Free Press. (Original work published 1916)

————. (1971). *How we think.* Chicago: Henry Regnery. (Original work published 1933)

————. (1972). The reflex arc concept in psychology. In J. Boydston (Ed.), *The early works: Vol. 5. 1895–98* (pp. 96–109). Carbondale: Southern Illinois University Press. (Original work published 1896)

————. (1980). *Art as experience.* New York: Perigee Books, G. P. Putnam. (Original work published 1934)

Dewey, J., & Bentley, A. (1949). *Knowing and the known.* Boston: Beacon Press.

Dialectics of Biology Group, The. (1982). *Against biological determinism.* London: Allison & Busby.

Dickens, C. (1962). *A tale of two cities.* Oxford: Oxford University Press. (Original work published 1859)

Dobzhansky, T. (1937). *Genetics and the origin of species.* New York: Columbia University Press.

Doll, W. E., Jr. (1972). A methodology of experience, Part I: An alternative to behavioral objectives. *Educational Theory, 22* (Summer), 309–324.

————. (1973). A methodology of experience, Part II: The process of inquiry. *Educational Theory, 23* (Winter), 56–73.

————. (1977). The role of contrast in the development of competence. In Alex Molner & John Zahorik (Eds.), *Curriculum theory* (pp. 50–63). Washington, DC: Association for Supervision and Curriculum Development.

————. (1983a). Curriculum and change: Piaget's organism origins. *Journal of Curriculum Theorizing, 5*(2), 4–61.

————. (1983b). A re-visioning of progressive education. *Theory Into Practice, 22* (Summer), 166–173.

————. (1984). Developing competence. In E. Short (Ed.), *Competence* (pp. 123–138). Lanham, MD: University Press of America.

————. (1988). Curriculum beyond stability: Schön, Prigogine, Piaget. In W. F. Pinar (Ed.), *Contemporary curriculum discourses* (pp. 114–133). Scottsdale, AZ: Gorsuch Scarisbrick.

————. (1989a). Complexity in the classroom. *Educational Leadership, 47,* 65–70.

————. (1989b). Teaching a post-modern curriculum. In J. Sears & D. Marshall (Eds.), *Teaching and thinking about curriculum* (pp. 39–47). New York: Teachers College Press.

————. (1991). Post-modernism's utopian vision. *Education and Society, 9*(1), 54–60.

Doll, W. E., Jr., & Robbins, P. M. (1986). Improving arithmetic skills. In Robert F. Nicely & Thomas F. Sigmund (Eds.), *Mathematics: Teaching and learning yearbook.* Pennsylvania Council of Teachers of Mathematics.

Donaldson, M. (1978). *Children's minds.* New York: W. W. Norton.

Donne, J. (1955). Devotions upon emergent occasions, Meditation XVII. In John Hayward (Ed.), *Complete poetry and selected poems.* London: Nonesuch Library. (Original work published 1624)

————. (1968). An anatomie of the world. In Herbert J. C. Grierson (Ed.), *The poems of John Donne* (vol. 1). Oxford: Clarendon Press. (Original work published 1633)

Doyle, M. A. (1992). Rethinking reading and writing. Unpublished dissertation, Louisiana State University.

Driesch, H. (1905). *Der vitalismus al gerschichte und als lehre.* Leipzig: J. A. Barth.
———. (1914). *The history and theory of vitalism.* London: Macmillan.
Dyke, C. (1985). Complexity and closure. In David J. Depew & Bruce H. Weber (Eds.), *Evolution at a crossroads: The new history and the new philosophy of science* (pp. 97–131). Cambridge, MA: MIT Press.
———. (1988). *The evolutionary dynamics of complex systems.* New York: Oxford University Press.
Dyson, F. (1971). Energy in the universe. *Scientific American, 225*(3), 50–59.
Eddington, A. (1928). *The nature of the physical world.* New York: Macmillan.
Einstein, A. (1952). *Relativity: The special and the general theory* (15th ed.) (R. W. Lawson, Trans.). New York: Bonanza Books. (Original work published 1905, 1916)
Eiseley, L. (1961). *Darwin's century: Evolution and the men who discovered it.* Garden City, NY: Doubleday, Anchor Books.
Eldredge, N. (1986). *Time frames: The rethinking of Darwinian evolution and the theory of punctuated equilibria.* New York: Simon & Schuster, Touchstone Books.
Eldredge, N., & Gould, S. J. (1972). Punctuated equilibria: An alternative to phyletic gradualism. In T. J. M. Schopf (Ed.), *Models in paleobiology* (pp. 82–115). San Francisco: W. H. Freeman.
Elyot, Sir Thomas (1962). *The book named the governor.* S. E. Lehmberg (Ed.), London: J. M. Dent & Sons, Ltd. (Original work published 1533)
Enuma Elish. (1982). In Joan O'Brien & Wilfred Major (Eds.), *In the beginning: Creation myths* (pp. 16–26). Chico, CA: Scholars Press.
Ernest, P. (1991). *The philosophy of mathematics education.* London: Falmer.
Evans, J. (1990). African-American Christianity and the postmodern condition. *Journal of the American Academy of Religion, 58*(2), 207–222.
Faculty Handbook. (1986). Jurcipa, California School District.
Fancher, R. (1979). *Pioneers of psychology.* New York: W. W. Norton.
Feyerabend, P. (1988). *Against method* (rev. ed.). New York: Verso.
Fienberg, R. T. (1992). COBE Confronts the Big Bang. *Sky & Telescope,* Vol 84, No. 1, July 1992, 34–35.
Ford, L. (Ed.). (1973). *Two process philosophers: Hartshorne's encounter with Whitehead.* Tallahassee, FL: American Academy of Religion.
———. (1984). *The emergence of Whitehead's metaphysics, 1925–1929.* Albany: SUNY Press.
Foster, H. (Ed.). (1983). *The anti-aesthetic.* Port Townsend, WA: Bay Press.
Frankena, W. K. (1939). The naturalistic fallacy. *Mind, 48*(192), 464–477.
Furth, H. G. (1981). *Piaget and knowledge: Theoretical foundations* (2nd ed.). Chicago: University of Chicago Press.
Gadamer, H-G. (1975). *Truth and method.* New York: Seabury Press.
Galilei, G. (1844). *Le opere di Galileo Galilei* (Tomo IV). Firenze: Societa Editrice Fiorentina.
Gardner, H. (1985). *The mind's new science.* New York: Basic Books.
Genre. (1987). 20(3–4).

Gerard, R. W. (1957). Units and concepts of biology. *Science, 125* (3244), 429–433.

Gleick, J. (1987). *Chaos: Making a new science.* New York: Viking Press.

Gödel, K. (1963). *Uber formal unentscheidbare satz der principia mathematici unter verwandte systeme I* (Bernard Meltzer, Trans.). In R. B. Braithewaite (Ed.), *On formally undecidable propositions in "principia mathematica" and related systems.* New York: Basic Books. (Reprinted from *Monatshefte fur Mathematik und Physik,* 1931, *38,* 173–198)

Goldberger, A. L., Bhargava, V., West, B., & Mandell, A. J. (1985). Nonlinear dynamics of the heartbeat. *Physica D, 17,* 207–214.

Golding, W. (1962). *Lord of the flies.* New York: Coward-McCann.

Good, R., Wandersee, J., & St. Julien, J. (1992). Cautionary notes on the appeal of the new "ism" (constructivism) in science education. In Ken Tobin (Ed.), *The practice of constructivism in science education.* Washington, D.C.: AAAS.

Gould, S. J. (1981). *The mismeasure of man.* New York: W. W. Norton.

———. (1982, April). Punctuated equilibrium—a different way of seeing. *New Scientist 94,* 137–141.

———. (1988, August). Kropotkin was no crackpot. *Natural History,* pp. 12–21.

———. (1989a, March). The wheel of fortune and the wedge of progress, *Natural History,* pp. 14–21.

———. (1989b, April). Tires to sandals. *Natural History,* pp. 8–15.

———. (1990, March). An earful of jaw. *Natural History,* pp. 12–23.

Gould, S. J., & Eldredge, N. (1977). Punctuated equilibria: The tempo and mode and evolution reconsidered. *Paleobiology 3,* 1977, 115–51.

Graubard, S. R. (1988). *The artificial intelligence debate.* Cambridge, MA: MIT Press.

Gribbin, J. (1984). *In search of Schrödinger's cat.* New York: Bantam Books.

Griffin, D. R. (Ed.). (1988a). *The reenchantment of science: Postmodern proposals.* Albany: SUNY Press.

———. (1988b). *Spirituality and society: Postmodern visions.* Albany: SUNY Press.

———. (1989). *God and religion in the postmodern world.* Albany: SUNY Press.

———. (1990). *Sacred interconnections: Postmodern spirituality, political economy, and art.* Albany: SUNY Press.

Griffin, D. R., Beardslee, William A., & Holland, J. (Eds.). (1989). *Varieties of postmodern theology.* Albany: SUNY Press.

Griffin, D. R., & Cobb, J. B., Jr. (1976). *Process theology: An introductory exposition.* Philadelphia: Westminster Press.

Griffin, D. R., & Smith, H. (Eds.). (1989). *Primordial truth and postmodern theology.* Albany: SUNY Press.

———. (1977). A review of Gadamer's *Truth and Method.* In R. Dallmayr and Thomas A. McCarthy, *Understanding and social inquiry* (335–363). Notre Dame, IN: University of Notre Dame Press.

Habermas, J. (1981). Modernity versus postmodernity. *New German Critique, 22* (Winter), 3–14.

———. (1983). Modernism—an incomplete project. In Hal Foster, ed. *The Anti-*

Aesthetic: Essays on postmodern culture (pp. 3–15). Port Townsend, WA: Bay Press.

Hahn, R. (1967). *Laplace as a Newtonian scientist.* Los Angeles: William Andrews Clark Memorial Library.

Harap, H. (1928). *The techniques of curriculum making.* New York: Macmillan.

Harris, W. T. (1891, December). Vocation versus culture; or the two aspects of education. *Education, XII,* 194–197.

Hartshorne, C. (1964). *A natural theology for our time.* La Salle, IL: Open Court.

————. (1981). *Whitehead's view of reality.* New York: Pilgrim Press.

Hayles, N. K. (1984). *The cosmic web.* Ithaca: Cornell University Press.

————. (1990). *Chaos bound.* Ithaca: Cornell University Press.

Heidegger, M. (1962). *Being and time* (John Macquarrie & Edward Robinson, Trans.). New York: Harper. (Original work published 1926)

Heisenberg, W. (1972). *Physics and beyond.* New York: Harper & Row.

Hendley, B. (1986). *Dewey, Russell, Whitehead: Philosophers as educators.* Carbondale: Southern Illinois University Press.

Heraclitus. (1987). *Heraclitus: Fragments* (Commentary by T. M. Robinson). Toronto: University of Toronto Press.

Herbart, J. F. (1901). *Outlines of educational doctrines.* New York: Macmillan.

Hesiod. (1982). *Theogony.* In Joan O'Brien & Wilfred Major (Eds.), *In the beginning: Creation myths* (pp. 54–62). Chico, CA: Scholars Press.

Hirsch, E. D., Jr. (1967). *Validity in interpretation.* New Haven: Yale University Press.

————. (1987). *Cultural literacy.* Boston: Houghton Mifflin.

Ho, M-W., & Saunders, P. T. (1984). *Beyond neo-Darwinism: An introduction to the new evolutionary paradigm.* Orlando, FL: Academic Press.

Hofstadter, D. (1985). Mathematical chaos and strange attractors. In Douglas Hofstadter (Ed.), *Metamagical themas: Questing for the essence of mind and pattern* (pp. 364–395). New York: Basic Books.

Hofstadter, D., & Dennet, D. C. (Eds.). (1981). *The mind's I.* New York: Basic Books.

Hunter, M. (1982). *Mastery teaching.* El Segundo, CA: TIP Publications.

Huxley, J. (1942). *Evolution, the modern synthesis.* London: Allen & Unwin.

Iltis, H. (1932). *Life of Mendel.* New York: W. W. Norton.

Iser, W. (1978). *The act of reading.* Baltimore: Johns Hopkins University Press.

Jacob, F. (1974). *The logic of living systems.* London: Allen Lane.

Jaeger, W. (1939–1944). *Paideia: The ideals of Greek culture* (2nd ed., Vols. 1–3). (G. Highet, Trans.). New York: Oxford University Press.

Jameson, F. (1991). *Postmodernism.* Durham, NC: Duke University Press.

Jantsch, E. (1980). *The self-organizing universe.* Oxford: Pergamon Press.

Jeffress, L. A. (Ed.). (1951). *Cerebral mechanisms in behavior: The Hixon symposium.* New York: John Wiley.

Jencks, C. (1987). *What is post-modernism?* (2nd enlarged, rev. ed.). New York: St. Martin's Press.

Jenkin, F. (1867). The origin of species. *North British Review,* (Vol. 42, pp. 149–171).

Jensen, A. (1981). *Straight talks about mental tests.* New York: Free Press.

Joachim, H. H. (1957). *Descartes' rules for the direction of the mind.* London: Allen & Unwin.

Joule, J P. (1963). On matter, living force, and heat. *Scientific Papers* (Vol. 1, pp. 265–276). London: Dawsons of Pall Mall.(Original work published 1887)

Journal for Research in Mathematics Education. (1990). Monograph No. 4: Constructivist views on the teaching and learning of mathematics. National Council of Teachers of Mathematics.

Keynes, R. D. (Ed.). (1979). *The Beagle record.* New York: Cambridge University Press.

Kierkegaard, S. (1941). *Fear and trembling and the sickness unto death* (Walter Lowrie, Trans.). Princeton, NJ: Princeton University Press. (Original work published 1843)

Kilpatrick, W. H. (1918). The project method. *Teachers College Record, 19*(4), 319–335.

———. (1925). *Foundations of method.* New York: Macmillan.

Kitchener, R. F. (1986). *Piaget's theory of knowledge: Genetic epistemology and scientific reason.* New Haven: Yale University Press.

———. (Ed.). (1988). *The world view of contemporary physics: Does it need a new metaphysics?* Albany: SUNY Press.

Kliebard, H. (1975a). Reappraisal: The Tyler rationale. In William Pinar (Ed.), *Curriculum theorizing* (pp. 70–83). Berkeley, CA: McCutchan. (Original work published 1970)

———. (1975b). The rise of scientific curriculum making and its aftermath. *Curriculum Theory Network, 5*(1), 27–37.

———. (1986). *The struggle for the American curriculum, 1893–1958.* Boston: Routledge and Kegan Paul.

Kline, M. (1980). *Mathematics: The loss of certainty.* New York: Oxford University Press.

Koestler, A., & Smythies, J. R. (1970). *Beyond reductionism: New perspectives in the life sciences.* New York: Macmillan.

Kolb, D. (1986). *The critique of pure modernity: Hegel, Heidegger, and after.* Chicago: University of Chicago Press.

Kuhn, T. (1959). *The Copernican revolution.* New York: Vintage Books.

———. (1970). *The structure of scientific revolutions* (2nd ed.). Chicago: University of Chicago Press.

———. (1977). *The essential tension: Selected studies in scientific traditions and change.* Chicago: University of Chicago Press.

Kundera, M. (1988). *The art of the novel* (Linda Asher, Trans.). New York: Grove Press. (Original work published 1986)

Küng, H. (1988). *Theology for a third millennium.* New York: Doubleday.

Kuntz, P. (1968). *The concept of order.* Seattle: University of Washington Press.

Lakatos, I., & Musgrave, A. (Eds.). (1970). *Criticism and the growth of knowledge.* Cambridge: Cambridge University Press.

Laplace, P. S. (1966). *Celestial mechanics* (Vols. 1–4) (N. Bowditch, Trans.). New York: Chelsea Publishing. (Original work published 1799–1805)

————. (1951). *A philosophical essay on probabilities* (3rd ed.) (F. W. Truscott & F. L. Emory, Trans.). NY: Dover Publications. (Original work published 1820)

Lashley, K. S. (1951). The problem of serial order in behavior. In L. A. Jeffress (Ed.), *Cerebral mechanisms in behavior: The Hixon symposium* (pp. 112–136). New York: John Wiley.

Leacock, S. (1929). Human interest put into mathematics. *The Mathematics Teacher, 22,* 302–304.

Levin, H. (1966). What was modernism? In (Ed.), *Refractions: Essays in comparative literature* (pp. 271–295). New York: Oxford University Press. (Original work published 1960)

Lieberman, J. (1970). *The tyranny of the experts: How professionals are closing the open society.* New York: Walker.

von Linne, C. (1964). *Carli Linnaei systema naturae* (Facsimile of 1st ed.) (M. S. J. Engel-Ledeboer & H. Engel, Trans.). Nieurwkopp: B. deGraff. (Original work published 1735)

Lockwood, M. (1965). The experimental utopia in America. In F. E. Manuel (Ed.), *Utopias and utopian thought* (pp. 183–200). Boston: Houghton Mifflin.

Lorenz, E. (1963). Deterministic nonperiodic flow. *Journal of the Atmospheric Sciences, 20,* 130–141.

————. (1979). On the prevalence of aperiodicity in simple systems. In Mgrmela & J. Marsden (Eds.), *Global analysis* (pp. 53–75). New York: Springer-Verlag.

Lovejoy, A. (1965). *The great chain of being.* New York: Harper Torchbooks. (Original work published 1936)

Lowe, V. (1962). *Understanding Whitehead.* Baltimore: The Johns Hopkins Press.

————. (1985). *Alfred North Whitehead: The man and his work* (Vol. II) (J. B. Schneewind, Ed.). Baltimore: Johns Hopkins University Press.

Lucas, C. (1985). Out at the edge: Notes on a paradigm shift. *Journal of Counseling and Development, 64,* 165.

Lucas, G. (1983). *The genesis of modern process thought.* Metuchen, NJ: Scarecrow Press.

————. (1989). *The rehabilitation of Whitehead.* Albany: SUNY Press.

Luria, A. R. (1961). *The role of speech in the regulation of normal and abnormal behavior.* New York: Liveright.

Lydon, A. (1992). Cosmology and curriculum. Unpublished dissertation, Louisiana State University.

Lyell, C. (1830–1833). *Principles of geology* (vols. 1–3). London: John Murray.

Lyotard, J-F. (1984). *The postmodern condition: A report on knowledge* (G. Bennington & B. Massumi, Trans.). Minneapolis: University of Minnesota Press.

Lynn, K. S. (1963). Introduction to "The professions." *Daedalus, 92* (Fall), 649–654.

Malthus, T. R. (1914). *Essay on the principle of population.* New York: Macmillan Co. (Original work published 1798)

van Manen, M. (1988). The relation between research and pedagogy. In W. F. Pinar (Ed.), *Contemporary curriculum discourses* (pp. 437–452). Scottsdale: Gorsuch Scarisbrick.

————. (1991). *The tact of teaching.* Albany: SUNY Press.

Mann, H. (1867). First Annual Report of the Secretary of the Board of Education. In *Lectures, and annual reports, on education* (pp. 384–432). Cambridge: George C. Rand and Avery.

Maran, S. P. (1992). Hubble illuminates the universe. *Sky & Telescope, 83*(12), 619–625.

Mathews, S. (1912). *Scientific management in the churches.* Chicago: University of Chicago Press.

Maturana, H., & Varela, F. (1980). *Autopoisesis and cognition.* Boston: D. Reidel Publishing.

Mayr, E. (1942). *Systematics and the origin of species.* New York: Columbia University Press.

———. (1982). *The growth of biological thought: Diversity, evolution, and inheritance.* Cambridge, MA: Belknap Press of Harvard University Press.

———. (1988). *Toward a new philosophy of biology: Observations of an evolutionist.* Cambridge, MA: Belknap Press of Harvard University Press.

———. (1991). *One long argument: Charles Darwin and the genesis of modern evolutionary thought.* Cambridge: Harvard University Press.

McGue, M. (1989, August 17). Nature—nurture and intelligence. *Nature, 340,* 507–508.

McMullin, E. (1968). Cosmic order in Plato and Aristotle. In P. Kurtz (Ed.). *The concept of order* (pp. 63–76). Seattle: University of Washington Press.

Mendelson, J. (1979). The Habermas–Gadamer debate. *New German Critique, 18,* 44–73.

Merchant, C. (1983). *The death of nature: Women, ecology, and the scientific revolution.* San Francisco: Harper & Row Torchbooks.

Miller, J. G. (1956). The magical number 7 plus or minus 2: Some limits on our capacity for processing information. *Psychological Review, 63,* 81–87.

———. (1978). *Living systems.* New York: McGraw-Hill.

Minsky, M. (1986). *The society of mind.* New York: Simon & Schuster.

Monod, J. (1972). *Chance and necessity.* New York: Vintage Books.

Munby, H. (1989). Reflection-in-action and reflection-on-action. *Current issues in education, 9* (Fall), 31–42.

Munby, H., & Russell, T. (1989). Educating the reflective teacher: An essay review of two books by Donald Schön. *Journal of Curriculum Studies, 21,* 71–80.

New German Critique. (1981). Special issue on modernism. D. Bird, B. Martin, R. Reinhart, & J. Steakley (Eds.). *22* (Winter).

New German Critique. (1984). *33* (Fall). Modernity and postmodernity. D. Bathrick, H. Fehervary, M. Hansen, A. Huyssen, A. G. Rabinbach, & J. Zipes (Eds.). *33* (Fall).

Newton, Isaac. (1962). *Philosophia naturalis principia mathematica* (3rd ed.) Trans. to English by A. Motte as *Mathematical principles of natural philosophy.* Trans. revised by F. Cajori. Berkeley: University of California Press. (Original work published 1729)

———. (1952). *Opticks* (4th ed.). New York: Dover Publications. (Original work published 1730)

Nicolis, G., & Prigogine, I. (1977). *Self-organization in non-equilibrium systems.* New York: John Wiley.

————. (1989). *Exploring complexity.* New York: W. H. Freeman.

Nielsen, K. (1991). *After the demise of the tradition: Rorty, critical theory, and the fate of philosophy.* Boulder: Westview Press.

Nietzsche, F. (1968). *The portable Nietzsche* (Walter Kaufman, Trans.). New York: Viking Press. (Original works published c. 1888–1895)

O'Brien, J., & Major, W. (1982). *In the beginning: Creation myths.* Chico, CA: Scholars Press.

Oliver, D. (1990, September). Grounded knowing: A postmodern perspective on teaching and learning. *Educational Leadership, 48,* 64–69.

Oliver, D. W., with Gershman, K. W. (1989). *Education, modernity, and fractured meaning: Toward a process theory of teaching and learning.* Albany: SUNY Press.

Ovid. (1976). *Metamorphoses.* (Sir Samuel Garth, Dryden, et al., Trans.). New York: Garland Publishing. (Original work published 1732)

Oxford English Dictionary (2nd ed., Vol. 3). (1989). (J. A. Simpson & E. S. C. Weiner, Eds.). Oxford: Clarendon Press.

Pagels, H. (1982). *The cosmic code: Quantum physics as the language of nature.* New York: Simon & Schuster.

————. (1985, January). Is the irreversibility we see a fundamental property of nature? *Physics Today, 38,* 97–99.

————. (1988). *Dreams of reason: The computer and the rise of the sciences of complexity.* New York: Simon & Schuster.

Paley, W. (1822). *Natural theology.* London:

Palmer, R. E. (1969). *Hermeneutics: Interpretation in Schleiermacher, Dilthy, Heidegger and Gadamer.* Evanston, IL: Northwestern University Press.

Pannenberg, W. (1986). Hermeneutics and universal history. In Brice R. Wachterhauser (Ed.), *Hermeneutics and modern philosophy* (pp. 111–146). Albany: SUNY Press. (Original work published 1967)

Parmenides. (1984). *Parmenides of Elea: Fragments.* Introduction by David Gallop. Toronto: Toronto University Press.

Pattee, H. H. (Ed.). (1973). *Hierarchy theory.* New York: George Braziller.

Peacocke, A. (1979). *Creation and the world of science.* New York: Oxford University Press.

————. (1983). *An introduction to the physical chemistry of biological organization.* Oxford: Clarendon Press.

————. (1986). *God and the new biology.* San Francisco: Harper & Row.

Peitgen, H-O., & Richter, Peter H. (1986). *The beauty of fractals.* New York: Springer-Verlag.

Peitgen, H-O., Jurgens, H., Saupe, D., Maletsky, E., Perciante, T., & Yunker, L. (1991). *Fractals for the classroom.* New York: Springer-Verlag.

Pekarsky, D. (1990). Dewey's conception of growth reconsidered. *Educational Theory, 40* (Summer), 283–294.

Perloff, M. (1987). Introduction. *Genre, 20* (Fall–Winter), 233–240.

Peters, M. (1989). Techno-science, rationality, and the university: Lyotard on the "postmodern condition." *Educational Theory, 39*(2), 93–105.

Peterson, I. (1988). *The mathematical tourist: Snapshots of modern mathematics*. New York: W. H. Freeman.

Phillips, D. C. (1987). *Philosophy, science, and social inquiry*. New York: Pergamon Press.

Piaget, J. (1952). Jean Piaget, an autobiographical essay. In E. G. Boring et al. (Eds.), *A history of psychology in autobiography* (Vol. 4, pp. 237–256). Worcester, MA: Clark University Press.

———. (1971a). *Biology and knowledge* (Beatrix Walsh, Trans.). Chicago: University of Chicago Press.

———. (1971b). *Science of education and the psychology of the child* (D. Coltman, Trans.). New York: Viking Press.

———. (1977a). Comments on mathematical education. In Howard Gruber & Jacques Voneche (Eds.), *The essential Piaget* (pp. 726–732). New York: Basic Books. (Original work published 1972)

———. (1977b). *The development of thought: Equilibration of cognitive structures* (A. Rosin, Trans.). New York: Viking Press.

———. (1978). *Behavior and evolution* (D. Nicholson-Smith, Trans.). New York: Pantheon Books.

Piatelli-Palmarini, M. (1980). *Language and learning: The debate between Jean Piaget and Noam Chomsky*. Cambridge: Harvard University Press.

Pinar, W. (1975). Currere: Toward reconceptualization. In William Pinar (Ed.), *Curriculum theorizing* (pp. 396–414). Berkeley: McCutchan.

Pittendreigh, C. S. (1958). Adaptation, natural selection, and behavior. In A. Roe & G. G. Simpson (Eds.), *Behavior and evolution*. New Haven: Yale University Press.

Plato. (1945). *The republic of Plato* (F. M. Cornford, Trans.). New York: Oxford University Press.

———. *Meno* (1949). (Benjamin Jowett, Trans.). New York: Liberal Arts Press.

———. *Timeaus* (1959). (F. M. Cornford, Trans.). New York: Liberal Arts Press.

———. (1961). *Cratylus* (Benjamin Jowett, Trans.). In Edith Hamilton & Hunington Cairns (Eds.), *The collected dialogues of Plato* (pp. 421–474). New York: Pantheon Books.

Polanyi, M. (1966). *The tacit dimension*. Garden City, NY: Doubleday & Co.

———. (1975). Order. In M. Polanyi & H. Prosch (Eds.), *Meaning* (pp. 161–181). Chicago: University of Chicago Press.

Pope, A. (1830). The dunciad. In Dr. Johnson (Ed.), *The poetical works of Alexander Pope, Esq.* Philadelphia: J. J. Woodward. (Original work published 1728)

Popper, K. R. (1968). *The logic of scientific discovery*. New York: Harper & Row.

———. (1982). *The open universe: An argument for indeterminism*. London: Hutchinson.

Prigogine, I. (1961). *Introduction to thermodynamics of irreversible processes* (2nd, rev. ed.). New York: John Wiley, Interscience.

———. (1980). *From being to becoming: Time and complexity in the physical sciences*. San Francisco: W. H. Freeman.

———. (1988). The rediscovery of time. In Richard F. Kitchener (Ed.), *The world view of contemporary physics: Does it need a new metaphysics?* (pp. 125–143). Albany: SUNY Press.

Prigogine, I., & Stengers, I. (1984). *Order out of chaos: Man's new dialogue with nature.* New York: Bantam Books.

Putnam, H. (1988). Much ado about not very much. In Stephen R. Graubard (Ed.), *The artificial intelligence debate* (pp. 269–282). Cambridge, MA: MIT Press.

Ralt, D., et al. (1991). Sperm attraction to a follicular factor(s) correlates with human egg fertilizability. *Proceedings of the National Academy of Science USA, 88*(7), 2840–2844.

Reichenbach, H. (1951). *The rise of scientific philosophy.* Berkeley: University of California Press.

Reynolds, W. (1987). *Implications of effective teacher research: Madeline Hunter's seven steps to educational paradise.* Paper presented at the AERA conference, Washington, DC.

Rice, J. M. (1969). *Public school system of the United States.* New York: Arno Press. (Original work published 1893)

———. (1969). *Scientific management in education.* New York: Arno Press. (Original work published 1914)

Ricouer, P. (1981). Hermeneutics and the critique of ideology. In John B. Thompson (Ed. and Trans.), *Paul Ricouer: Hermeneutics and the human sciences* pp. 63–100). Cambridge: Cambridge University Press.

Rorty, R. (1980). *Philosophy and the mirror of nature.* Princeton: Princeton University Press.

———. (1982). *Consequences of pragmatism.* Minneapolis: University of Minnesota Press.

———. (1985). Habermas and Lyotard on postmodernity. In Richard Bernstein (Ed.), *Habermas and modernity* (pp. 161–175). Cambridge, MA: MIT Press.

———. (1986). The contingency of selfhood. *London Review of Books* (pp. 11–15).

———. (1989). *Contingency, irony, and solidarity.* Cambridge: Cambridge University Press.

———. (1990). The dangers of over-philosophication. *Educational Theory, 40*(1), 41–44.

Rousseau, J. J. (1900). *Julie ou la nouvelle Heloise, tome premier.* Paris: Flammarion. (Original work published 1761)

———. (1969). *Emile* (B. Foxley, Trans.). New York: Dutton. (Original work published 1762)

Rugg, H., et al. (1969). *The foundations of curriculum-making: The twenty-sixth yearbook of the National Society for the Study of Education, Part II.* New York: Arno Press. (Original work published 1927)

Russell, B. (1903). The free man's worship. In Richard Rempel, Andrew Brinky, & Margaret Moran (Eds.), *The collected papers of Bertrand Russell: Vol. 12. Contemplation and action 1902–14.* London: Allen & Unwin.

Russell, B., (1957). *Why I am not a Christian.* New York: Allen & Unwin.

Russell, T., & Munby, H. (1991). Reframing: The role of experience in developing teachers' professional knowledge. In Donald Schön (Ed.), *The reflective turn* (pp. 164–187). New York: Teachers College Press.

Ryle, G. (1949). *The concept of mind.* London: Hutchinson.

Comte de Saint-Simon, H. (1952). New Christianity. F. M. H. Markham (Ed. and Trans.), *Henri Comte de Saint-Simon (1760–1825): Selected writings* (pp. 81–116). New York: Macmillan. (Original work published 1825)

Schieve, W., & Allen, P. (1982). *Self-organization and dissipative structures.* Austin: University of Texas Press.

Schilpp, P. A. (Ed.). (1941). *The philosophy of Alfred North Whitehead.* Evanston, IL: Northwestern University.

Schmittau, J. (1991). Mathematics education in the 1990's: Can it afford to ignore its historical and philosophical foundations? *Educational Theory, 41* (Spring), 121–133.

Schön, D. (1983). *The reflective practitioner: How professionals think in action.* New York: Basic Books.

———. (1987). *Educating the reflective practitioner.* San Francisco: Jossey-Bass.

———. (1991). *The reflective turn: Case studies in and on educational practice.* New York: Teachers College Press.

Schrödinger, E. (1945). *What is life?* New York: Macmillan.

Schubert, W. H. (1986). *Curriculum: Perspective, paradigm, and possibility.* New York: Macmillan.

Schwab, J. (1978a). The practical: A language for curriculum. In I. Westbury & N. J. Wilkof (Eds.), *Science, curriculum, and liberal education: Selected essays* (pp. 287–321). Chicago: University of Chicago Press. (Original work published 1970)

———. (1978b). The practical: Arts of eclectic. In I. Westbury & N. J. Wilkof (Eds.), *Science, curriculum, and liberal education: Selected essays* (pp. 322–364). Chicago: University of Chicago Press. (Original work published 1971)

———. (1978c). The practical: Translation into curriculum. In I. Westbury & N. J. Wilkof (Eds.), *Science, curriculum, and liberal education: Selected essays* (pp. 365–383). Chicago: University of Chicago Press. (Original work published 1973)

———. (1983). The practical 4: Something for curriculum professors to do. *Curriculum Inquiry, 13* (Fall), 239–266.

Serres, M. (1983). *Hermes: Literature, science, philosophy.* Josué V. Harari & David F. Bell (Eds.) Baltimore: Johns Hopkins University Press.

Shakespeare, W. (1903). *Venus and adonis.* London: J. M. Dent. (Original work published 1593)

———. (1936). Troilus and cressida. In W. Aldis (Ed.), *The complete works of William Shakespeare* (pp. 819–860). Philadelphia: Blakeston. (Original work published c. 1603).

———. (1962). *Othello.* (M. R. Redley, Ed.). Cambridge: Harvard University Press. (Original work published 1603.)

Skinner, B. F. (1948). *Walden two*. New York: Macmillan.

———. (1953). *Science and human behavior*. New York: Macmillan.

———. (1957). *Verbal behavior*. New York: Appleton-Century-Crofts.

———. (1968). *The technology of teaching*. Englewood Cliffs, NJ: Prentice-Hall.

Sloan Foundation Report. (1976). Proposed particular program in cognitive sciences. New York: Sloan Foundation.

Smith, H. (1982). *Beyond the post-modern mind*. Wheaton, IL: Theosophical Publishing.

Snow, C. P. (1964). *The two cultures: And a second look*. Cambridge: Cambridge University Press.

Soltis, J. (1990). The hermeneutics/interpretative tradition and its virtues. (Paper presented at AERA, conference, Boston.)

Spencer, H. O. (1929). What knowledge is of most worth? In Herbert O. Spencer (Ed.), *Education: Intellectual, moral, and physical* (pp. 1–87). New York: D. Appleton. (Original work published 1859.)

Sproul, B. (1979). *Primal myths: Creating the world*. San Francisco: Harper & Row.

Stevens, W. (1947). *Poems*. New York: Vintage Books. (Original work published 1938)

Taylor, F. W. (1947). *Scientific management*. New York: Harper and Brothers. (Original work published 1911)

Tennyson, A. L. (1975). *In memoriam* (Arthur Hallam, Ed.). London: The Folio Society. (Original work published 1850)

Thomas, L. (1980, September–October). On the uncertainty in science. *Harvard Magazine*, pp. 19–22.

Thorndike, E. L. (1913). *Educational psychology* (rev. and enlarged into 3 volumes, based on 1903 volume). New York: Teachers College, Columbia University.

———. (1921). *The teacher's word book*. New York: Teachers College, Columbia University.

Torshen, K. (1977). *The mastery approach to competency-based education*. New York: Academic Press.

Toulmin, S. (1982). *The return to cosmology*. Berkeley: University of California Press.

———. (1990). *Cosmopolis*. New York: Free Press.

Tyack, D. (1974). *The one best system: A history of American urban education*. Cambridge, MA: Harvard University Press.

Tyler, R. (1950). *Basic principles of curriculum and instruction*. Chicago: University of Chicago Press.

Wachterhauser, B. R. (1986). *Hermeneutics and modern philosophy*. Albany: SUNY Press.

Waddington, C. H. (1957). *The strategy of the genes: A discussion of some aspects of theoretical biology*. New York: Macmillan.

———. (1968–1972). *Toward a theoretical biology* (Vols. I and II). Chicago: Aldine Publishing.

————. (1975). *The evolution of an evolutionist.* Ithaca, NY: Cornell University Press.

Wallace, A. R. (1905). *My life: A record of events and opinions.* New York: Dodd, Mead, & Co.

Wallack, F. B. (1980). *The epochal nature of process in Whitehead's metaphysics.* Albany: SUNY Press.

Waters, B. (1986). Ministry and the university in a postmodern world. *Religion and Intellectual Life, 4* (Fall), 113–122.

Watson, J. B. (1913). Psychology as the behaviorist views it. *The Psychological Review, 20,* 158–177.

————. (1916). The place of the conditional reflex in psychology. *The Psychological Review, 23,* 89–116.

————. (1936). Autobiography. In Carl Murchison (Ed.), *A history of psychology in autobiography* (Vol III, pp. 271–281). Worcester, MA: Clark University Press.

Weiss, P. (1970). The living system. In A. Koestler & J. R. Smythies (Eds.). *Beyond reductionism: New perspectives in the life sciences* (pp. 192–216). New York: Macmillan.

West, C. (1989). *The American evasion of philosophy.* Madison: University of Wisconsin Press.

Westfall, R. (1968). Newton's concept of order. In P. Kuntz (Ed.), *The concept of order* (pp. 77–88). Seattle: Washington University Press.

Whitehead, A. N. (1898). *A treatise on universal algebra, with application.* Cambridge: Cambridge University Press.

————. (1906). On mathematical concepts of the material world. *Philosophical Transactions of Royal Society of London* (Ser. A), *205,* 465–525.

————. (1911). *Introduction to mathematics.* London: Williams and Norgate.

————. (1933). *Adventures of ideas.* New York: Macmillan.

————. (1938). *Modes of thought.* New York: Macmillan.

————. (1948). *Essays in science and philosophy.* New York: Philosophical Library.

————. (1967a). *The aims of education.* New York: Free Press. (Original work published 1929)

————. (1967b). *Science and the modern world.* New York: Free Press. (Original work published 1925)

————. (1971). *The axioms of projective geometry.* New York: Hafner Publishing. (Original work published 1906)

————. (1978). *Process and reality: An essay in cosmology* (Corrected ed.) (David R. Griffin & Donald W. Sherburne, Eds.). New York: Free Press. (Original work published 1929)

Whitehead, A. N., with Russell, B. (1910–1913). *Principia mathematica* (Vols. I–III). Cambridge: Cambridge University Press.

Wicken, J. (1987). *Evolution, thermodynamics, and information: Extending the Darwinian program.* New York: Oxford University Press.

Wiener, N. (1961). *Cybernetics, or control and communication in the animal and the machine* (2nd ed.). Cambridge, MA: MIT Press.

Winograd, T., & Flores, F. (1987). *Understanding computers and cognition.* Reading, MA: Addison-Wesley.

Witherell, C., & Noddings, N. (1991). *Stories lives tell: Narrative and dialogue in education.* New York: Teachers College Press.

Woodger, J. H. (1948). *Biological principles.* London: Routledge and Kegan Paul.

Yale Report. (1828). Original papers in relation to a course of liberal education. *American Journal of Science and Arts, xv* (2), 297–340.

Zygon. (1984, December). Order and disorder: Thermodynamics, creation and values. E. Peters & K. Peters (Eds.). *19*(4).

Index

About the Author

William E. Doll, Jr. is an associate professor in the Department of Curriculum and Instruction at Louisiana State University. A native Bostonian, he has taught school there, in Denver, and in Baltimore. He received his doctorate from Johns Hopkins University and has taught in and chaired the Elementary Education department at SUNY-Oswego. At the University of Redlands, in California, he was director of Teacher Education.

Dr. Doll has written numerous articles for national and international journals. This is his first book.